THE 1ᴼᵀ EARL'S GR
WAS A PLAITFORD

BRIDGE FOOT.

HISTORY OF FACTS, EVENTS AND PEOPLE

OF

PLAITFORD

&

MELCHET PARK

GEOFF CUELL

WITH

SHEILA CUELL & CATHERINE SHUTLER

ISBN 978-0-9927210-0-8

Published by
Geoff Cuell
Haz,
Sherfield English Road
Landford
Salisbury
Wiltshire
SP5 2BD

Acknowledgements

Firstly, we would like to thank the residents past and present who contributed towards this book with documents, memories and photographs.
Our thanks also to local historian Stephen Ings for allowing us tap into his vast knowledge of the history of the surrounding area.

We would also like to thank:
British Newspapers online; Mary Cook; Dorset County History Centre; Google Books; Hampshire County Record Office and Museum Service - Winchester Museum; Isle of Wight Record Office; Eric Kemish; LTVAS (Lower Test Valley Archaeological Study Group); National Archives; Peter Osman; Pembrokeshire Record Office; Romsey Reference Library and online eResources; Salisbury Museum; Salisbury Reference Library; Michael Sleigh - Wellow History Society; Southampton City Council - City Archives and Southampton Museum; The Duke of Cornwall Light Infantry Museum: The National Horse Racing Museum; The Romsey Advertiser Newspaper; The Royal Hampshire Regiment Museum; Wiltshire & Swindon History Centre,

List of Illustrations

Bridgefoot Ford, late 1920s. Left is "Dickie" Tutt with three of the Rogers children from Bridgefoot Farm. The youngest is Kenneth Rogers born 1926   Front Cover

Contents

Introduction

Plaitford is one of the smaller villages in Hampshire on the county border with Wiltshire. Its history shows that it is a New Forest Village with most of its farms still having forest grazing rights. With the advent of the New Forest National Park and the decision to make the A36 Southampton to Salisbury trunk road its northern boundary, the village has been split with approximately one third, including Plaitford Common, within the National Park and the remaining more populated part outside.

Recorded in *Victoria County History 1911,* 'Plaitford covers an area consisting of five acres of land covered by water and 1,323 acres of which 382 acres was arable, 247.5 permanent grass land and 136.5 was woodland. The parish was generally low-lying, reaching nowhere a greater height than 140 ft'.

Prior to county boundary changes in 1895, Plaitford, along with West Wellow and Melchet Park, was in Wiltshire, with Melchet Park being part of Whiteparish. Melchet was made a separate civil parish until 1932 when, under a government review, it was joined with Plaitford and became the Parish of Melchet Park and Plaitford, as it is today.

We have archaeological finds from the Mesolithic Period (10,000 to 4,001 BC) and the Bronze Age (2,200 to 801 BC). These finds give a good indication that Plaitford has been a settlement for between six and twelve thousand years. Directories from the 1800's also mention that Plaitford and Landford were Roman settlements.

We have delved into the history of Plaitford as far back as we can and have managed from various documents to name some of the people from the past, these include from the Domesday Survey of 1086, Eadric the Blind, Grimbold the Goldsmith and Wulfric the Huntsman, and on the list of tax payers in1332, John, son of Andrew de Grymestede, Michael Ballarde and William le Bone. With the help of the Internet and local record offices we are able to look at wills of Plaitford residents as far back as the mid sixteenth century. Although these are all just names of faceless people, they all played a part in the history of Plaitford.

Well into the twentieth century, the village was very much a farming community, with well over a dozen farms and smallholdings.

However, as with many rural villages in the late nineteenth century, Plaitford saw a fall in population. In 1861, the population was around 330 and by 1891 it had fallen to 164. This was due to modern farming methods needing less manpower, low farm wages and better prospects in the industrialized towns and cities. In February 2010, the electoral roll, including Melchet Park, stood at 250 plus children.

In living memory, prominent names from the nineteenth and twentieth century such as Biddlecombe, Bungay, Fielder, Hood, Hutchings, Moore, Noble and Tutt, though still found in the locality, no longer reside in Plaitford. These older families with many generations of history in the area are becoming few. Their children and grandchildren have, through necessity and with the help of modern transport, moved away to seek work outside the area.

The Bowles families are the longest standing still living in Plaitford. Their history in the village can be traced back ten generations to the 1740's when John Bowles came to Gauntletts Farm from Downton. Another is the Curtis family whose roots in Plaitford go back to the mid nineteenth century.

Other than the short stretch of the A36, Plaitford has not changed. The large farm working community that existed until the Second World War has long gone. Many of the old farm houses are no longer lived in by farmers and now only stand as a reminder of those bygone days.

This book will, we hope, give you a sense of the history of the parish based on historical facts, events and the people who lived here.

We have only touched on the social history of the periods covered, there are many far more qualified who have written on the subject over the years. Our aim has been to produce a useful reference for those who wish to discover the history of their property or their ancestry in the village.

We have attempted to be as accurate as possible in transferring to paper the information we have been given and discovered through our own research.

We have not made assumptions nor have we made up pieces to fit the plot. We have, however, made one or two educated guesses where there is a good chance that the evidence surrounding a particular subject showed a high amount of probability.

Where possible we have tried to confirm individual memories with others to ensure accuracy.

Chapter 1
Pre-history and Plaitford Common
By Catherine Shutler (nee Hocking)

The earliest known settlement in Plaitford comes from the Mesolithic period. Mesolithic means 'middle Stone Age' 10,000BC - 4000BC, between 6,000 and 12,000 years. In 1965 a Mesolithic flint axe or adze head was discovered in a gravel washer at a gravel pit at The Slings, on the Plaitford side of the ford in Church/Giles Lane. The Axe Head was deposited with Southampton City Museum.
During the Mesolithic period, Britain was still joined to Europe until about 6500BC. The people of this period were nomadic, and plants and animals, other than dogs were yet to be domesticated.
Next we have Neolithic (new Stone Age), 4000-2200BC. Farming, new tools and pottery were introduced from Europe, and wooded areas were cleared to make fields for crops and animals. Large ceremonial monuments ceased to be built, and individual burials became more widespread.
The Neolithic period was followed by the Bronze Age, 2200-800BC. During this period tools, weapons and ornaments were made from an alloy of copper and tin – bronze. Most people occupied small farmsteads and cleared woodland to create field systems using low stone and earth walls. Plaitford's most prolific discovery of pre-history artifacts date from this period. Fragments of a Bronze Age dagger and shards of an urn with an eight inch (20cm) rim were also discovered in 1965 in a gravel washer at The Slings. These items were deposited with Southampton City Museum.
A Bronze Age hoard was discovered in a sandpit at Bowers Farm in 1928 and consisted of two twisted bronze neck torcs, one nine inches (23cm), the other seven an a half inches (19cm) in diameter and three sections of an eight and a quarter inch (21cm) decorative pin. Also found close to the bronze hoard were the shards of a complete Deverel-Rimsbury globular type pot and a two-pound (0.9kg) cylindrical clay loom weight. All the items found at Bowers Farm were deposited with Winchester Museum Service.
We continue this chapter with some interesting facts about Plaitford Common from pre-history to the twenty- first century. We start with more proof of a Mesolithic settlement with the discovery of Mesolithic tools during excavations for an Esso pipeline across the common in 1962. Over the years more discoveries of Bronze Age occupation have also been found on the common.

Bronze Age human cremations were buried beneath round barrows. Plaitford Common has at least two round barrows. One known as the "Plaitford Barrow" situated at grid reference SU 278185 was excavated by J.P Preston in 1929 and produced two Deverel-Rimbury Cremation urns. These urns can be seen in Salisbury Museum. The Barrow is quite elaborate for the New Forest area, and it is possible that the two urns contained the remains of a chieftain and his wife. The Landford Barrow near Sturtmoor pond was excavated at the same time and was found to have nineteen burials. No grave goods were found in either barrow. More possible barrows have been identified on the common but have not been excavated.

The Bronze Age was one of the first cultures to really leave their mark on the common. Many boiling mounds can still be found, one in particular is especially well preserved and you can clearly see where the trough is, as it still fills with water today. Boiling Mounds, found close to a water source, are a bit of a mystery. They were made to boil water by digging a 'trough' and lining it with wood and probably animal skins. The trough was then filled with water. A fire was then lit, and large flints were put into the fire to heat up. When they were hot enough, they would be put into the cold water in the trough. The water would then be heated by hot flint. Due to the sudden extreme temperature change, the flint would explode into much smaller pieces. These small pieces of burnt flint would be discarded next to the trough and eventually a mound of discarded flint would form, hence the term boiling mound. No one is sure what the water was used for. Theories include cooking, washing and other chores, or bathing. A sauna has also been suggested, and there would have been a hut over the top of the site. Another suggestion is for getting yeast activated for brewing beer! Burnt flint is easily recognizable. It is normally grey in colour and has a 'mosaic' pattern on it.

From the Bronze Age we move into the Iron Age, 800BC-43AD. Iron replaced bronze as the main metal. Most Iron Age Britons continued to live a rural life farming animals and growing crops in large communities or tribes, and field systems began to appear. There are some large and substantial banks on Plaitford Common that may form part of an Iron Age field system. The banks would have been topped with posts to make a boundary fence or a hedge.

After the Iron Age we see the Romans from AD43-410. In the 1st Century AD, the British Isles were populated by a variety of tribes living in scattered settlements led by Kings or Chiefs. In AD 43, a conquering Roman Army arrived on the south coast from Gaul (modern day France). This invasion began almost 400 years of

Roman rule. Rome controlled Britain by means of a civil administration headed by a governor, and backed up by a military army. In spite of the occasional rebellion, Britain was peaceful and prosperous for long periods. The Romans transformed British society, and the landscape. An extensive network of roads linked well-planned towns with water supplies. Large, well-furnished villas dotted the countryside. By AD 410, when the Romans abandoned Britain, the people had been introduced to a new way of life. That included new systems of government, literacy and two new religions, one in particular was Christianity. The Kellys Directories of the nineteenth century list Plaitford along with Landford as being Roman Settlements. Other than the reputed discovery of a Roman drain at Redhouse Farm in 1968, of which there appears to be no recorded evidence, Plaitford is devoid of any recorded Roman finds.

The New Forest area did have Roman Villas close by at Rockbourne and Downton, and also at East Dean. Roman potteries and kilns have also been found in the forest at Sloden and Linwood.

There is evidence of many ancient tracks ways that criss-cross the common. It is believed that a section of the Cloven Way runs across the common north of Deazle Wood. The Cloven Way is reputed to be the route Cerdic, the first King of Wessex (519-534), took from where he landed on the south coast at Eling to Old Sarum and beyond.

There are no obvious signs of settlement on the common, but it was definitely used by our ancestors, as we have seen with the field systems, burial mounds, boiling mounds and track ways. There is also the possibility of an animal pound. Traces of a bank with internal and external ditches are to be seen surrounding a natural hill on the northwestern part of the common.

The bank may have had posts in it to provide fencing. This is a rather unusual enclosure having ditches on either side. Normally, banks would have either external ditches for defensive purposes to keep things out, or internal ditches like an animal pound to keep things in. The enclosure in this case is likely to be medieval or before.

At the bottom of this hill, is a well. Again we are not too sure of its origins. It is not mentioned on any old map. Normally wells would be clearly identified.

This is where the common stops showing us what it has, and we now have to refer to documents, newspapers, photos and word of mouth. There are many more lumps, bumps and mysterious holes on the common for which there are no obvious explanations.

The Common from the eighteenth century

In 1790, [1]Geologist William Smith, the 'Godfather' of British Geology examined the soils and circumstances with the boring of coal in the New Forest, opposite the Shoe alehouse at Plaitford and 83 years later, on May 17 1873, the Hampshire Advertiser reported the following:

"COAL. - A number of men are now engaged in making excavations near the Shoe Inn, Plaitford, it being anticipated that coal is to be found there. Already the men have gone to a depth of nearly one hundred feet, and it is stated that some pieces of coal have been found, and being tested, burn exceedingly well. We trust the expectations of those carrying out the boring may be realised, and that a plentiful supply of "Black Diamonds" may be found"

It is recorded that in September 1872, approx. 4000 soldiers returning from the 'Autumn Maneuvers' camped on Plaitford Common for two days. They were heading back to barracks in Southampton, Gosport and Portsmouth. They couldn't all arrive home at once, and so they all left in their individual troops.

Sports were played regularly on the Common (see chapter 7 - Plaitford Races).

In 1877 it was proposed that the Common became an enclosure by the Earl of Ilchester, who owned the Manor of Plaitford. A belt of trees and a fence was to be put around it, and the use would be confined to the freeholders and fourteen life holders. A protest was held by Mr. Briscoe Eyre, Mr. Hunter (a solicitor) and others, who were representing the rights of the inhabitants of Plaitford, parts of Wellow and Landford, who used the Common to graze their livestock and had rights to collect firewood etc.

The people of Plaitford won the case, and thankfully the Common remained. If not, today may be a totally different story…

A modern feature of the landscape on Plaitford common is the National Grid electricity pylons that replaced pylons erected in 1932. Erected in 1965, they form part of the Nursling to Mannington line. They are known as the 4YB Super towers, with 400kv running through the wires! The pylons are tower numbers 83 - closest to Sturtmoor pond, 84 - in the middle of the common and 85 - stands in Plaitford Mire (bog). There are two further pylons in the parish of Plaitford, 86 – in the grounds of the nursery opposite the village hall and 87 - in Gore Copse on Pyesmead Farm.

Over the years since the pylons were erected, there have been many stories concerning vehicles disappearing into Plaitford Mire. They include a Landrover and a Fordson tractor. It is also said that one of the workers fell off the top of one of the towers. We have been unable to substantiate these rumours and we have spoken to two men who were involved with the towers in the 1960's and they don't recall any of these things happening.

There is also another story of a crawler tractor used in the erection of the original pylons in 1932 being lost. It is said that it had got stuck and was left overnight and by the following morning it had disappeared!

While we are on the subject of objects disappearing in boggy areas, it is also rumoured that an American army tank sank on Plaitford Common during the last war. However, we have found no evidence of this, and it is surprising just how many tanks supposedly disappeared in bogs all over the New Forest!!

There is a water pipe running across the common from Blacksmith's bog to the other side and on out towards Landford.

The Esso pipeline, from Fawley to Bristol also runs across Plaitford Common. For a period of five days in October 1970, two small flair stacks appeared on the common. The stacks were to burn off Ethylene Gas from the pipe line, which had to be removed by the Esso Petroleum Company to allow works to start in the latter end of 1971 on the Cadnam Section of the M27 South Coast Motorway.

[1]William Smith: Map of the Strata of England and Wales. John Phillips, 1844.

Ownership

The Common was part of Plaitford Manor, originally part of the Manors of West Grimstead and Minstead. After being passed through several generations of the de Grimstead, Berkley and Compton families, it was sold to Sir Stephen Fox in 1679. When he died in 1716, it passed to his son, Stephen, who was made the Earl of Ilchester in 1756. The Earls of Ilchester held title to Plaitford manor until it was sold in 1911. The Briscoe Eyre's bought the Common and in 1928, 136 acres were given to the National Trust, and in 1930, Mrs. Briscoe Eyre gave the remaining Common to the National Trust, totaling 460.543 acres. In 1934, Gerard Bonham-Carter (who Owned Barford Farm), gave 7 acres, known as Closed Copse, and Deazle Wood.

Today, Plaitford Common and Clayford Common are still in the ownership of the National Trust. The northern part of the common is also within the New Forest National Park Boundary. Although it is not Crown Land, it is an adjacent common. The common is a Site of Special Scientific Interest (SSSI).

Plaitford Common as part of the New Forest was fenced along the southern side of the A36 in the 1970s. Unfortunately this action put an end to animals roaming the village keeping the road side verges trimmed and in particular keeping the vegetation under control on the National Trust land on the opposite side of the main road. Readers who attended Plaitford School will remember the open green areas and the clear access to the back gate of the school. Over the past 40 years the area from Botleys ford to Border Garage has been neglected and is now just a jungle of brambles and silver birch trees.

The new forest including, Plaitford Common became a national park in 2005 and the A36 became the parks northern boundary.

Chapter 2
Domesday Survey 1086 to 1800

Plaitford or Pleiteford as it is spelt in the Domesday Survey (the name probably derives from the old English word for play "plega"). Therefore, the name Plaitford could mean a ford where play or sport took place.

The Domesday Survey of 1086 tells us that Edmund held Plaitford, this consisted of two virgates (approx. 60 acres) of ploughed land, a mill rendering 10 pence annual rent to the manor and woodland three furlongs long and three furlongs wide. One virgate was held by Algar prior to the Norman Conquest.

Edmond, a Saxon Noble and son of Aiulf, held West Grimstead at the time of the Survey. Aiulf was probably either the son or brother of Algar who held Plaitford in the reign of Edward the Confessor.

Plaitford was in the possession of a powerful family and was annexed to the Alderbury Hundred[2] though it is situated within the [1]Frustfield Hundred that included Bramshaw, Landford and Whiteparish.

Plaitford later became a member of the Manor of West Grimstead. The manor subsequently passed to the family de Grimstead who took their name from their chief manor at West Grimstead.

[1]Alderbury & Frustfield Hundred: Modern History of Wiltshire 1844.
[2]Hundreds were originally introduced by the Saxons as administration areas with enough land to sustain approximately 100 households.

The people of Pleiteford from the Great Domesday Book.

"Aelfhild; Aellic; Aethelwulf; Algar; Alweald; Alwig; Alwine; Asgot; Eadric; Eadric the Blind; Ealdhild; Aubrey de Coucy, Earl of Northumbria; Edgar the priest; Edmund; Edmund, son of Aethelwulf; Edward; Edward of Salisbury, the sheriff; Edwin; Erlking; Esbern; Father of Edward; Father of Godric the huntsmam; Father of Oda; Father of Osweard; Father of Saewulf; Father of Swein; Father of Thorkil; Father of Wulfnoth; Father of Wulfric; Foresters of King William; Gestr brother of Saeric; Gode; Godric; Godric the huntsman; Godwine; Godwine Clec; Grimbold the goldsmith; Hearding; Husband of Aelfhild; Husband of Ealdhild; Husband of Leofgyth; King Edward as lord; King William as landholder; Lang; Langa; Leofgyth; Lidhsman; Oda; Odolina; Ordweald; Osweard; Ragnburh; Saegifu; Saeric; Saeweard; Saewulf; Swein; Thorkil; Ulf; Wado; Wife of Wynsige; Wulfgeat; Wulfgeat the huntsman; Wulfnoth; Wulfric Waula; Wulfric the huntsman; Wulfweard; Wulfweard, the kings purveyor; Wynsige".

The manor of Plaitford was held by the King for the service of keeping the park of Melchet. It is thought that a medieval hunting lodge, probably built between 1250 and 1350, may have stood on an island surrounded by a moat opposite Manor Farm (not to be confused with the large lake to the left, towards the church, created in the 1980s). Small scale excavations from the moat have revealed $12^{th}/13^{th}$ century glazed pottery. Large boulders and flint nodules appear on the island and may represent part of the original fabric of a building. Two boulders near the thatched staddle barn opposite Manor Farm could indicate an entrance to the site or may be a result of farm buildings that stood in this area in the mid nineteenth century as indicated on the 1844 Tithe Survey map. This particular site, one of very few to have survived in Hampshire, is recognized as a Scheduled Monument and protected as such by English Heritage.

It is most likely the de Grimstead family would have kept a presence in Plaitford. From the following tax list of 1322, John son of Andrew de Grymstede is recorded as paying the highest figure in tax. Did he occupy a property at the moat site?

A tax list for Pleytford in the year 1332, in the reign of Edward III:
"John Alisaundra eight shillings; William Russel five shillings; William la Bone twelve pence; Richard Roddoke eighteen pence; Richard la Frere twelve pence; Michael Ballarde twelve pence; Richard Bawden eight pence; John le Clerke two shillings; Benet Ballarde eight pence; William Kubbel twelve pence; Michael la bone twelve pence; Richard Alwyne two shillings; Richard Payn two shillings; William Russel three shillings and four pence; Thomas Arnalde four shillings; John son of Andrew de Grymstede six shillings and eight pence."

The de Grimstead family held title to Plaitford manor until 1361 when John de Grimstead died leaving his title to Reginald Perot, son of Isobel, sister of Adam de Grimstead, John's father. Reginald died in 1370 and was succeeded by his infant son Ralph. In 1406, Ralph Perot released all claim to Sir John de Berkley.

It would appear that for a short period in 1361, Plaitford Manor became separated from West Grimstead as follows:

Before his death, in 1361, John de Grimstead granted a reversion of the manor of West Grimstead after the death of Eleanor, the widow of his grandfather, to John de Batteshorn. The manor of Plaitford was apparently not included, although the same year John de Batteshorn was pardoned for acquiring lands in Plaitford. The fact that Plaitford was a member of West Grimstead seems to have led to some confusion. In 1402, Sir John de Berkley, who had married Elizabeth,

John de Batteshorn's daughter, claimed lands and tenements in Plaitford, appurtenant to his manor in West Grimstead. Sir John de Berkley did not finally acquire the manor of Plaitford until 1406. From that time, the manor followed the same descendants as that of the Manor of Minstead until 1679, when it was sold by Richard Compton to Sir Stephen Fox.

Sir Stephen Fox was born in Farley near Salisbury on 27 March 1627 to William and Elizabeth Fox, daughter of Thomas Pavey of Plaitford.

Sir Stephen Fox 1627-1716
The text below the portrait reads:
The Right Hon[our]able S[i]r Stephen Fox Kn[igh]t. Domestic Servant to King Charles ye 2ᵈ during his Exile & one of the Lord Commissioners of ye Treasury for 22 years in his s[ai]d Maj[es]ties & three successive reigns.
Aged 75 Anno [Domini] 1701.

Sir Stephen was present with the royalist army at the battle of Worcester during the civil war (1642-1649). He later accompanied King Charles II in his exile to the continent and had charge of all the expenses of the royal household. Knighted in 1665, Sir Stephen had three terms as Member of Parliament for Salisbury 1661, 1685 and 1713. He died in 1716 and in his will he bequeathed £10 to each of the villages of Plaitford, West Grimstead and Whaddon to support the poor. It is his distinction to have founded Chelsea hospital and to have contributed £13,000 in aid of this laudable public work. Unlike other statesmen of his day, he grew rich in the service of the nation without being suspected of corruption, and without forfeiting the esteem of his contemporaries. He was twice married (1651 and 1703) and by his first wife, Elizabeth Whittle, he had seven sons, who predeceased him, and three daughters. By his second wife, Christiana Hope, he had two sons and two daughters. The elder son by the second marriage, Stephen (1704-1776), was created Lord Ilchester and Stavordale in 1747 and Earl of Ilchester in 1756. In 1758, he took the additional name of Strangeways. The Earls of Ilchester held title to the manor until 1911 when it was split up and sold by the 6th Earl. It is important to note that the grandmother of the first Earl of Ilchester, Elizabeth Fox, nee Pavey, came from Plaitford and the dynasty continues today with Robin Maurice Fox–Strangeways, 10th Earl of Ilchester, born 1942.

The oldest detailed map of the Manor of Plaitford we have found was produced in 1729. The map forms part of a detailed survey carried out for the Hon. Stephen Fox, later to become the 1st Earl of Ilchester. We have managed to find buildings indicated on the map in the area of a building that still exist today, they are:

Bowers Farmhouse, Bridgefoot Farmhouse, Sweet Briar Cottage (formerly Gardeners Farmhouse), Gunsfield Cottage, Holly Cottage, Manor Farmhouse, Meadow Cottage (formerly Bowles Farmhouse), Pickernals Farmhouse, Redhouse Farmhouse, Shoe Cottage, The Drove, The Milestone and the thatched part of The Shoe Inn. Because of their age, there is a very good chance that the properties today are the same or part of the structures shown on the 1729 survey map. More details on the 1729 survey can be found in chapter's 10, Plaitford Farms and 11, Cottages and Houses.

A mill existed at Plaitford at the time of the Domesday Survey and is mentioned again in 1338-9. It was thought until recently that no further reference could be found. With the help of the Isle of Wight Record Office, two documents, a lease and release between John Harcourt-Powell Snr and John Harcourt-Powell Jnr (landowners) and

James White, both dated November 1812, include land and a water mill in the parish of Plaitford. A rough location for the mill is on the Plaitford bank of the River Blackwater, upstream towards Landford, near the ford in Giles Lane.

John Harcourt-Powell Jnr came from a long line of landowners in Landford, Plaitford and West Wellow. The first references are William and Rice Powell in May 1664, Thomas Powell, August 1706 to May 1716 and Simon, Lord Harcourt in 1716 and Harcourt-Powell from around 1776. Most of the land they owned in Plaitford was around the area of Powells Farm on Plaitford Common and Hobbs Copse Farm, just into Landford to the left of Sherfield English Road. On the 1842 Tithe Award Map for Plaitford, John Harcourt-Powell Jnr still held land in the area of Powells Farm. A notice in the Hampshire Advertiser of April 19 1873 advertised an auction to be held in May of that year. The property, a Small Freehold Estate, in the ownership of Thomas Harcourt-Powell, with frontage to the Salisbury and Southampton turnpike and the highway from Plaitford to Sherfield, comprised approximately 83 acres. This would appear to be the last mention of the Harcourt-Powell family in Plaitford.

The Pembrokeshire Powell family made various astute marriages and ended up with extensive property in sixteen English counties and in Pennsylvania USA. The Harcourt and later the Harcourt-Powell family seat was Drinkstone Park in the county of Suffolk from 1518 to 1867.

During the seventeenth century, Stephen March (1617) and later Lewis March, both of Shambler (Newport) on the Isle of Wight owned property in Landford, Plaitford and West Wellow. In 1664, some property was sold to William and Rice Powell. In 1671, Mary Powell of Pembroke in Wales, spinster, is mentioned and by 1682, Lewis March and his wife Mary (possibly Mary Powell) had moved to Pembroke, the home of the Powell family. Between 1694 and 1716, it would appear that Mary March, now a widow, transferred title of her remaining property in this area to the Powell family.

In 1549, during the reign of Edward VI, two uprisings occurred. Firstly, against the enclosure of land and involved the most common protest of "throwing down the hedges". Secondly, the introduction of the Book of Common Prayer. The unrest occurred throughout the country with two major rebellions in Devon (the Western Rising) and Norfolk (Ketts Rebellion). For their involvement in the rebellion in October 1549, nine rebels including [1]Thomas Richardson, a clerk from Plaitford were imprisoned in the Tower of London. All were presumably interrogated at length and beside the name of each prisoner the letter *J* was inscribed. The mark would seem to imply that each man was indited, tried and perhaps executed, but only evidence of one execution out of the nine has survived: that of Robert Bell who was hung, drawn and quartered at Tyburn on the 10 February 1550. Four of the nine were released from the tower in April 1550. There is no record as to the fate of Thomas Richardson.

[1]Thomas Richardson: Rebellion and Riot (Popular Disorder in the reign of Edward VI). Barrett L. Beer, 2005

Chidiock Wardour, 1542-1611, first son of William Wardour of Plaitford and Mary, daughter of Edward Bampfield of Poltimore, Devon was a member of Parliament with a family seat at Plaitford and a second constituency in Lugershaw to which he was elected in 1593. From 1570 he held the office of Clerk of the Pells (rolls of parchment) in the Exchequer, and was also a Middlesex J.P. On two occasions in 1588 and 1602, he petitioned Queen Elizabeth I for parity between his position as official responsible for the rolls of receipts and issues and that of writers of the tallies. The first failed but the second was successful. He was buried at Chiswick church in London.

A mystery to recent generations of local residents has been the origin of the name of [1]Botley's or Botly's ford. The ford across the stream that marks the Wilts/Hants border can be crossed when entering Plaitford Common from Sherfield English Road. A recent discovery of a survey map of Plaitford Manor, produced in 1729, for the Hon. Stephen Fox Esq, shows Botleys Lane running from Sherfield English Road, through the ford towards Powells Farm. A search through the wills of Plaitford residents has shown that the name Botley appears quite regularly from the late sixteenth to the early eighteenth century. The earliest mention is of a Father Botley in the will of William Rolffe of Plaitford in 1573. There is a gravestone in Plaitford Churchyard to a William Botly who died March 28 1703 aged 53 years. In 1727, another William Botley held a lease to land in Plaitford. From 1785 to 1890, various people leased a property in Plaitford known as Botley's. There appears to be no further record of the name Botley after 1727 and certainly not after 1785 when the lease went to a Richard Goodden.

Interestingly, the 1844 Tithe Survey for Plaitford makes no reference to Botley's, The Tithe Survey map does, however, indicate a pound for animals on the Plaitford side of the stream.

Two pieces of land, Botley's and Lower Botley's are indicated on the 1840 tithe map for Landford under the ownership of John Harcourt

Powell and leased by James Cocks, landlord of the Shoe Inn. They were situated on the right of Sherfield English Road, between "Botleys Lane" and Bridgefoot Cottages.

From the Wellow Register for 5 July 1596, Joane Botley married Summers Shanson and 2 December 1604, Milisent Hutchens married Wyliam Botley. There is also an entry of a baptism of John Botly on 11 November 1638 and a burial of "Mrs." Botley 1638.

[1]Botley or Botly: Ilchester Estate Archive, Dorset History Centre

The 1700's saw the increased popularity of coach travel. The Shoe Inn became an important posting inn and in 1753, the Sarum and Eling Turnpike trust came into operation allowing for a toll to be paid by road users towards the maintenance of the turnpike. More on the turnpike can be found in the chapter on the Shoe Inn.

Something amusing to end this chapter from the Salisbury and Winchester Journal, Monday 8 September 1788: *"Last Tuesday Rachel Martin, of Plaitford, was committed to Fisherton Gaol, by the sitting Justices at the **Parade Coffee-house**, for neglecting to work up certain woolen materials, which had been delivered to her; and for suffering herself to be employed by another master before she had completed her said work."*

Rachel Martin, daughter of Thomas and Anne, was baptised in Plaitford on 24 January 1762. Baptism records show that she had three children out of wedlock: Ann, baptised 15 May 1785, John, born on 28 October 1787 baptised 11 November (Bastardy Order states this child was a female! and the father was John Humby, labourer of Plaitford) and Hannah, born 08 December 1790 and baptised 26 December (the father was Thomas Williams of Plaitford). Rachel lived until her 70th year. She died in Wellow and was buried at Plaitford on 16 September 1832.

Chapter 3
St Peter's Church

Many early documents refer to St Peter's as a Church. It was in fact a Chapel attached to West Grimstead until Plaitford became a rectory in its own right in1866.

St Peter's church, with its external flint walls and ironstone quoins, consists of a south vestry, west gallery, and north porch and west bell turret. The church was built in the middle of the thirteenth century and restored in 1856. Some of the original thirteenth century features are still visible, which includes the chamfered pointed doorway, the chancel and nave, the piscina (a shallow basin for washing communion vessels) and sedile (priest's seat) on the south side of the sanctuary. The south vestry appears to have been a small chapel and contains the only original window, which faces south. The font is a modern restoration from part of a thirteenth century font. As well as the north door there was a corresponding south door, behind the organ, now blocked up. At the back of the sedile a number of medieval floor tiles were set in the wall during the restoration in 1856. There are seven different designs including one on the top right, which was also found at the Royal Palace at Clarendon, near Salisbury and is dated from about 1250. This may suggest the date of the church construction. Until the restoration the tiles were set in the floor. Sir Richard Colt Hoare of Stourehead, writing in 1835, speaks of them as *"some old painted tiles in the pavement"*, adding that they *"indicate a better state of things from former times"*, a comment which suggests that the building was in poor repair in the second quarter of the 19th century.

A churchwarden's presentment by Richard Russell dated 3 January 1631 in preparation for the Archdeacons Visitation, reports that the church is in a very poor state of repair. He states that the roof, probably thatched, is in decay and the timbers in the belfry are rotten. The ingress of rain through the roof is decaying the main wall. Water has been getting into the porch and the church for four or five years. The doors are rotten, the windows and the pavements in the church are in decay. He also mentions that there is no bearer fit to carry the dead to church. Richard Russell, husbandman lived in Plaitford and died in 1659.

Donald A. Spaeth mentions in his book The Church in an Age of Danger. Parsons and Parishioners 1660-1740:

'An incident in Plaitford in the early eighteenth century demonstrates the difficulties parishioners might encounter in scheduling a funeral,

when the minister insisted for reasons of personal convenience upon performing the burial in the same day that he came to the parish or chapelry to read divine service.

The resulting misunderstanding offended both Lay and Clerical properties and might lead to worsening of relations between them. William Richman of Plaitford, died one Saturday in October 1713, and his friends and relatives planned his funeral the following Tuesday, to give them time to enough to get a coffin and to make other arrangements. When the parish clerk notified the rector of West Grimsread, John Foot, of the funeral at prayers the following day, Foot expressed his displeasure at these plans. He refused to come on Tuesday to perform the funeral, telling the parish clerk 'that since they had not brought him to be buried on that day being Sunday, they might get someone else to bury the said corpse'. On Tuesday Richman's body was never the less carried to the chapel yard at Plaitford to be interred, accompanied by 'the greatest part of the parishioners'. Foot was not there 'to do his duty' and since the parishioners had not found anyone to replace him, the body had to be left in the chapel for two days until the minister next visited Plaitford. When he finally came, the minister performed the funeral quickly, instructing that the body be carried to the grave without first reading the church service. Only six people including the widow and parish clerk were able to attend the funeral. Foot's behavior offended lay sensibilities in several respects. His absence meant the body had to be left for two nights in the chapel, after neighbours would have ensured that the deceased was attended during final sickness and after death. His unexpected arrival meant that most of the parish was unable to attend the hastily arranged funeral, violating the social nature of the ceremony. Foots omission of sections of the funeral service did not escape the notice of the parish clerk'

A case of brawling in Plaitford Church appeared before the Episcopal Consistorial court of Sarum in the autumn of 1755. Stephen Whitlock of Plaitford was excommunicated and condemned in expenses (fined) for attacking John Petty of Plaitford during a service in the church on Sunday 21 September.

John Bullar on a tour round Southampton, visited St Peter's in 1801, he wrote: '*The church is a scarce half a mile from the road. It is an ancient structure principally built with flints; and consists only of a nave and chancel; excepting a pew on the south side, long since erected to accommodate a parishioner of consequence. The wall is decorated with awkward daubings intended to represent the baptism of Christ and his ascension. Between them in large letters, is*

inscribed, "This seat was erected by Thomas Pavy, for the yous (use)
*of Sir Stephen Fox and family." The other pews are ancient, as also
is the font. At the west end, part of the pavement is decorated with
curious bricks, each about five inches square, ornamented with
devices in white. Some of these appear to represent a fox and goat,
with a fleur-de-lis between them, supporting a coat-of-arms, but is
too small to preserve, in such kind of work, distinctness in the figures.
On several are a fox and a cock; on others a man in armour,
attacking a beast. No inscription is to be seen; nor, is there a single
monument in the church.*

*These armorial bearings are most probably connected with the name
Fox. Sir Stephen Fox, in consideration for his good and faithful
service, had a special grant to him and his heirs, from Charles II, to
bear, in their coat-of-arms, a fleur-de-lis in a canton* (division of a
shield). *This is still to be seen in the arms of the Earl of Ilchester and
Lord Holland who are descended from Sir Stephen Fox'.*

As mentioned above, extensive repairs and improvements took place
in 1856. According to the Church Wardens accounts 1855-1904, at
the April Vestry meeting in 1855 it was agreed that a tax of four
pennies in the pound was to be levied against all the parishioners of
Plaitford to help pay for the forthcoming repairs. The total tax
collected was six pound eleven shillings and four pence half penny
The work was carried out by John and James Petty of West Wellow
and took several months and involved putting in drainage around the
church, retiling the whole roof and belfry, placing two stone steps in
the chancel, concreting part of chancel and aisle, raising the west end
and tiling with red and black 6in tiles. Other work included raising
the vestry floor and fitting a door, new step and paving to south
doorway, repair to the door and stone dressings. Wooden floors on
brick foundations and seats (pews) were installed. A new oak north
door was fitted and stone dressings to the doorway. In the account
from John and James Petty they mention new stone quoins for repair
to the porch walls along with new paving and roof tiles. This would
indicate that the porch[1] was of an earlier build and not erected as part
of these improvements as previously recorded. The cost of the work
carried out by the Petty's was £178.8s.2p (equivalent to £14,000 at
today's rates). The account does not appear to mention materials
used. A newspaper report on the reopening of the church mentions
Messrs Petty as the contractors responsible for the improvements.
They may well have invoiced the materials separately. The church
reopened on Sunday 16 November 1856 with a service by the Rev.

Thomas Morse. The Earl of Ilchester munificently contributed (donated money) towards the cost of the restoration.

[1]History of Modern Wiltshire, Colt Hoar 1837, mentions a porch of wooden construction.

In July 1856, the Rev. Morse sought license from the Bishop of Salisbury to use the National School Room for the performance of Devine Service and the Administration of Holy Sacraments during such time as the chapel was closed for repairs.

The south doorway and door, renovated in 1856, was later blocked off. We can find no mention of when or why this work was carried out. We have, however, found an entry in the Church Warden accounts 1855-1904 for June 1900 where a sum of seven pound three shillings was paid to William Trodd for various repairs to the church including a repair of the church wall. We know from the Victoria County History, The History of the County of Hampshire that the south door had been blocked sometime before the volume was published in 1911. After also checking the Church Warden accounts 1904-1967, the payment entry to William Trodd was one of only two large payments made by the Church Wardens between 1855 and 1911. The other was for a shed built by W. Petty in 1883, see later in this chapter.

It is recorded in 1863 that the church had a harmonium that had been tuned by Mr. Chiznell at a cost of seven shillings and six pence.

The gallery at the west end dates from the late eighteenth century or early nineteenth century and has its original pews. Traces of early wall paintings can be found on either side of the gallery. In October 1971, a structural report on the gallery floor, requested by the then Rector, the Rev. Paul Bunday, advised that the gallery was only suitable for a maximum of ten persons, well distributed and that a "restricted use" notice should be displayed. The gallery was subsequently strengthened.

The organ, installed in 1967, of which there are only two known examples, was made by Flight and Robinson and dates from about 1830. The organ replaced the harmonium, installed in1924 that stood below the altar to the left of the vestry door.

Church Organists

Margaret Hart still continues to play the church organ at services as she has done since moving to the village in 1969. We have managed to list some of her predecessors: 1896-1903 Joseph Griffin (ST[1]); 1903-1914 John Travis Holmes (ST); 1914-1921 Mrs. Mary Eliza Holmes (ST); 1922-1941 Mrs. Creeth (ST), Miss H Brooke, Lena Hutchings, R Scurlock, Miss Fancourt; 1942-1948 Miss Fanstone,

Mr. Pinder, Miss Dyer, Miss Turner (ST), Mr. Scurlock; 1950's Mrs. Doris Hawker, Mrs. Willoughby and c1958-1972 Miss Brightmore.

¹ST = School Teacher at Plaitford School.

The east window, showing St. Peter, St. Paul and Christ the good shepherd, was made by Lavers, Barraud and Westlake in the 1870's. Plaitford's war memorial is represented by a plaque on the south wall and commemorates three Plaitford men who fell in the Great War, 1914-1918. They are Robert Vincent Bowles and brothers John and James Simmonds.

Electricity was connected to the church in 1955 and central heating installed in 1965.

In June 1965, a Priest's desk and chair were presented to the church in memory of Sidney, Amabel and Susanna Simmons of Plaitford house for their service to the Parish by their nephew Lt. Col. J.T Palmer.

In 1979, the area under the gallery was converted to provide an area for the Sunday school.

The Horizon Parish Magazine for July 1999 reports of the acquisition of an oak registry table to commemorate the new Millennium.

The church had a further upgrade in 2005/6, with the addition of a small kitchen area under the gallery, and a single toilet was built outside with disabled access and baby changing facility.

Exterior of the church.

On the outside below the triple stepped lancet window on the east side, there is evidence of a 17th century stepped brick plinth.

A hand written note in the memoranda at the back of the parish register, 1715-1812, states, *'A new roof erected unto the parish church of Plaitford in the year 1784'*

In the same volume there is also a mention that, *'Wheat was so dear in 1795 it sold for twelve shillings and sixpence per bushel and in 1800 it was one pound'*. Entries were made by William Newell, Churchwarden.

In June 1883, W. Petty erected a new building at the rear of the church for the accommodation of the bier etc. (A bier is a cart for transporting the dead to church). He also fitted a new window blind at the west end of the church. All for the sum of six pound nineteen shillings. It is thought this shed later stored fuel for the heating stoves.

At the Easter Vestry meeting in 1900 the question of re-tiling the church roof, which was in a very bad state, was discussed. Subscriptions were sought and by February 1901 the sum of

£32.18s.9p was collected from parishioners and friends of the church. It would appear the work was carried out as a later document entitled 'Plaitford Memorial Lamps Account' dated 24 October 1902 shows a Balance from the Church Roof of nine shillings and seven pence in the receipt column. The Memorial Lamps mentioned no longer exist and no record has been found that mentions the quantity or for what reason they were being purchased. The date would indicate that they were probably in memory of Queen Victoria. In photographs from around the turn of the nineteenth and twentieth century there is a white lamp sitting in the top of the arch over the church gate. This may have been one of the lamps in question.

At the Easter Vestry meeting on 27 April 1905 the Rector, the Rev. Roberts, warmly thanked the churchwardens for their help with the new eastern extension of the churchyard, which was given by the Earl of Ilchester and Mrs. Fryer. He also stated that it would soon be ready for consecration which took place on Sunday 6 August and was carried out by the Lord Bishop of Salisbury.

The spire and belfry was re-built in1958 at a cost of £614 and is smaller than the previous with a less ornate spire. The original had a larger square section below an octagonal spire and had six arched vents on each side. The new version has large louvre vents on three sides. Photographs from the early 20th Century show the original spire topped with a cross set in a diamond shape

Photographed before the first war the earlier more ornate belfry and spire can be seen and one of the memorial lamps purchased in 1902 is shown set into the top of the metal arch over the church gate.

An earlier black iron weather vane showing a cockerel above a banner inscribed 1744 had hung in the church for many years but was stolen in 1987.

Five years after the spire and belfry was rebuilt, J.W. Gray & Son Ltd, Salisbury successfully tendered to replace 46 of the spire shingles, damaged by woodpeckers. The tender dated August 1963 was for £37.0s.0p. The woodpeckers didn't appear to take the hint as in 2005 the wooden shingles (tiles) on the spire were again replaced. A quotation from Hall, Wardle & Sons, Ltd, Roofing Contractors, Bournemouth dated 19 July 1965, would indicate that the roof was again in need of repair. The figure quoted to re-felt, batten and retile the complete roof was £571.12s.6p. To replace defective lead would be extra.

The ornate semi-circular wrought iron arch over the entrance gate at one time contained a lamp that sat in the square section at the top.

Plaitford was a chapelry annexed to the church of West Grimstead until 1866, when it was declared a rectory in the gift of the Earl of Ilchester. The advowson (the right of nominating a clergyman to a vacant position) seems to have passed with the manor until 1361, when it was sold with the manor of West Grimstead by John de Grimstead to John de Batteshorn, who died in 1399, when it passed to his daughter Elizabeth wife of Sir John de Berkley. Sir John acquired the manor in 1406, and the decent of the advowson from that time was identical with that of the manor.

The decision to separate Plaitford from West Grimstead appears to have been decided as early as 1855, the year before the church was renovated. In a letter from the Bishop of Salisbury to Lord Ilchester dated February 1855, the Bishop advises that the separation of the Chapelry of Plaitford from West Grimstead can be affected without much cost (about £25) or delay. He mentions that the effect of the separation would mean that Plaitford would need a house (Rectory). The bishop finishes his letter as follows: '*This Chapelry has been connected with W'Grimstead from the earliest of time – in the taxation of Pope Nicholas AD 1288 so be it subordinate to West Grimstead.*'

At the time that Plaitford was made a Rectory in 1866, the Rev. James Barton, then Curate, became Rector and resided in the new rectory in Pound Lane that was completed in 1865. In 1871, the Rev Alfred Gay became the first fully appointed Rector.

Plaitford's independence only lasted fifty-one years. After the departure of The Rev. Hulme in 1917 the dioceses decided, much to the annoyance of the local people, that Plaitford should share a parson with Landford. According to tradition, the bishop of Salisbury, after taking tea at Landford Rectory, suggested that he and the new incumbent should walk across the fields to the induction service at Plaitford. When they arrived they had to make their way to an empty church between two rows of irate Plaitford parishioners who expressed their indignation by shaking their fists as the bishop and new rector passed by.[2]

The new rector was the Rev. Herbert Montague Davies and although he took on the roll as Plaitford rector in 1917, a United Benefice of Landford and Plaitford did not come into operation until 1924. Almost 60 years later in 1983, an order for the creation of the new United Benefice of Bramshaw and Landford with Plaitford was established.

[2]Stephen Ings, Hampshire Magazine, August 1981.

The 1842 Tithe Award map for Plaitford shows glebe land owned by the church as being the churchyard, close and barn, an arable field of just over two acres, and Parsonage Mead, a meadow of just over three acres. These two pieces of land were just beyond the church, alongside the road on the left and now belong to Manor Farm. This land is also mentioned in a Churchwarden's Church Glebe Terrier (boundary of private land) of 1608 that mentions four acres or thereabouts bounded by the highway on the north side, farm meadow on the south side, church litton (graveyard) on the east side and farm barton (buildings) on the west side. Another terrier from 1704/5 mentions a two room dwelling house and garden with a barn and stable and two fields adjoining consisting of five acres. In 1785, a small brick and thatched dwelling house with garden adjoining glebe land of four and half acres. Today, we do not know where the dwelling house stood. The field known as Close and Barn may indicate a possible position of its location. The 1844 tithe map positions the barn close to the road at the Manor Farm end of the field.

Over the years other property and land have been owned by and bequeathed to the church. Sydney and Evelyn Cottages on the A36 were built by the Rev. Alfred Gay, rector of Plaitford 1871-1899, and named after two of his children. Evelyn Cottage still belongs to the church. Others were Forest View and Lavender Cottage, both on Plaitford Common and the allotment gardens that later became Purley Way.

The churchyard contains the usual cluster of family graves containing many generations of names that are sadly no longer associated with Plaitford.

The oldest known gravestones are those of William Botly, who died on 28 March 1703 aged 53 years and Jane, wife of Richard Gauntlett, who died 19 November 1710 aged 73 years.

In the hope of finding an ancient yew tree, we measured the large yew opposite the church door to try to determine its age. The girth measured 3.7 metres at 1.3 metres above root level. Unlike most other trees, the yew does not conform to any regular growth pattern. Yew trees are exceptionally slow growing and may have periods of dormancy as they become very old. We have found many growth charts online that all appear to use the following formula: for example, a yew tree with a girth of 3 metres will be 242 years old, 4 metres – 292 years and 5 metres – 700 years. All figures are given as approximations. Using these charts we have calculated Plaitford's tree to be anything between 270 and 300 years old. This would tie in with the earliest graves marked 1703 and 1710 and the earliest church records. Another small yew stands on the northern edge of the eastern end of the graveyard. We think this tree was planted in 1905 when this part of the churchyard was extended and consecrated in August of that year.

A visitor to the churchyard in 1826 wrote in The Times newspaper that there were 28 tombstones. The inscriptions on many of them were not legible, but on those that were, there were inscribed the names and ages of 14 individuals, whose united years amount to 1,121, or an average of 80 years.

The Rectory later Plaitford House

Built in 1865, the rectory in Pound Lane was occupied by the rectors of Plaitford for fifty one years from 1866 to 1917. During this time only five rectors lived in the rectory James Barton 1866-1870; Alfred Henry Gay 1871-1899; Richard Roberts 1899-1908; Guy S Whitaker 1909-1914 and Walter S Hulme 1915-1917.

The 1901 census, records Elsie Albury a domestic servant aged eighteen working at the rectory. At the time her parents were living in Landford but her place of birth is recorded on the census as the Falkland Islands, South Atlantic. The next census in 1911 records her younger sister Phoebe as cook. She was also born on the Faulkland Islands and is recorded as a British subject by parentage. A further look at the same census we found her parents David and Emma

Albury living next door at Plaitford Rectory Lodge. David was employed as a groom.

After The Rev. Hulme left in 1917, the rectory ceased to be a residence for the rectors or Plaitford. The property was rented out by Salisbury Diocese until February 1924. An auction notice in the Western Gazette on 1 February 1924 describes the property as follows:

"A WELL-BUILT FREEHOLD RESIDENCE
Knows As PLAITFORD RECTORY
Together with Pleasure Grounds and Gardens, Garage, Stabling, Lodge and Pasture Lands embracing a total of about 6acres 3rod 24perch."

The notice went on to say that the tenant had given notice to quit expiring on 22 February and the auction was to take place at the British Legion Club in Salisbury on 25 February 1924. A further notice in the Western Gazette dated 29th February records - *"The bidding failed to reach the moderate reserve. The property has, however, since been disposed of at a satisfactory figure."*

We think the tenants mentioned may have been James and Henrietta Curtis as they are recorded on the 1922 and 1923 electoral rolls as living at the rectory. The 1925 electoral roll records the first mention of the property as Plaitford House with the Rev. Roberts[1] and family living there. He may have been the person who purchased the property in1924? In 1927, brother and sister Sidney and Susanna Simmons were living in the house. They were later joined by their sister, Amabel, and they continued to live in Plaitford House until the early 1960s. During the Second World War, the house was used as the Air Raid Precautions (ARP) headquarters and the First Aid centre for Plaitford. First Aid training was given at the house to residents from the local area by Susanna Simmons. William and Mary Yeo lived at Plaitford House from c1967 to the 1990s. During this time Plaitford Art Gallery and art restoration business was run from the house.

[1]Not the Rev. Roberts 1899-1908 he died in 1908.

Sunday school

The earliest Sunday school recorded in Plaitford comes from the House of Commons papers of 1835 that included the '1833 Abstract of Education Returns'. It mentions:

One Sunday school (commenced 1823) of 14 males and 13 females, is supported by subscription'.

In the early 1900's, Sunday school was held in the Rectory School at the rectory in Pound Lane and was conducted by the Rev. and Mrs. Roberts.

A reference to the school room at the rectory can be found on the inside front cover of the 1904-1968 Church Warden Accounts for Plaitford. A statement written by the Rev. Guy Whitaker rector of Plaitford 1909-1914 and dated 20 September 1916:

"Having paid the late Rev. Roberts for the furniture viz. 4 iron wood desks and two wooden forms and for the fixtures, viz. 2 fire grates and wooden shelves in small room in the school-room adjoining the stables at Plaitford Rectory and having received nothing from the Rev. W.S Hulme, the above mentioned furniture and fixtures are my property, and I hereby give and bequeath them to the churchwardens of St Peter's, Plaitford for the use of the parish". The statement was signed by Guy Whitaker, late Rector of Plaitford and churchwardens, Charles E Brooke and Ernest C Bowles.

A footnote mentions that Sydney Simmons purchased the items in March 1935 for three pounds. Sidney Simmons lived at Plaitford House, formerly the rectory, with his sisters, Susanna and Amabel. From the late 1920's to the late 1940's, Sunday school was held at Plaitford House with Miss Susie Simmonds in charge.

A conversion of the area under the gallery at the west end of the church took place in 1979 to make a suitable area for the Sunday school and other meetings.

Sunday school outings took place until the mid 1980's and we have found an early report in the Romsey Advertiser of one that took place in September 1905:

'A Sunday school treat to Bournemouth was arranged by the Rev. Roberts. Mr. Brooke and Mr. Hurst provided "Wagon" transport to and from Totton where a train was caught to Bournemouth. Shops, gardens, trams and sand were the attractions. Inspector Hood, a native of Plaitford, provided their tea at the "Quadrant". Everyone went home highly delighted for the glorious day out although it was rather showery'.

In the 1950's, Miss Hedges, Sunday school teacher and the Rector the Rev. Freeman arranged Sunday school outings to Bognor Regis, Hayling Island and Swanage with as many as three coaches travelling, come rain or shine!

The 1970's and 80's saw annual Sunday school outings to Sandbanks arranged by Gwen Bowles. The coach belonging to Red Rufus Coaches and driven by Elrad Matthews was always full. The last outing took place in 1986.

Rectors or West Grimstead and Plaitford:

1306 William de Budesden; 1315 Andrew de Grymstede;
1349 Thomas Goyn; 1352 Lamburt de Threkyngham; 1379 Robert
Bartalot; 1382 Thomas Englys; 1399 John Fysshere; 1401 John
Wyltuneshurst; 1404 Thomas Wardecopp & John Colefote;
1416 Richard Huphulle; 1418 John Hasard; 1420 Henry Walbrond;
1450 Richard Curteys; 1476 John Moren; 1479 Robert Swyfte;
1508 John Brockersby; 1519 Gul Bowman; 1552 John Billinge; 1608
Richard Wall; 1625 Edward Hyde de Bosbombe; 1630 William
Barlow; 1637 Edward Hyde;1666 Richard Page; 1679 John Foot;
1717 Thomas Reading; 1741 John Field; 1763 James Lewis; 1768
Neville Wells; 1801 John Griffith; 1817-1855 Henry Strangeways;
1855-1864 Thomas Daniel Cox-Morse;1864 William Edward
Brendon[1].

[1]Appointed in August 1864 died in October the same year.

Rectors of Plaitford from 1866:

1866-1870 James Barton[1]; 1871-1899 Alfred Henry Gay[2];
1899-1908 Richard Roberts; 1909-1914 Guy S Whitaker; 1915-1917
Walter S Hulme.

[1]James Barton was Curate from 1865. He became Rector when Plaitford became a rectory in its own right in 1866. He was suspended for abusive behavior in 1871. For more information see chapter 5, Nineteenth Century.
[2]Alfred Gay was the first fully appointed rector of Plaitford.

Rectors of Landford and Plaitford: [1]

1917-1945 Herbert Montague Davies[2]; 1945-1952 William Walters;
1953-1965 Shirley Becket-Freeman[3]; 1966-1976 Paul Bunday; 1976
1981 Ben Elliott.

[1]The two parishes became a United Benefice in 1924.
[2]Rector of Landford he took on Plaitford after Walter Hulme and continued to live at Landford Rectory
[3]Shirley Becket Freeman killed his wife in 1988. For full report see chapter 12, Twentieth Century.

Rectors of Bramshaw Landford and Plaitford: [1]

1981-1987 Harry chant; 1987-2004 Derek Clacey; 2004-present
David Bacon.

[1]The three parishes became a United Benefice in 1983. Bramshaw rectory became the residence of the Rector

Chapter 4
The Shoe Inn & the Sarum to Eling Turnpike

This age-old inn today stands proud alongside the busy A36 Salisbury to Southampton trunk road. The original thatched property now stands at the rear and would have fronted the road, which is now the gravel track running behind the existing building.

It is very difficult to date the original thatched part of the inn. Legend has it that it dates back to the early fifteenth century. We have found no evidence of this. We can possibly obtain a rough date from the construction of Shoe Cottage, the thatched cottage that stands to the left of the inn. It would appear that the chimney on this cottage is a later addition to the original building. This would date Shoe Cottage and possibly the original Shoe Inn to be earlier than the mid sixteenth century (1500s) when brick chimneys were introduced.

We have no evidence to doubt that for many, if not hundreds of years, there may well have been an ale house on the site of The Shoe. Situated on the main road from Salisbury to Southampton, it was in a prime position as a stop off point and could well have supplied a drink to thirsty travellers.

It would be wrong if we did not print the findings of our research in these pages as follows: A survey and map of the Manor of Plaitford carried out in 1729 for the Honourable Stephen Fox indicates a cottage on the site of the current inn. The survey records that this cottage was leased by Widow Batler and there is no mention of the cottage being an inn! Nothing is known of its early history and there appear to be no records to support the existence of an inn or ale house prior to the second half of the eighteenth century.

The Sarum to Eling Turnpike Trust was formed in 1753 to enable tolls to be charged for the use of the road from Salisbury to Southampton and again for its position half way between the two cities, The Shoe was ideally situated to be upgraded to a posting inn[1]. There has always been some speculation as to when the existing building alongside the main road was built. Recently discovered evidence appears to point toward the second half of the eighteenth century. Two lease documents from the Earl of Ilchester to John Latham in 1816 and James Cocks in 1824 for a cottage, *for many years past called and known as the Shoe Inn, and built by John Beavis*, suggest this to be the case. An earlier abstract of title document dated 12 July 1797 between John Latham and Ann Butt, widow of William Butt contains the following: "*All that said dwelling house then since converted into a public house called the*

Shoe Inn". The word converted may refer to the work carried out by John Beavis somewhen between 1765 and 1775. Plaitford Manor Rent Rolls for 1765 to 1775 show that John Beavis[2], a carpenter was Innkeeper at The Shoe. He married Mary Martin in Plaitford on 15 February 1765. The enlarging of the inn at this time coincided with the extra traffic generated by the Sarum to Eling Turnpike road and the need for extra accommodation for travellers. It would probably have been during this period that the main road was re-aligned to where it is now.

A further discovery was of a transfer lease from The Earl of Ilchester to Charlotte Hatchett of a cottage and garden known as the "Old Shoe Inn" dated June 1841. The original lease to her husband, William, was dated April 1826 and appears to suggest that the oldest thatched part of the inn was, by the first half of the nineteenth century, separated from the building at the front we know today.

[1]The meaning of post house and posting inn had very little to do with the movement of mail, it refers to a place where post horses were kept at each post station or stage on the travelling route, for hiring out to those who travelled by post-chaise, a 4 wheeled carriage.
[2]John Beavis is first mentioned paying rent on Lady-day, 25 March 1765

An advertisement placed in the Salisbury & Winchester Journal by William Newell, landlord of The Shoe, on 3 August 1801, advises his patrons that he had recently built a good coach-house and additional stalled stables. This may well have been the brick-built building to the right of the pub and the large wooden building that can be seen in photographs well into the twentieth century. William Newell was a member of the jury of the Plaitford Manor Court from 1794 to 1836 and held the post of chairman on and off during that period. The manor court met each April and passed judgment on matters arising in the Manor of Plaitford on behalf of the Earl of Ilchester. All jurors were sworn in and were selected from men of good standing. James Cocks, mentioned later in this chapter, also sat on the manor court jury from 1815 to 1857 and as foreman from 1844.

It is thought The Shoe got its name from cavalry troops who frequented the inn on their way from Salisbury to the military port at Marchwood. Their horses may well have been re-shoed in the vicinity of the Inn?

It is fair to say that Plaitford became quite well known during the latter half of the eighteenth and first half of the nineteenth centuries. This was down to the importance of The Shoe, ideally placed as a posting inn halfway between Southampton and Salisbury where coaches could change their horses for the onward journey and the popularity of the annual Plaitford races. The races took place between

1825 and 1848 coinciding with the years that James Cocks was the landlord.

As far as we know, James Cocks took over the lease on the inn from John Lathum in 1824. Somewhat confusingly, he is recorded as innkeeper on baptism records in 1821. James Cocks was postmaster at the Shoe Inn from 1813 to December 1818 when he announced in the Salisbury & Winchester Journal on the seventh of that month that he was transferring his posting business to the Vine Inn at Ower.

This occupation along with yeoman (farmer) was recorded on two baptism records in 1817 and 1818. The next, in 1821, records him as inn keeper, a position he held until his death in 1862, aged 75. His wife, Margaret Anne, died on passage home from America on board the Hannibal in August 1834, aged 46. She had been to America in an endeavour to settle one of her sons.

From 1840 until his death in 1846, aged 33, Robert Clayton, James Cocks' son was innkeeper of the White Horse in Romsey and his uncle Samuel the elder brother of James was postmaster living in a property adjacent to the White Horse.

As well as being an innkeeper, James Cocks also farmed land on Plaitford Common as a tenant to Lord Ilchester, and land known as Hobbs (later known as Furze Farm), part of which is now Hobbs Copse Farm and Powells Farm as a tenant of John Harcourt Powell. He also had land of his own.

During his last 20 years as landlord, James Cocks saw the decline of the coaching era and the beginning of the end for The Shoe as a posting inn. With the ever expanding railways in the 1840s, coaching started to decline. A sale notice from March 1847 mentions a sale of coach horses and carriages at the Shoe.

This decline can be noted by the reduction of staff in subsequent census returns. On the census for 1841 the inn's prosperity and importance as a coaching inn can clearly be seen. Besides Mary Cocks, his niece, there were three female servants and five male servants, of which some were probably his farm workers, living at the inn. The return for 1851 shows a decline as a coaching inn and records James Cocks as innkeeper and farmer of 60 acres employing four labourers along with a gardener, hostler and housekeeper there is now only one female servant aged twelve years and six agricultural laboures living at the inn.

The following advertisement in the Hampshire Advertiser and Salisbury Journal, dated March 13 1847 sums up the situation:

'*To Coach and Postmasters, Farmers, Flymen and Others.*
MR. GEORGE JENVEY is instructed to offer by PUBLIC AUCTION,
on Wednesday, the 17th March 1847, on the premised at the Shoe Inn,
Plaitford, (at one o'clock precisely,) the valuable COACH HORSES
and CARRIAGES, the property of Mr. James Cocks.
The Horses are in number 12 to 15, and in good working condition,
together with 5 colts, ranging in age from 1-year old to 4 years old,
(the 4 year old colts are worthy of the attention of any gentleman as
hackneys,) a light Post-Charlot in good condition; a neat Fly,
adapted for on or two horses; several sets of Harness and saddles; a
light spring cart, nearly new, and other articles.
The Auctioneer respectfully calls the attention of his friends and the
public to this sale, as from the Railway from Bishopstoke to Salisbury
being opened, the necessity of Mr. Cocks discontinuing to keep the
establishment as usual is apparent.'

The 1861 and 1871 census returns tell a similar story. In fact in
1871, Samuel Edward, who succeeded James Cocks as Landlord,
only had one servant and a cow boy.

The following newspaper report from The Hampshire Advertiser and
Salisbury Guardian July 3 1852 again confirms the dwindling
popularity of Plaitford as a posting station.

"The Coronation Party at Plaitford -
Since the decline of coaching and the discontinuance of the once
popular Plaitford Races, that village has been getting out of
knowledge. The worthy host of the Shoe Inn, Mr. Cocks has, however,
for some few years past pleasantly excited his parish by assembling
on the coronation day his kinsfolk of the first and second generation,
with guests young and old, amounting to nearly a hundred, for whom
and particularly for the young, he lavishly provided the material for
the complete holiday. The programme closes with an exhibition of
fireworks; and in fine weather few fetes are more enjoyed by those
who are present than that provided by the fine old English patriarch
at Plaitford"

We previously mentioned that James Cocks leased The Shoe from the
Earl of Ilchester in 1824. By the time of the Tithe Survey for
Plaitford in 1844 James Cocks is recorded as leasing the Shoe as a
lifeholder. We came across a notice in the Hampshire Advertiser,
dated June 14 1862. The notice advertised an instruction from the
executors of the will of Mr. James Cocks deceased to sell by auction
the leasehold property known as the Shoe Inn, with extensive stabling
and coach house accommodation. The sale also included a brewery

and plant attached thereto, two large gardens and four plots of good pasture land. The auction was held at The Shoe on July 2 1862.

In 1871, at the time Samuel Edwards was landlord, the rate book records that the Shoe was leased by Francis Ashby who from 1857 was owner of Ashby's Eling Brewery Co Ltd, 60-62 Rumbridge Street, Totton. Founded in 1824, the business was acquired by Strong & Co Romsey Ltd in 1920.

Following are a few historical facts about the Shoe Inn:

James Cocks' daughter, Harriet, born at the Shoe in 1815 and later married Josiah Allsop, of Wellow, at Plaitford Church in 1837, would throughout her lifetime recount how Queen Victoria as a young princess along with her mother the Duchess of Kent took tea at the inn whilst waiting for their post horses to be changed. It is difficult to vouch for the authenticity of this claim. However, we can be sure that Harriet would have talked of this happening during her father's lifetime! It could be said that with his standing in the community he would have quelled such a claim had it not been true. On the other hand, if it were not true, he may have let her tell her story as a way of attracting more business. We will never know!

We do know that in 1832 at the age of thirteen Princess Victoria went on a grand tour of Britain accompanied by her mother, the Duchess of Kent. A stop off at The Shoe may well have taken place during that tour.

We do not have a date for when the last New Forest Highwayman, John Taylor or Reynolds was caught whilst drinking at the inn. Legend has it that after a brief trial at the Red Rover in West Wellow, he was publicly hanged on Plaitford Common. Without wanting to in anyway discredit the legend, we make the following observations based on similar documented situations:

If he had been drinking at the inn, he would have been among friends and would have been known in the area, this would discount a mock trial followed by a mob lynching. It is more likely that he was caught and taken to Salisbury gaol, then sent for trial to Winchester, sentenced to death and hanged. His body may well have been returned to Plaitford Common and hung in a gibbet (a body shaped metal cage) for a long period as a deterrent against other would-be highwaymen. We have been unable to find any evidence of a John Taylor or John Reynolds. It is possible that this legend refers to John Biddlecombe, whose story can be found in a separate chapter. Over the years Chinese whispers have probably embellished the story and may well have effected a name change.

During the nineteenth century, convicts were transported between Ilchester Gaol and the hulks (prison ships) at Portsmouth for transportation to the colonies.

William Bridle, the keeper of Ilchester Gaol recalled a time, between 1808 and 1821, when he and two assistants were transporting twenty two men and they stopped and took breakfast at a lone house, The Shoe, at Plaitford, during which time they sat by the kitchen fire. On leaving, he treated them to a walk of a full mile. The present Governor of Bristol Gaol was there with fewer convicts whom he did not trust to leave their coach.

In January1816, one John Tull or Tute, a 'Whipper In' to Mr. Gilbert's hounds was taken ill at the inn and died two days later aged about 70. It is said his wig hung above the bar until 1989.

In March 1818, the ostler of The Shoe Inn sought out and captured the notorious John Biddlecomb (See chapter on John Biddlecomb), taking his prisoner back to The Shoe from where he was taken to Fisherton Gaol in Salisbury

After some race meetings held on Plaitford race course, during the second quarter of the 19th century, around 100 persons would attend a dinner at the Shoe Inn.

An advertisement from the Hampshire Advertiser, September 13 1862:

'TO INVALIDS AND OTHERS – BOARD AND LODGING, with superior accommodation at the SHOE INN, PLAITFORD, most delightfully situated midway between Southampton and Salisbury on the border of the New Forest.

N.B. – Excellent Post Horses and Carriages, let on hire. Good Livery and Bait Stable and lock-up Coach Houses. Charges moderate.'

At Salisbury Petty Sessions on September 12 1863 Superintendent Matthews apposed a license application from Jacob Rutter Wells, Landlord of The Shoe Inn. A report states: *'Letters had been submitted by Captain Berners,* Manor Farm*, complaining of the conduct of the house, and Sergeant Ghy deposed that he had seen the defendant drunk twice since 21 March. On 28 July he saw a woman who represented herself as Mrs. Wells fighting with a man in front of the house. On 28 August Mr. Wells was in the taproom, behaving himself like a madman'.*

Mr. Wells regretted his actions and stated that he had been a total abstainer for four months. The report continues: *'General Buckley remarked that a landlord who could not conduct himself with propriety was not fit to have charge of a public-house in a **rough*** *neighbourhood. A careful landlord was all the more necessary in such a place.'*

In January 1865, two French Sailors, Emilie Vincent Kern and Pierre Julien Beranger, members of the crew of a Peruvian Corvette of fourteen guns lying at Falmouth, committed a robbery at 13, Marsh Lane, Southampton. Kern was apprehended shortly after in Richmond Street. Beranger was caught in the Plaitford Hotel (Shoe Inn) the following morning. The captain, along with his crew, had been discharged from the corvette at Falmouth and was heading home to France via Southampton. The captain paid their fine and the two offenders were allowed to continue their journey with the rest of the crew.

Over the years The Shoe has been an important venue for meetings and auctions - including property. Newspaper advertisements from the late 1700s and throughout the 1800s, advised that auctions of timber and standing trees were to be held. Also from 1796 to 1803, it was the venue for meetings of the aborted Southampton & Salisbury Canal. Between 1837 and 1844, regular meetings of the Sarum and Eling Turnpike trust were held at the inn. It is also recorded that between 1825 and 1896 the New Forest Foxhounds held seasonal meets at The Shoe. Residents can remember this continuing up to the 1950s and 1960s. Also it was a venue for inquests such as that in 1837 of George Mussel, aged 3, whose clothes had caught fire and after lingering for a week he died from the injuries received. We have evidence that from 1838, James Cocks and William Jennings chaired meetings held at the inn on the Commutation of the 1844 Tithes for the Parish of Plaitford. As Churchwarden, James Cocks was a signatory of the Parish Rate Book. A copy of the 1855 -1857 book is held at the Shoe. The Plaitford Cricket club held their meetings at The Shoe in the late 19th and early 20th century. The current landlords still hold a copy of the 1904 Cricket Scoring Book along with a copy of the 1911 "Register of Castrator of Swine" with entries from 1912 to1915. The castrator was Thomas Westbrook, stepfather of landlord William Peck.

As Plaitford did not have a village hall until 1970, the school was used as the venue for village activities, and until 1961 chairs and tables were stored at The Shoe and transported to the school when needed, after 1961 they were stored at Powells Farm.

Some readers will remember Harry Lovell who used to cut hair at the pub during the 1940s and 50s, usually on a Sunday when working on the Sabbath was illegal!

In 1911, The Shoe was sold as part of the Manor of Plaitford, held by successive Earls of Ilchester since the seventeenth century. It was bought by the Romsey Brewers, Strong & Co, who had held the lease on the property since 1903. Following Strong's acquisition, the building was given the Tudor style half- timbered appearance it has today.

A full list of known landlords of The Shoe from 1765 can be found at the end of this chapter. Here we mention a few who have given the longest service. After James Cocks died in 1862 after 47 years, Samuel Edwards became landlord a post he held until the summer of 1891. He was followed by brother and sister, William and Arabella Peck. William died in August 1914. Arabella died in August 1934. Alfred Gradidge became landlord 1916. His son, Alfred Thomas, was killed in action on 26 October 1918, sixteen days before the armistice, aged 29. He left a son, Thomas, born in 1915 who, was now an orphan as his mother, Alice Mary, had died earlier. Young Thomas was brought up by his grand parents at The Shoe. Alfred Snr. continued as landlord until his death in December 1936. His second son, John (Jack), succeeded his father as landlord until his retirement in1959. He moved to New Road, Landford and died in March 1970, aged 79.

George Gibbs and his wife, Grace (Gay), came to the pub from London in 1968. Before moving to Plaitford, George sold fruit and vegetables in London, and after he and Gay retired in the 1987/8, they moved to Wellow and opened a greengrocers business in Frank Moody's old shop between Slab Lane and the Post Office. Later they moved to Totton and opened a similar shop there. George and Gay died in 2004 and are commemorated at Plaitford.

Robin (Smiler) Huntley was landlord from 1987. A gifted magician and a member of the Magic Circle he appeared with and was a friend of the late comedian and magician Tommy Cooper.

Aart and Jenny Noordijic arrived at The Shoe in 1997. They extended the property adding extra bed and breakfast facilities. Jenny, a keen horsewoman, could often be seen riding her horse around the lanes. They moved away in 2009.

James Cocks held the post for 47 years; the Gradidge family the 43 years; Samuel Edwards 28 years; the Peck family 24 years and George Gibb 20 years.

We are able to account for 25 innkeepers and landlords of The Shoe from the current Pete and Ghislaine Kirkland back 248 years to John Beavis in 1765.

The Shoe Inn c1900. The men in the picture from left to right could be William Peck, landlord 1891-1914, Frederick his nephew and Thomas Westbrook

Photographed in the early 1930's, note the Tudor Style façade added after Strong & Co Brewery purchased the inn in 1911. You can just make out the old coach-house and stables on the right of the picture. Note the change of road surface at the county boundary.

Inn Keepers & Landlords of the Shoe Inn 1765-2013

John Beavis 1765-1772

John Beavis is first recorded paying rent on Lady-day, 25 March 1765

Betty Roberts 1773-1774

Betty Roberts shown on 1773 rent roll as paying rent for John Beavis

Roger Rose 1774-1775

Roger Rose shown in 1774/5 as paying rent for John Beavis

Roger Rose 1776-1789

Elizabeth Rose 1789-?

Wife of Roger Rose formerly Betty Roberts

Michael Williams. ?   ?

William & Ann Butt ?-1797

John Latham 1797-?

William Newell 1801-1816

John Latham 1816-1824

John Latham was involved in other interests besides the Shoe Inn

George Green 1817-1818

George Green married Mary Cook in Romsey in March 1817. He is recorded as Landlord of the Shoe Inn.

James Cocks 1824-1862

James Cocks Jnr. April 1863

James Cocks Jnr took on the license for a brief period after his father died.

Jacob Rutter-Wells September 1863

Samuel Edwards 1863- 1891

Samuel Edwards shown on census records (1871/81/91) as landlord/innkeeper

Jacob Rutter-Wells 1883-1891

Jacob Rutter-Wells recorded on manor rent rolls as paying rent for the shoe.

William & Arabella Peck 1891-1914

William & Arabella were brother and sister

Frederick Peck 1914-1915

Frederick was Arabella's son he enlisted in the army on 3 March 1916

Charles Fanstone 1915

Alfred Gradidge1916-1936

John H Gradidge 1936-1959

Frederick Carvey 1960-1966

Arthur Oakden 1966-1968

Thomas Stewart 1968-1969

George Gibb 1969-1987/8

Robin Huntley 1987/8-1998/9

Arte & Jenifer Noordijic 1998/9-2009

Kevin & Kerry Wall 2009-2013

Pete & Ghislaine Kirkland 2013

Sarum & Eling Turnpike to A36 Trunk Road

In the 17th century some counties were able by means of an Act of Parliament to levy a charge or toll from road users to pay for maintenance, and this was paid at the tollgate or turnpike. Other counties, including Wiltshire, petitioned for acts to establish Turnpike Trusts. In 1706, an act was passed that served as a model for the next 130 years.

It wasn't until the 5th June 1753 that commissioners and trustees were elected and took the oath to execute the following act, passed in the last session of parliament entitled " *The act for widening the roads leading from Lobcomb Corner in the parish of Winterslow to Harnham Bridge in the county of Wilts and from the west corner of St Ann's Street in the City of New Sarum to the parishes of Landford and Brook and from hence to Eling and from Landford aforesaid through Ower to Eling aforesaid in the county of Southampton"* The last paragraph went on to say *"To qualify us to act as Commissioners and Trustees for putting the said act into execution."* This was followed by a long list of signatures including John Bowles of Plaitford. The road became known as the Sarum to Eling Turnpike with the section from Salisbury to Southampton passing through Plaitford and Ower. It was probably during the second half of the 18th century that the road was re-aligned from what is now the rear of The Shoe to its position today. We are led to believe that the old road would have forded the stream on the Shoe side of the current road bridge.

In 1840, the turnpike had eight main toll gates, including, Tolgate Road in Saisbury, Brickworth Corner- Whiteparish, the junction with Lyndhurst Road, Landford and one opposite The Shoe, and four side tollgates with bar along its route. The tolls at The Shoe were collected by the innkeeper.

By the second half the eighteenth century, the stage coach was well established means of transport. The industrial revolution was in full flow and the need for travel on the increase ensured that over the next seventy years The Shoe Inn, now a posting inn, was the most important inn on the road between Salisbury and Southampton. Being half way between these two cities it was ideally situated, as coach operators needed a change of post horses every ten miles or so. Between 1766 and 1775, the front of the building as we know it today was built to cater for the increase in trade from the turnpike.

During the first half of the nineteenth century, at the height of stage coach travel, James Cocks was innkeeper at The Shoe Inn.

His own stage coach, 'The Packet', ran a daily service between Salisbury and Southampton, leaving Salisbury at 8am and arriving in Southampton at 4pm. A rival also ran 'The Rover' on the same route. Long distance coaches such as the Red Rover - Bristol to Brighton, Celerity - Bristol to Portsmouth, Little Magnet – Southampton to Taunton, Telegraph – Southampton to Yeovil and Phoenix - Southampton to Cheltenham, along with their return journeys, on alternate days, all changed their horses at The Shoe. These operators would stable their own teams of horses at the inn alongside the innkeepers post horses that were available for hire. During this period there were at least two blacksmiths in close proximity to The Shoe. During the mid 1800s, meetings of the Turnpike Trust were regularly held at The Shoe.

We have found a reference to Esther Sarah Hutchins (1826-1906, later to become Esther Brooke) of Gauntletts Farm, who at the ages of seventeen and eighteen made two trips to London by stagecoach. Her journey started at The Shoe and she would probably have changed coaches in Southampton or Salisbury.

In his 1794 publication on agriculture in Wiltshire, Thomas Davis, Steward to the Marquess of Bath at Longleat writes: *"There are few counties in this kingdom in which turnpike roads are so numerous, as in Wiltshire."* He continued *"And to the credit of the county, it may be remarked, that there are few parts of the kingdom in which the system of making and keeping turnpike roads in repair, is so well known and practiced."*

The upkeep of the turnpike was important, and the following extract is of an advertisement that appeared in 1865 and 1868 asking for farmers and others willing to contract for the *"supply and delivery by the cubic yard, of properly prepared materials, to be delivered and measured by the road side, for repairing the roads comprised in the following sections:-*

Section No. 1. - From Lobcombe Corner in the Parish of Winterslow, to the city of New Sarum.

Section No. 2. - From the city of New Sarum to the Shoe Inn, at Plaitford.

Section No. 3. - From the Shoe Inn, at Plaitford, to Eling, and from Totton gate to the 15th mile mark at Cadnam.

Section No. 4 - From the junction of the road at Landford through Bramshaw to Cadnam, and thence to Lyndhurst Bar, including also the cross road at Lamb's corner".

Another advertisement from 1868 gave builders and others a chance to either tender for the repair of the whole of the turnpike road or any of 23 individual lots along its length, most covering one mile. For instance, lot 8 ran from the tenth mile to the eleventh, at the Shoe Inn, Plaitford, and lot 9 from the eleventh mile to the twelfth etc.

From these advertisements it gives us an idea in the route of the turnpike.

Using the roads of today, it would have started at Lopscombe (known then as Lobcombe) Corner on the A30 into Salisbury to St Ann's Street. From the city it would take the A36 through Aderbury (in those days), over Pepperbox Hill, through Brickworth to its junction with Lyndhurst Road, Earldoms. This is where the turnpike split. One route continues via Plaitford, Ower and Totton to its terminus at Eling Quay. The other took the Lyndhurst Road through Landford, Bramshaw, Cadnam, Netley Marsh and Totton to Eling Quay.

In the late 1860s the end was in sight for Turnpike Trusts. A parliamentary committee on "Turnpike Act Continuance" sitting on May 5 1869, chaired by Lord George Cavendish resolved that the Sarum and Eling Turnpike Trust should not continue.

Changes started to happen quite quickly as recorded in an auction notice from March 1870, advising the sale of Toll Houses on the Sarum to Eling Turnpike at Testwood, Totton and Netley Marsh.

An ancient milestone, Sarum 11m Soton 11m, still stands outside the house of the same name, alongside the A36, seventy yards to the east towards Southampton from The Shoe Inn.

In February 1930, The Times newspaper in its "state of the roads advice to motorists" reports, among other road works throughout the country, "The Southampton-Ower-Salisbury road is being widened at Testwood and reconstructed at Plaitford. The road was widened from Plaitford to Ower in 1934/5 and was one of the first stretches of road in Hampshire to receive a tarmacadam surface.

At the time of the turnpike and right up to the 1970s the road to Salisbury was not the reasonably straight road it is today. Starting from the first visible section of the old road - the lay-by by Golden Acres Nursery, the road went up over the rise in front of The Poacher public house. From this point most properties on either side, now set back and slightly lower than the existing road, at one time fronted the old road. Turning left into Northlands and the Cedars Nursing Home takes you onto a piece the old road. Further on turn right to Whiteparish, just past Jewson Builders Merchants the road swings left. At this point you can see the old road coming in from the right. On towards Salisbury, the next two large lay-bys on both sides of the road were part of the old road. Where the traffic lights are at Brickworth there was a sharp bend. On over Pepperbox Hill, as you drop down the other side towards Whaddon, the old road is over to your left and ran the other side of the Three Crowns Pub, from where it wound its way on through Alderbury to Petersfinger and Salisbury. Throughout time, animals of the New Forest roamed freely across the main Southampton to Salisbury road onto the common behind the school/village hall and into the village. This was stopped in the 1970s, when the forest was fenced off alongside the southern edge of the main road.

Over the years, the A36 trunk road that now runs through Plaitford over the old turnpike road has become one of the busiest roads in the country, linking Southampton with Bristol. In 1992, a proposal was put forward to build a bypass around Wellow. Three routes, green, purple and yellow, were put forward, all of which would start at Ower and bypass Wellow to the north then re-join the A36 at Earldoms. The most southerly green route was to run parallel to the purple from Ower to Kings Farm in Wellow. At this point the routes split with the purple heading north-west (more later) and the green heading south-west to pass through Plaitford at Pyesmead Farm, severing Sherfield English Road and Giles Lane then turning north-west through Landford Wood to Earldoms. The most northerly yellow route ran through Embley Wood continuing south of Wellow church to Boxes Lane, Wellow where it merged with the north east section of the purple route. They would then run parallel through Plaitford over land belonging to Gardeners Farm, Bowles Farm and Manor Farm; on through Plaitford Wood, Melchet Court Farm to Earldoms. An alternative section of the yellow route would run north of Wellow Church from Embley Wood to Boxes Lane. The estimated cost was between £20 and 23.5 million. After many public consultations, the proposals were eventually scrapped.

Because the A36 is relatively narrow through Plaitford and Wellow compared with other trunk roads, it is difficult with the size of modern machinery to maintain or resurface without the road having to be closed. For a two month period in the early spring of 2002, the road was closed from Hants/Wilts border, near The Shoe Inn, to the roundabout at Wellow, for digging up and resurfacing. It was the first time a major trunk road had to be completely closed for maintenance in England.

Chapter 5
Nineteenth Century

The rural hardships and social life of the nineteenth century are well documented. It is our intention in this chapter to cover the important known historical facts about Plaitford. Because of their importance we have dedicated separate chapters to John Biddlecombe, The Race Course and The Shoe Inn and Sarum to Eling Turnpike Road.

At the start of the nineteenth Century, England was again at war with France and between 1803 and 1805 we were under threat of invasion by Napoleon's army. In 1803, emergency arrangements to anticipate the possibility of an invasion were put into operation. In this part of Wiltshire, parishes within a twelve mile radius of Salisbury were required to submit a return of inhabitants willing to loan fire arms to the government. Among the Wiltshire Lieutenancy papers held at Wiltshire & Swindon Record Office is a return from Plaitford as follows:

'Plaitford December 12 1803
A return of Arms in the Parish and tithing of Plaitford in the county of Wilts.
John Osborn Esq. 1 Gun
Mr. Wolf. 1 Gun
Wm. Newell. 1 Gun out of repair and not worth repairing
There are more guns in some of the Farmers possession in the parish and tithing of Plaitford they say that they keep them for the defense of their own property or Bird keeping and for the defense of their house.
I am Sir your Most Obedient and Humble Servant
Wm. Newell Superintendent'

William Newell was Innkeeper at the Shoe Inn c1801 to 1816.

The fire arm returns from other local parishes: Landford five Guns; Whiteparish nine Guns, six Pistols and two Swords; East and West Grimstead along with West Dean would not loan any fire arms as the inhabitants, mostly farmers like Plaitford, wished to keep their guns to protect themselves in the event of an emergency. Most of the returns appear to be addressed to Major John Osborne at Melchet Park, who was the area Inspector.

Other than this threat of invasion and the earlier introduction of the Sarum to Eling Turnpike road in 1753, Plaitford had not changed very much since the seventeenth century. The village was predominantly a farming community with agricultural labourers moving from farm to farm in the area seeking full time or seasonal work. In the mid 1800's, it is recorded that the village had many scattered mud walled dwellings on common ground occupied by squatters.

Disillusioned by the reduction in wages and the introduction of new mechanized farming equipment, which was threatening their livelihood, rural workers, mostly impoverished and landless agricultural labourers, rioted against landowners. The "Captain Swing[1]" or "Swing Riots" as they were known took place throughout the country in 1830/32. Plaitford and Melchet Park, as with many villages in the country were effected by these riots. Three disturbances are recorded in the area:

On four occasions between midnight and noon on 24 November 1830 a mob eventually numbering between 200 and 300[2] attacked the farm of Mr. William Gray at Plaitford (location unknown). Mr. Gray, armed with a gun, succeeded in keeping the mob at bay, until their last attempt when some of the rioters entered Mr. Gray's house and forced him to go with them. On the same day, about 30 men and boys visited the farm (probably on Plaitford Common in the area of Powells Farm) of Mr. James Cocks, Landlord of The Shoe Inn. They were armed with hammers and axes and destroyed Mr. Cocks Chaff Cutting Machine before joining the rest of the mob.

At Melchet Park on 22 November 1830, a threshing machine, the property of Mr. Richard Webb was damaged by a mob, numbered at between 200 and 300.

Rioters were identified and charged, and the trials took place on 8 January 1831. In one case Isaac Roberts (1841 Census, Farm Labourer, Plaitford) and John Martin (1841/1851 Census, Farm Labourer, Plaitford Common) were found guilty of riot and assault on Mr. Gray. They were sentenced to 12 months hard labour and had to enter into recognizance of £50, to keep the peace for two years.

On the same day, Michael Hood (1841-1881 Census, Wheelwright, Plaitford Common) and Joseph Martin (unknown) were found guilty of rioting and destroying the chaff cutter belonging to Mr. James Cocks. They were sentenced to 12 months hard labour.

The Swing Riots helped to bring about the introduction of the Reform Act in 1832 and the Poor Law Amendment Act in 1834.

[1]The name Captain Swing was appended to several of the threatening letters sent to farmers, magistrates, parsons and others. The "swing Letters" were first mentioned in The Times on 21 October 1830. Captain Swing has never been identified, and many people believe he never existed, having been created by workers as a fictional figurehead who could function as a safe target for their opponents.

[2]Mob numbers were probably greatly exaggerated by the press of the time.

Poor Relief

The 1834 Poor Law Act required parishes to combine into unions. Although Plaitford and West Wellow were in Wiltshire at the time, they formed part of the Romsey Union. Each union was supervised by a Board of Guardians. Guardians elected to represent Plaitford included Captain Hugh Berners who leased Manor Farm, George Curtis, Powells Farm and The Rev Alfred Gay. The majority of Paupers were forced into the Romsey workhouse, some stayed in their cottages and were given out-door relief. We have managed to extract the following sections from a very fragile Romsey Union Out-Door Relief list for November 1837:

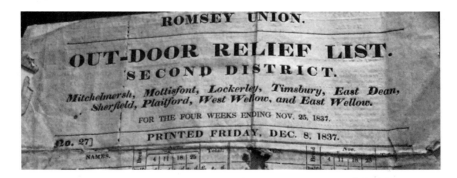

From the top picture you can make out five columns, the first on the left is headed bread[1], columns two to four show the week commencing dates (4, 11, 18 & 25) and the fifth is the total for the month.

The lower picture records the number of loaves of bread per month in column one, and the weekly amount of poor relief in shillings and pence in the next four columns and the total on the right.
Example: Catherine Joy aged 48 with four children received twenty loaves in November and one shilling and ten pence per week, a total of seven shillings and four pence for the month. Hannah Gough and Sarah Humby only received four loaves of bread each and no money. The document also records there was only one person from Plaitford in the Romsey Workhouse in November 1837.
¹Size of the loaves of bread is recorder as half gallon

As the century progressed, the way of life in Plaitford continued to change, particularly during the second half. New mechanized agricultural practices continued to reduce the need for farm labourers. Low farm wages and the attraction of better wages in the towns and cities would see the population of Plaitford almost half between 1861 and 1891. Also in the same period, the introduction of the railways saw a decline in the need for long distance stage and mail coaches, thus changing The Shoe Inn from an important posting inn to a village public house.
The comparison given below will give an indication of the sharp decline in the population, particularly from Plaitford Wood and Plaitford Common, between the Census of 1851 and 1891.
The Census for 1851 records 67 occupied properties of which 27 were north of the River Blackwater (eleven in Plaitford Wood and sixteen others) and 40 south of the river (27 on the common and thirteen others).
The Census for 1891 records 37 occupied properties of which 13 were north of the river (two on Plaitford Wood and eleven others) and 24 south* of the river (thirteen on the common and eleven others).
*The south side of the River Blackwater on the 1891 Census include Pickernalls, Powells and Redhouse Farm's, The Shoe, the School, six properties on Southampton Road and thirteen entered as The Common with no distinction between Common Side/Claypits Common and Plaitford Common.
Most if not all the cottages in Plaitford Wood and on Plaitford Common would have been pretty miserable and would have had mud walls with a thatched roof. Once the cottages became unoccupied, they would rapidly deteriorate. The roof and timbers would have rotted allowing the walls to be washed away leaving no trace today of their existence.

Some villagers rented cottages and land from the church but most were rented from the Earls of Ilchester. Other land owners were the Harcourt-Powell family.

Rents were normally paid at Michaelmas (29 September) each year when a representative of the Earl of Ilchester would collect the rents from farmers and cottagers and provide them with a meal at The Shoe Inn.

Some changes for the good would take place during the middle and second half of the century. In 1845, the Earl of Ilchester gave the village land to build a school and school house which opened in 1846. The church was restored in 1856 became an independent rectory in 1866. A rectory was built in Pound Lane in 1865.

Blacksmiths

Records start in the early 1800's and Plaitford appears to have had only two families of blacksmiths. Both forges were located on Plaitford Common, close to The Shoe Inn which as a coaching inn was probably a good source of income.

We will start with the three brothers of the Tutt family who are recorded in the Plaitford baptism records as blacksmiths. They were, George and Lydia 1814, John and Elizabeth 1816 and Alexander and Jane 1834.

Our next record starts with the first ten year census in 1841, which mentions John Tutt who we think had his forge on the common behind the village hall, in the area of the properties Wateravons and Witchwood. In 1851, John is briefly joined by his younger brother, George. John's son, Edwin, was working with him in1861 and by the 1871 census they were joined by Alexander, Edwin's elder brother. Edwin committed suicide in September 1875 (See September 1875 later in this chapter) and the 1881 census records that Alexander had been admitted to Wilts County Lunatic Asylum in Devises, and John died in August 1880. The 1881 census makes no mention of the Tutt Family as blacksmiths in the village. Alexander Tutt had returned to Plaitford by the time of the 1891 census, he died in January 1901. His grandson, Henry Frank Lovell, took over the business and is the only blacksmith in Plaitford on the 1901 census. We move forward to the mid 1900's where we find Kenneth Tutt, great grandson of Alexander the younger brother of John and George, working with Walter Hutchings at the forge where Border Garage, Wellow Vehicle Sales, now stands.

The other recorded Plaitford blacksmiths were the Pearce/Perman/Hutchings family; they can be traced back via parish baptism records to James and Ann[e] Pearce living in Plaitford from 1813-1826. Moving forward to the 1841 census there is a brief mention of [1]George and Martha Pearce who by the 1844 tithe survey were living in a cottage where Appledoor and Orchard cottages now stand.

The next census in 1851 mentions Charles Permain (Perman), his forge was in the area of Border Garage, Vehicle Sales alongside the A36. George Pearce died in June 1845 and by the 1851 census his widow, Martha, had married Charles Perman. It is possible that George Pearce's forge may have been located at Border Garage and Charles Perman had worked for him. Charles Perman was still recorded as a blacksmith on the 1891 census, aged 75, and he was living at Brook Cottage, built in 1872[2], that stood behind his forge. Living at the same address were two of his grandsons, William Hutchings, aged fourteen, also a blacksmith and his brother, Frank, aged eleven, a scholar. Charles Perman died in April 1901 and by the 1911 census we find William Hutchings living at Brook Cottage and running the forge with his brother, Frank. William Hutchings died in December 1920, and later his son, Walter, would take on the business. With the reduction in the use of horses and the need for a forge, diversification became necessary and Walter Hutchings opened Plaitford's one and only petrol station in the 1930's which remained open until the 1960's.

[1]George Pearce may be the son of James and Ann[e]. There are five baptisms, all girls, recorded in Plaitford and two boys in Wellow - one is George, born in 1806, which by 1841 would make him 35 years of age. The 1841 census records him as 25.
[2]Brook Cottage was knocked down in the late 1960's early 70's.

Walter Hutchings second left at his forge in the 1920's with Brook Cottage in the back ground.

Bakers, Grocers and Shopkeepers

The only record we have of shops in the village comes from the ten year census returns from 1841-1911 and the Kellys and Post Office directories from 1855.

Some of the early shopkeepers would have offered basic items for sale from one room in their mud wall and thatch cottages. Two businesses became reasonably well established: Esther Brooke, in the north of the village at Gardeners Farm traded for 34 years, and Robert and Ann Gough, in the south on Plaitford common, 38 years.

1841 and 1851: Henry Green is listed as a baker but by 1861 he was a farmer with his wife, Sarah, at Bowers Farm. The Kellys directory for 1867 records Henry Green as a farmer and baker.

1851: Clemence Noble a widow and shopkeeper at The Drove at Bridgefoot where she was living with her husband, Mark, in 1841.

1851-1889: Robert and Ann Gough, baker and grocer, in the area of Plaitford Common. Robert Gough was buried at Plaitford in September 1877. The Kellys directory for 1885 records Ann Gough still running the business, she died in June 1889.

1851: John and Martha Hurst, shopkeepers, in the area of Common Side.

1859: Isaac Roberts, shopkeeper. Could this have been the ironmongers reputed to have existed in the Plaitford Green/Wood area? An Isaac Roberts was living with his wife, Sarah, in Plaitford Wood in 1851 and is recorded as a gardener.

1861-1895: Oliver Brooke is recorded as a farmer and grocer at Gardeners Farm, after his death in May 1867, his wife, Esther, continued to operate the business along with a bakery.

1871: James Fielder, aged 79, shopkeeper in the area of Plaitford Common. This could be the same James Fielder who at 59 along with his wife, Mary, is recorded on the 1851 census as farming at Bridgefoot Farm, where they lived until April 1861. Kellys directories of 1855, 1864 and 1867 record John Fielder as a shopkeeper and baker, but there is no mention of him on the 1861 census.

1891: John Hutchings, grocer, Salisbury Road.

1901: Sarah, wife of William Hurst, is recorded as having a shop at Fielder Farm. There is no mention made of the shop on the 1911 census. Sarah, still living at Fielders Farm, died in April 1915, and her shop appears to be the last to be recorded in Plaitford. There are no bakers, grocers or shopkeepers recorded on the 1911 census or the Kellys directories from 1903 to 1939.

Gardeners Farm (now Sweet Briar Cottage) in the early 1950's, other than what appears to be a new thatched roof, the property probably still looked as it did at the time Esther Brook ran a shop, bakery and farm from the premises.

Police

In 1839, the rural Constabulary Act meant that county Police Forces could be set up in any of the 54 counties in England, This was optional and by 1850 only 36 counties had done so. It would appear that Wiltshire was one, because two policemen are recorded as living in Plaitford: George Hill 1848-1852 and John Phillips in 1855. The 1851 census shows George Hill as living in the area of the common.

Romsey Labourers Encouragement Society

Held annually from 1854 until 1878, the Labourers Encouragement Society was set up as an incentive to farm labourers from Romsey and the surrounding area. The following report from the Romsey Register (predecessor to the Romsey Advertiser), November 1854 sets out the objectives:

"After a substantial dinner of beef and plum pudding, about 100 candidates received money Prizes from the Right Horourable Viscount Palmerston (President).

Awards were made to: Shepherds, Teamsmen, Ploughmen, Seedsmen and Drillmen, Rick Makers and Thatchers, Turnip hoers, Labourers with neat tidy cottages, and others who had been for a long series of years in one service, and had educated and 'got out' their families without Parish Aid".

It would appear that until his death in 1862, James Cocks, farmer and landlord of The Shoe Inn, encouraged his employees to enter as most of the farming and long service award winners from Plaitford were in his employ. The same can be said for Captain Berners and his bailiffs, Henry Feltham and Samuel Andrews at Manor Farm.

Over the 24 years many awards were presented to labourers from Plaitford, we have selected just a few:

1854: John Hutchins, servant to Mr. Cocks (farmer and landlord of The Shoe Inn) for thatching a corn rick in the neatest and best manner – 20 shillings.

1854: John Hutchins for having lived in the service of Mr. Cocks for 40 years and 'got out' his family respectably, only being relieved by illness – 40 shillings.

1858, George Bungay and his wife (Margaret), for the neatest and cleanest cottage and garden – 20 shillings.

1861: Richard Harnett and wife (Anne) for allotment and gardens – 20 shillings. (Anne Harnett died in 1863, Richard married Ann Bowles widow of Frederick in 1867).

1869: Richard Joy, ploughman to Captain Berners (Manor Farm) joint third place – ten shillings.

1876: Edward Hutchings champion ploughman – fifty shillings and a greatcoat.

1878: James Bungay for regular church attendance – prayer book.

Child Mortality

Child mortality was high in the nineteenth century and one Plaitford family stands out not just for their loss but also for the father's determination to have a son named after him.

George and Mary Bungay had ten children before Mary died in January 1847, aged 37. Their first born, George, died in March 1835, aged four. The fourth born also baptized George in October 1835 died in 1837, aged three. The family was to lose three more children; Fanny in 1848, aged nine, Henry in 1847, aged three, and Jane in 1846, aged three months.

George now a widower married Dinah Hood in September 1847. Their son was baptized at Plaitford on 8 December 1850 and was given the name George. One could say it was third time lucky for George Snr as George Jnr was to later marry Sophia Jane Bundy and between them produce seven children.

Another tragedy was to strike the family in September 1852 when George and Mary's second born, Thomas, aged 20, was accidentally shot by John Moore whilst poaching. (See September 1852 in the following section on newspaper reports.)

Between 1801 and 1899, 106 children under the age of five were buried at Plaitford Church compared to 22 between 1900 and 1994.

During our research we have discovered many newspaper reports, articles both local and national that refer to people from and about happenings in Plaitford during the nineteenth century. Some are amusing, some tragic:

November 1806: The Romsey Advertiser carried the following notice: "*I WILLIAM Bowles of Plaitford in the county of Wilts, do hereby caution the public not to give credit to Rebecca, my wife, (who is living apart from me,) for any money or goods, as I will not be answerable for payment of any debts which she has already contracted or may hereafter contract. - Witness my hand the thirtieth day of October 1806*". They must have made up because their son Vincent was born in 1809 and when William died he left his estate to Rebecca.

October 1823 Extract from the Morning Post**:** Remarkably Fine Stag Hunt in the New Forest. The hunt met at Markway Bottom, five miles from Lyndhurst, on the Christchurch road. They were to hunt a fine stag, known to farmers in the neighbourhood of Burley as a trespasser. The stag was roused from his hiding place at Viney Ridge. The chase followed a route towards Bolderwood, crossing the Ringwood Road at Bratley Bridge, over Fritham Plain, past Iworth Lodge, doubling back to Brook, past Bramble Hill Lodge, through Bramshaw Wood and eventually, after many changes in direction, through Hampworth[1] Common. 'The stag then inclined to his right to Wellow, turning to the left through Plaitford, through fields, through farm yards and gardens, driving every body in his way; some of the poor woman that had not time to get to their houses took refuge in the pig-sty; he crossed the Salisbury road, ran towards Whiteparish, turned back through Landford, took to Lanford[1] Water, run up to Hampworth, when the hounds came up to him'. The stag was eventually caught on North Common. 'To end the sport the stag was laid in a cart and taken to Bramble Hill Lodge, the shoulders were taken to the Fox and Hounds, Lyndhurst, and served up in good style by Mrs. Redford, to a large party of sportsmen, and the evening was spent in harmony'.

January 1834 Hampshire Telegraph: *"Attempted Robbery on the Highway. Attempt by Footpads* ¹*. - On Monday, an eminent botanist, and florist from Exeter. left Southampton at half-past five in the evening, on his return to Salisbury, accompanied by his son, between eight and nine years of age. On reaching Plaitford the air becoming very heavy and the night boisterous, he placed the youth under the apron of the gig, the carriage having lamps; the little boy observed two men jump from the hedge near Landford, which he momentarily communicated to his father, the rascals rushed forward and desired the travellers to stop, and follow them a considerable distance, but the travellers considered these worthies had no fair business to transact at so late an hour of the night in their line, caused their steed to put on a quicker pace and escaped".*

¹Footpads were highway robbers on foot, whereas Highwaymen were usually mounted

April 1837: Hampshire Advertiser: *"On Tuesday 18 April, an inquest was heard at the Shoe Inn on the body of George Mussel, three years of age. The clothes of the deceased caught fire whilst his father was in the garden, and although he promptly came to its assistance on hearing the baby cry, and procured the best medical advice, the child after lingering for nearly a week, died from the injury received".*

George Mussel's parents were Charles, an agricultural labourer, and Sarah, a needlewoman, who are recorded on the 1841 census as living in Plaitford with five children. By 1851 they had a further four children.

February 1851 Hampshire Advertiser and Salisbury Journal: *"Frederick Noble was brought up in custody to the County Magistrates' Office in Winchester on a charge of having committed an aggravated assault on a police-constable named Hill, when he took Noble into custody at Plaitford on a charge of stealing underwood. The prisoner had just come out of gaol, having undergone two month's imprisonment for robbery; and was now sent back for another month in default of paying £5 and costs".*

The 1851 census records Frederick Noble agricultural labourer as living as a lodger at The Shoe inn.

October 1852 The Cottager's Monthly Visitor:
"Fatal Effect of Poaching. - An inquest was held lately by Mr. R M Wilson, coroner, on the body of Thomas Bungay, of Plaitford. It appeared that the deceased who was aged 20, went out with a lad three years younger than himself, named John Moore, each armed with a gun, for the purpose of poaching, on Sunday

*afternoon. Having found a covey of partridge in a field in the
occupation of Farmer Noble, they marked down a single bird in the
hedgerow, and both fired at the birds rising, John Moore lodging the
contents of his gun in his companions left side. Bungay called out
"John, what did you shoot me for?" and upon Moore's replying, "I
didn't know that I did," Bungay answered, "Yes you did though;"
and, after walking two or three yards, fell down and expired in a few
minutes. From the position of the wound it seemed probable that the
charge lodged in his heart. Verdict, "Homicide by misadventure".*
Thomas Bungay, a ploughboy, aged 20, was the son of George and
Mary. At the time of the 1851 census he was living with his
stepmother, Dinah, on Plaitford Common. He was buried at Plaitford
on 8 September 1852. John Moore, also a ploughboy, born in
Brokenhurst, is recorded in the 1851 census as living with his mother,
Ann, on Plaitford Common Side.

1856: A story of Hardship. The following is a copy of a letter from
the Rev, Thomas S. Hill, Chaplain of Salisbury Infirmary to the Poor
Law Board, relating to the relief of the Poor in Extra-parochial
Places, including No-Man's- Land (Hants).
*"High Street, Salisbury, 4 March 1856
Sir
I would take the liberty of laying the following case before you, which
seem to be a case of hardship, asking you to be kind enough to let me
know whether anything can be done to alleviate it. James Reynolds
was born at Landford, about nine or ten miles from Salisbury, and
became a parishioner of Plaitford, by being a carter to Farmer
Noble, boarding and sleeping in his house for three years. He then
lived in the parish of Whiteparish for eight years, carter to Mr. Webb,
in one of his cottages (there he married); then at Plaitford in a
cottage for seven years; then back to Landford, living in a cottage for
seven years; then for one year living in Plaitford, whilst working in
Whiteparish; then went to Downton parish (six miles from the
village) as carter to Squire Bradburn, working for him for 11 years,
till March 1855; he was then taken ill, lived in the house until
Michaelmas, receiving relief during that time for self, wife and three
youngest children from Downton. At Michaelmas he was turned out
of his house; his master wanted it for his new carter. He could get no
other house in that part of Downton, and took one in No-Man's-Land
(a piece of land that belongs to no parish). From that time to this he
has not been able to get relief from any parish. He has occasionally
been able to work a little; but at present he is a patient in Salisbury
Infirmary. His wife has applied to Bramshaw, Romsey and Alderbury*

*Unions; from none can she get relief. She applied at Alderbury on 22
February last; she could get no relief from it, as she had left
Downton (their present cottage is about 300yds from their late
cottage, which stands in Downton parish). She applied to Romsey
Union (which includes Plaitford, of which the husband is a
parishioner) on February 25, and was refused relief. She was then
advised to sleep in Plaitford, and then apply to Romsey; she did so on
Sunday last, March 2, and applied again yesterday, March 3, and
was again refused. She slept at the house of James Jones. I am afraid
I have made a long story; but I have tried to make all things clear;
and I shall feel much obliged if you will be kind enough to tell me
whether the man can get any relief, and how he or his wife must act
so as to get it; for he is very ill, and his wife and three children
cannot live on nothing.*
I remain, &c. Thomas S. Hill, Chaplain of the Infirmary"
Extract from: Accounts and Papers of the House of Commons 1857.

James and Sarah Reynolds had three sons baptized in Plaitford
Church: James 1832, George 1834 and William 1837.

July 1867 Western Gazette: *"Salisbury County Petty Session: Mary
Ann Bungay, of Plaitford was summoned for assaulting Mary Ann
Winter, but as there evidently faults on both sides, the bench properly
bound both Woman over in the sum of £5 to keep the peace for 6
months".*

Mary Ann Bungay a needlewoman was the wife of George Bungay,
agricultural labourer. On the 1851 to 1871 census, they were living in
area of the Plaitford Common and Bridgefoot. We have no record of
Mary Jane Winter.

December 1867 Hampshire Advertiser: *"Andrew Hutchings of
Plaitford, Wilts was summoned for riding a Timber carrier without
reins on the Sarum to Eling Turnpike road, on 21 November, and was
fined 5 shillings and costs".*

The 1871 census records Andrew Hutchings, agricultural labourer,
aged 23, and his wife, Mary, also 23, and two daughters as living at
Bowers Farm. By 1880 a further four children had been baptised at
Plaitford. Before the 1881 census they had moved to Surrey.

April 1868 Salisbury & Winchester Journal: *"Charles Arter, who did
not appear, was summoned for illegally taking six trout from a
stream belonging to the Earl of Ilchester, at Plaitford. He was fined
50 shillings and costs or two months imprisonment and Lord
Folkestone said it might as well be known that the defendant was
liable to a penalty of £5 for each fish; but as the defendant was not*

known to the police as a regular offender, he was only fined 50 shillings and costs or in default three weeks hard labour".

May 1868 Hampshire Telegraph: The following is reminiscent of a Keystone Cops movie! *"ATTEMPTED PRIZE FIGHT. - On Monday morning last a party of the 'fancy' among whom was 'Nat Langham*[1]*' came down from London. The Police had heard on Sunday, on reliable authority, that they intended coming to Hampshire on Monday, for the purpose of fighting, and when the train, in which the pugilists were, arrived at Winchester, the "Blues" were waiting for them; and on seeing these unwelcome gentlemen, they decided to go further. At Bishopstoke, Chandlers-ford and Romsey they alighted, and so did the police, each time both parties returning to the carriage. At Dunbridge all turned out and here a break and several other vehicles were waiting for them. Into these they jumped as soon as possible, and proceeded through Lockerley to Plaitford, the police following on foot. At Plaitford (Wiltshire) they also found police waiting for them, but they pursued the same course to Downton. Here also the "blue jackets" were found. They then turned back and came to Sherfield, where they attempted to pitch a ring, but the police came upon the scene here also, and relieved them of the ropes and staves. Thus ending a fruitless attempt to carry out one of those disgraceful sights called a 'prize fight,' the pugilists and their friends returning to London in the evening, greatly disappointed."*

[1] Nat Langham, 1820-1871 was British Bare Knuckle Middleweight Champion 1846-1853.

January 1871 Extract from the Hampshire Telegraph: A Clergyman Fined – At the Southampton Petty Sessions on Thursday 5 January, James Barton, a Clergyman of Plaitford, was fined five shillings and costs, or three days imprisonment in default for drunk and disorderly conduct in the streets on Wednesday 4 January. The fine was paid.

April 1871 Extract from the Salisbury and Winchester Journal: 'Serious charge against a Clergyman - The Rev. James Barton, late rector of Plaitford, was defendant in an action, before Salisbury Magistrates, on Tuesday, for "using foul and abusive language" towards a Mr. George Peter Dodson, a retired solicitor, in which he cut a rather discreditable figure. It was proved that he had used most disgusting language; in fact swore like a trooper. He was ordered to enter into his own recognisances in the sum of £100, and to find two sureties in £50 each, to be of good behaviour for twelve months'.

In a longer report about the same case, it is mentioned that after Mr. Dodson had experienced various problems with Rev, Barton, he had reported him to the Bishop. As a result, Rev. Barton was suspended for two years. This suspension fuelled more abusive behaviour towards Mr. Dodson, hence the above action.

The Reverend Barton came to Plaitford as a Curate and became Rector in 1866.

September 1875 Western Gazette: *"An inquest was held by Mr. Wilson on Monday, on the body of Martha Hurst, a widow, aged 58 years, who died on Saturday evening. It would appear that the deceased was milking a cow when she suddenly fell from the stool on which she had been sitting and died in a few minutes. Mr. Nunn, Surgeon, stated that the deceased had complained to him lately of palpitations of the heart, and we doubt not her death was attributed to heart disease. Verdict 'died by the visitation of God"*

Martha Hurst was the wife of John Hurst a shopkeeper and agricultural labourer, and between them they had nine children. Martha was buried at Plaitford on 8 September 1975.

September 1875 Western Gazette: *"PLAITFORD - An Inquest was held in this village on Wednesday, before Mr. R A Wilson, Deputy Coroner on the body of Edwin Tutt, Blacksmith. Deceased had been staying with his parents for the benefit of his health, and had been in a low and desponding state of mind. On Tuesday morning deceased came down stairs with blood flowing from his throat, and when he got to the bottom he fell down and expired. On examination it was found that the windpipe and the principal arteries had been completely severed, it was supposed by a razor. The jury returned a verdict of suicide whilst in a state of temporary insanity".*

He was buried at Plaitford on 17 September 1875, aged 48.

One of the possible reasons for Edwin Tutt's state of mind comes from a report in the Hampshire Advertiser dated 16 November 1867 of a petition for bankruptcy. Edwin Tutt, Blacksmith of Plaitford, Wilts, horse-nail maker and shoeing-smith. At the time of the petition he was living at No 2, Chapel Place, Turnham Green, London, and was assistant to a shoeing-smith. The report goes on to say that he had moved to London to avoid paying £172.12s.2p owed to nineteen creditors in Salisbury, Romsey and Plaitford. The hearing decided the better course would be to transfer proceedings to the Romsey County Court…

A further report in the Salisbury & Winchester Journal from January 1868: *"Romsey, Edwin Tutt's Bankruptcy. - At the county court was heard the case of Edwin Tutt, which had been transferred from London. The bankrupt was described as of Turnham Green, Middlesex, and formerly of Cherville-street, Romsey, horse-shoe nail maker. The bankrupt was opposed by several creditors. There were no assets. The case was dismissed for twelve months, without protection".*

It would appear that Edwin Tutt had married between 1851 and 1861. He and his wife, Arabella, had two sons, Edwin, born 1852, and James, born 1858. By the time of the 1861census he was a widower and as with the 1871 census he was living with his father, mother and two sons in Plaitford. In May 1875, Edwin Jnr. a blacksmith, married Fanny Mitchell in Oakwood, Surrey. At the time of the 1881 census, they had settled in Leatherhead, and James also a blacksmith was lodging nearby in the same town.

March 1878 Hampshire Advertiser**: "ALARMING ACCIDENT. -** *An accident which might have been afflicting but which, happily, was attended with no very serious consequences, took place on Tuesday, in Bell-street, near Mr. George's brewery. The governess in the family of the Rev, A. H. Gay, of Plaitford, accompanied with two of his children, was driving out of Romsey in a pony-carriage of char-a-banc fashion, when the vehicle came into sharp contact with a horse and gravel cart, by which both shafts of the pony-carriage were broken, and its occupants thrown out, the young lady and the children falling between the pony's heels and the trap. Fortunately, immediate assistance was at hand. The governess was slightly bruised, but no bodily injury was suffered by the children".*

The Reverend Alfred Gay was Rector of Plaitford from1871-1899.

1887: Lady Ashburton invited all the people of Plaitford to a feast at Melchet Court to celebrate the Golden Jubilee of Queen Victoria.

September 1894 Romsey Advertiser: *"At Romsey Borough Bench, William Hurst a dealer from Plaitford was charged with using a cart in the borough without having his name on it. The Mayor examined the cart and the case was proved and the defendant fined five shillings with four shillings costs – defendant said he could pay and had a bit left to lend the Mayor if he wanted it. He was otherwise very insolent and the Mayor fined him a further five shillings for contempt of court – defendant refused to pay the second fine. He was told if he refused to pay he would go to prison for fourteen days. He left the court without paying anything"*

On the 1891 census, William Hurst, dealer and farmer, aged 40, lived with his wife, Sarah Annie, aged 41, and five children at Fielders Farm.

December 1894: To the Editor of The Standard -A ONE-SIDED DISTRICT ELECTION. *'Sir,- Two candidates were nominated for Plaitford, a small village in the Romsey Union - vis., Mr. Wm Hurst,* *dealer, and Mr. George Curtis, Farmer. At the close of the day's polling is was found that twenty-three persons had cast their votes, After the count the poll was declared as follows: Geo. Curtis, 23: William Hurst, nil. As this election is certainly unique, perhaps you may be able to find space for this in the columns of The Standard'.*

1895: County Boundary changes. See introduction.

October 1895 Extract from the Hampshire Advertiser: At Romsey County Bench, John Simmonds, Plaitford, a labourer, was charged for stealing 43 crown pieces from his father, a total of £10.15s. After purchasing a watch and chain in Romsey, he travelled to Aldershot. He got drunk and stayed with some girls and had met up with a Mrs. Farmer to whom he had given the watch and chain. He then travelled to Portsmouth where he claimed he had lost the rest of the money. When he gave himself up, he only had nine pennies left on him. He was sentenced to 3 months' hard labour.

John was the son of John and Eliza Simmonds who from 1911 would live at The Drove. John Jnr would later become a casualty of the Great War.

1898/1899: Bridgefoot Cottages were built by the Earl of Ilchester on land leased to George Curtis as part of Powells Farm. The land on which they stand, known as Stony Lands, was situated next to a large gravel pit. The first record of occupation is the Lovell family recorded on the baptism record of their daughter, Annie, as living at Bridgefoot Cottages in May 1900. They lived at number three.

October 1899 Hampshire Advertiser: "*Jacob Noyce of Plaitford, pleaded guilty of stealing some cultivated mushrooms at Plaitford on 5 October, of the value six pence; the property of the executors of the late Walter Curtis, - he was ordered to pay two shillings fine, six pence damage and six shillings and six pence costs*".

Jacob Noyce, a farm labourer, aged 46, and his wife, Susanna, aged 35, were living at Rectory Lodge in Pound Lane on the 1901 census.

The Railways that were never built!

Early in July 1845, the Wilts, Somerset and Southampton Junction Railway publicly announced a plan to build a broad gauge railway from Fisherton Anger Station in Salisbury to the Royal Pier in Southampton. Already having a line from Bristol to Salisbury, the plan was to connect the Bristol Channel to the English Channel. The proposed 21 mile route was carefully surveyed and there appeared to be no engineering or other difficulties. It was reported that all the chief landowners were all favourable. Lord Ilchester and James

Pearce, Plaitford Parish Clerk had leased part of Plaitford Common to the railway company.

The estimate for the complete works was £350,000 and this included the construction of a "spacious terminus" on the waste shore near the Royal Pier. The directors offered 14,000 shares at £25 each with a deposit of £1 7s 6d per share. The interest was such that on the 17 July, the directors decided that no further applications for shares would be accepted after 24 July.

To quote the London Morning Chronicle of 9 July 1845 – "*The route of the proposed line will pass through common lands of little value; it will proceed from the station of the Wilts, Somerset and Weymouth Railway, at Fisherton Anger and proceed by or near Downton, Plaitford, over Hampworth[1] and East Willow[1] Commons by Bramshaw to Redbridge, taking the line of the old canal at Millbrook, and crossing the Mudlands to the Royal Pier, Southampton, contiguous to which, and on the present waste shore, it is proposed to erect a spacious terminus, the cost of which is included in the estimate*"

[1] As spelt in the article.

The sections of the plans of the proposed route (available at the Wiltshire records Office) of interest to the local area are the nine to thirteen mile sections from Southampton, that would run through Half Moon Common, across Blackhill Road at Furzeley, through Wicksmoor Farm, across Plaitford Common, over the New Road, Lyndhurst Road and Nomansland crossroads in Landford, across the bottom of School Road, Nomansland, over Hamptworth Common and through Lyburn Farm.

Wilts, Somerset, and Southampton Junction Railway.

The Parish of PLAITFORD, in the County of WILTS

Description of Property.	Owner or Reputed Owner.	Lessee.	Occupiers.
Parish Boundary		.. ..	
Heath	Lord Ilchester, Dorset-shire	.. ..	

Lord of the Manor, Lord ILCHESTER.

JAMES PEARCE, Plaitford, ParishC

A photograph of part of a document from the 1845 railway plans, showing the owner of the section of Plaitford Common the railway would cross.

Records show that by November the proposed line had been cancelled, probably as a result of the following:

In 1845, a Royal Commission looked in to the subject of the railway gauge. After a long investigation it was decided to recommend the standard gauge, which we have today. The decision was somewhat swayed by there being eight times more standard gauge in existence at the time than broad gauge. The Gauge Act passed in 1846 made standard gauge compulsory for all new railways. However, the Great Western retained its broad gauge until 1892, when it converted to standard gauge.

Eleven years later in October 1856, a public meeting was held in Guildhall in Southampton in consequence of a requisition to the mayor, signed by 140 of the principal merchants and tradesmen from the town, to consider the advisability of supporting the Bristol and South Wales Railway from Southampton to Salisbury. Again this would be on broad gauge and again the line had the consent of all the land owners. At the time of the meeting out of a 30,000 share issue only 8000 remained to be applied for.

In the report there appears to be some confusion to the exact route of the line. It does, however, mention a possibility of it passing Plaitford and Wellow.

The outcome of the meeting appeared to support the proposal and a committee was appointed to prepare petitions to both houses of Parliament.

Move on 26 years to November 1882. The Hampshire Advertiser, dated 18th November 1882 reports that the Pewsey, Salisbury and Southampton Railway company is intending to apply to Parliament in the next session in 1883 for leave to bring in a bill for the following:

Railway 1: Pewsey to Salisbury.

Railway 2: Salisbury to Southampton which would start from Fisherton Anger and terminate at Millbrook, Nr Southampton at the junction with the newly authorized Didcot, Newbury and Southampton Junction Railway. The line was to follow a similar route as the 1845 proposed railway.

The report states - " *The line will pass from and through, in, or into the following townships, parishes, extra parochial and other places or some of them (that is to say); Fisherton Anger, Milford, Laverstock, The Liberty of Clarendon Park, Alderbury, Downton, Redlynch, Standlynch, Landford, Plaitford, West Wellow in Wiltshire, and East Wellow, Eling, Nursling, Romsey and Millbrook in Hampshire".*

The bill was to give the railway company the power "*To purchase or acquire lands, houses and other property, compulsorily or by agreement, for the purpose of the said intended railway and works, and particularly to purchase compulsorily about nine acres of the common known as Plaitford Common, in the parish of Plaitford, and about five acres of the common known as West Wellow Common in the parish of West Wellow*"

Had any of these proposed railways been built, it may well still be running today or at least into living memory, having been axed by Dr Beeching in the 1960's!

Chapter 6
John Biddlecombe

'That notorious character, Biddlecombe, who has long carried out his depredations, to the terror of many of the inhabitants of the new forest and its vicinity, and for whom a great reward has been offered, is at length taken. This desperado has long eluded the vigilance of the officers'
From Jacksons Oxford Journal, 28 March 1818 and the Morning Chronicle (London) 11 April 1818

John Biddlecombe's parents, John and Peggy (Clark) married in Landford on February 13 1792. John, their eldest son was born on 21 August 1793 and was baptized in Landford on 25 August 1793. John junior was to follow a career that would end with him being hanged at Gallows Hill, Winchester on August 1 1818, aged 25 years. He was buried at Plaitford on August 2, the day after his execution.
It would appear from records that John Jnr had been in and out of trouble most of his adult life.
We have managed, through research and the help of his four times [1]great nephew, to obtain documents relating to some of his criminal activities that eventually led to his downfall:
John Biddlecombe, together with Daniel Biddlecombe, Edward Andrews and James Mussell were sentenced at the Wiltshire Quarter Sessions on 13 July 1815 to one month's imprisonment in Fisherton Gaol, Salisbury for assisting to kill game (poaching) without a license.
At the Wiltshire Quarter Sessions held on 16 July 1816, John was again sentenced to three months' imprisonment for having committed an offence against the game laws (poaching).
We have a copy of an indictment at Wiltshire Quarter Sessions on John Biddlecombe that relates to a robbery that took place on 9 May 1817 at the property of Mark Noble at Plaitford. From the County of Wilts Calendar of Prisoners for July 1817, John Biddlecombe Snr was charged for this offence and found not guilty. Did the court realize a mistake had been made by discovering that John Jnr should have been charged with this offence? The reason behind this thinking is the crossing through of the words "the elder" in three places after John Biddlecombe's name on the hand written indictment, indicating an error.
John junior was also thought to be involved in a "Daring Robbery" reported in the Salisbury and Winchester Journal, 25 August 1817

"Early on Sunday morning the 17th inst, between the hours of two and three o'clock, as Stephen Eldridge, a carrier, was returning to the city from Portsmouth, with his horse and cart, he was stopped near the public house called "The Fighting Cocks", at Ower by four men, who threw him down, and robbed him of three guineas, three £1 notes (two of them Portsmouth Notes) two 7sh[illing] pieces and three or four pounds in silver. They then robbed an elderly man, a passenger in the cart, of 26sh[illings] in silver, and demanded money of a female passenger who gave them 2½d [pennies] saying it was all she had. (This was not the case, for she had considerable property about her which she fortunately had concealed) The villains made use of dreadful implications during the robbery, and threw back the woman's halfpence into the cart, they then made off towards Ower. Eldridge has offered a reward of ten guineas for the apprehension and conviction of the robbers and every possible exertion has been made and is now making to take them. There is great reason to suppose that the four robbers who stopped Eldridge belong to a gang of bad characters who reside in the New Forest, and subsist entirely by plunder. In searching for them two caverns were discovered, in which it is conjectured that villains of this description often secrete themselves. Three men have been apprehended and are now in custody on strong suspicion of having committed the above robbery. Their names are Wm Hood, Edward Andrews and ----[Thomas] Noyce. A young man named John Biddlecombe about 22yrs old and about 5ft 9ins. is also strongly suspected, and a strict search is making after him".

The following month, September 1817, John Biddlecombe was again involved in a robbery, this time in Highclere. The Truman's Exeter Flying Post, 2 October 1817 reports: *"BURGLARY AND A ROBBER SHOT, - The dwelling house of John Bolton, at Highclere, in the county of Hants, was early in the morning of Friday se'n night broken open by three men, named Henry Knott, Thomas Pocock the younger, and John Biddlecombe, who dragged Bolton from his bed, and threatened to murder him if he did not tell where his money was. In the meantime, his wife escaped unperceived by the robbers out the back window and alarmed the neighbours, a party of whom arrived just as the robbers were leaving the house. A scuffle ensued, when after a severe struggle, Pocock (a bricklayer of East Woodhay) was shot dead by Mr. Batten. Knott was taken into custody, and Biddlecombe escaped with a bundle containing an old gold ring, some guineas, three £1 notes &c. Biddlecombe (for whose apprehension a handsome reward is offered) is about 5feet 11inches,*

26yrs of age, stout made, sandy beard, dark hair and complexion, wore a fustian thickset corduroy waistcoat with sleeves, red waistcoat underneath, and corduroy breeches."

Current opinion is that Biddlecome had been evading capture since his father had been found not guilty of robbing Mark Noble the previous July and the highway robbery of Stephen Eldridge in August and the robbery of John Bolton at Highclere in September. A handsome reward was offered for his apprehension and for a long period he managed to elude the vigilance of the officers and secreted himself in a wood near Plaitford. At some period before 18 March 1818, the ostler of The Shoe Inn, Plaitford came across Biddlecomb's hideout and managed to overpower him and take him as his prisoner to The Shoe, from where he was taken to Fisherton Gaol in Salisbury. On 31 March 1818, he was committed and charged on the oath of Thomas Cooper of Bramshaw with having broken open his fowl house and with feloniously stealing therein one fowl. Hand written against the entry on the calendar the words-"*For the Assizes*". We have no record of a verdict for this charge. This offence was carried out on the night of 27 January 1818, and a warrant was raised on 18 March, after John had been apprehended.

At the Winchester Summer Assizes on Tuesday 14 July 1818, John Biddlecombe was on the calendar for trial. He was charged with burglary and robbery in the house of John Bolton in Highclere on the night of 18 September 1817.

The following day, Wednesday 15 July, the death sentence was passed on twenty-one prisoners, including Biddlecombe for burglary and robbery as charged.

Of the twenty-one prisoners sentenced to death, eighteen were reprieved and three, including John Biddlecomb, were left for execution on Saturday 1 August.

Although we have no supporting evidence, it is possible that the burglary at the property of Mark Noble and the stealing of the fowl, which was put forward *for the assizes,* and the other offences, may well have been taken into consideration by the court.

It is reported that a few days before his execution John Biddlecomb had sent a letter to his father and family, '*Entreating them to take warning by his example - to observe the Sabbath – to be regular at church – and to abstain from Cricket Matches, and all other games on that sacred day; attributing his own melancholy end chiefly to the neglect of his religious duties'.*

The report on his execution by the Hampshire Telegraph and Sussex Chronicle dated 3 August 1818: '*This morning, soon after eight o'clock, John Biddlecomb, aged 25 years; Nathaniel Carter, 21; and James Williams, 28, were taken from the goal to the place of execution, where having joined the Chaplain in prayer, about nine o'clock, they were launched into eternity'*

The newspaper goes on to say: *'He conducted himself with propriety since condemnation – in appearance Biddlecomb was a fine, tall, powerful young man'*

Nathaniel Carter and James Williams were convicted of stealing four sheep.

A sermon preached in the Bridewell at Winchester and published by the Rev. Chaplin of the county of Hampshire, demonstrates the fatal consequences of poaching: The sermon was printed in newspapers across the south of England in January 1827. The following is taken from the Salisbury and Winchester Journal:

"About 7 years ago John Biddlecombe was found guilty and executed for house breaking, under the most aggravated circumstances of violence and cruelty. He commenced his career, as he told me with his own lips, by playing cricket and other games on the Sabbath day, which games ended by retiring to the alehouse when he frequently became intoxicated, and was thereby unfitted for this customary employment on the Monday. In a short time, Labor was irksome to him, and for his support, he had to recourse to killing, as he expressed himself, a few birds. This could not last long, poultry his next object of attack, and every species of cattle-stealing followed. At length, neither the person or the property of his neighbours were held sacred: "His hand was against every man" and such was the desperate daring with which he perpetrated his crimes that "everyman's hand was against him". Unable to face the light of the sun, for a while he lurked unseen by day, and wandering as a vagabond by night. Justice at last overtook him, and he ended a life of iniquity in sin, by a death of ignominy and disgrace".

With the help of research carried out by John Biddlecombe's four times great nephew we are able to give an account of the outcome of the trials of four of John Biddlecome's accomplices, three of which were from the local area.

For the assault and robbery of Stephen Eldridge near the "Fighting Cocks" at Ower, William Hood, Edward Andrews and Thomas Noyce were arrested and stood trial at the Hampshire Lent Quarter Sessions, March 1818. William Hood, who was baptised in Plaitford on 5 January 1799, was acquitted having "admitted the evidence". No further convictions have been found. The 1851 and 1861 census, records him as living with his unmarried sister Elizabeth, in New Milton, where he was employed as a wheelwright.

Edward Andrews and Thomas Noyce were both convicted of "robbery on the highway" and sentenced to death. Their sentence was later reduced to a conditional discharge; to be "transported for life". They were both removed to the Prison Hulk "Laurel" in Portsmouth Harbour on 13 May. In July they were transferred to the transport ship "General Stuart"[2] at Southampton. They arrived in New South Wales, Australia in December 1818.

Edward Andrews, born in Landford on 25 December 1791, is described in his record as a labourer, 5ft 4ins tall, dark and sallow with brown hair and hazel eyes. After serving a period of eight to ten years, Andrews would have been given a" ticket of leave". Ticket of leave men were permitted to marry, or bring their families from Britain (at their own expense), and to acquire a property. Records show that Andrews held a ticket of leave from 1838 to 1844. A convict who observed the conditions of his ticket of leave until completion of one half of his sentence was entitled to apply for a conditional pardon. Andrews made an application and was granted a pardon in July 1846 on the condition of not returning to the country from where he was transported.

Thomas Noyce, baptized in Wellow on 4 September 1796 was recorded as a handyman, 5ft 9ins tall with a fair/pale complexion, brown hair and hazel eyes. Unfortunately, there are no further records of his time in Australia.

Henry Knott, aged 43 from Sussex was charged with robbery of John Bolton in Highclere and sentenced to death. The sentence was later commuted to deportation for life. As with Edward Andrews and Thomas Noyce, he was taken to the prison hulk "Laurel". The list of prisoners held aboard the Laurel record Noyce as number 1882, Knott 1883 and Andrews 1893. They all sailed together on the transport ship "General Stuart". After being in Australia for almost two years, Knott was sentenced in November 1820 to two years for an unknown misdemeanor and sent to Newcastle, a harsh penal work prison. In July 1824, he was given a punishment of seven days on a treadmill for being drunk and disorderly in his master's service. At the age of 59, Henry Knott applied to marry Ann White, and permission was granted on 11 June 1834.

John Biddlecombe senior and his wife Peggy had twelve children, of which the first seven were baptized in Landford between 1792 and 1804, and the remaining five in Plaitford between 1807 and 1816.

John senior was buried at Plaitford on 30 January 1820, aged 51. In 1843, his wife Peggy was living on Plaitford Common and on the 1851 Census she was head of the family and a pauper living on Plaitford Common with her daughter, Sarah, aged 53, a charwoman. Peggy was buried at Plaitford on 1 August 1851, aged 78 and Sarah on 26 June 1876, aged 79.

[1]Peter Osman four times great grand nephew of John Biddlecomb
[2]The ship General Steward sailed with 250 prisoners of which 123 had life sentences.

Chapter 7
Plaitford Races

Head east from the Shoe Inn along the A36 and you will find Plaitford's one and only ancient mile stone, right opposite is Plaitford Racecourse, an avenue of trees heading out towards the open common.

Our research has discovered that races were held over a twenty four year period from 1825 to 1848 inclusive. From newspaper reports and other records we have been able to account for twenty three years. We have been unable to find any records of races held in 1831. The events all took place around Whitsun time and until 1840 were known as the Plaitford Amusements.

The Hampshire Chronicle dated 11 June 1827 writes: *"Plaitford Amusements on Monday were numerously attended. The saddle and bridle were won by Mr. Freeman's pony, after three good heats. A large party of gentlemen dined on the green, and the day past in the most cheerful manner"*

In their report on the 1840 meeting, The Hampshire Advertiser & Salisbury Guardian, 13 June, write that they compared the attraction of this humble meeting to the immediate area with that of Epsom's "Derby Day", Doncaster's "St Leger" and Ascot's "Cup". The article also mentions that races were run over one and a half miles.

Most of the race meetings appear to be part of a country fair with circus acts, penny peep-shows and open fronted stalls offering gingerbread, winkles and nuts. This can be seen from the following newspaper advertisement from 1848:

'PLAITFORD RACES - To come off on Friday next.
Take notice - The ground will be let for Booths and Standings on Thursday, June 15th, between the hours of nine and four o'clock, and which must be paid for at the same time.
N.B – On no account will any Publican be allowed to erect Booths for sale of Spirituous or other Liquors'

After the races in the 1840's around 100 persons would attend a dinner at the Shoe inn.

What would appear to have been the last race day and the one that attracted the most publicity took place on Friday 16 June 1848. This was the one and only meeting under the jurisdiction of the Jockey Club. Extensive research on our behalf by The National Horseracing Museum has only found this one race shown on Racing Calendars of the 19th century.

This being said, during the 1840's the importance of Plaitford as a racing venue can be found in some of the national sporting publications of the time, such as The Era, New Sporting Magazine and Sports Review, which all included Plaitford Races in their national listing of races to take place in the country.

Why the meeting in 1848 is the last recorded, we do not know. A newspaper report on the races states, '*The running was the best since the establishment of the races. The course was crowded with a full and fashionable company. These meetings are certainly much on the improve.*' From this report it would appear that the meetings were expected to continue, but so far we can find no evidence of this. In 1852, it is recorded, alongside the decline of coaching and the discontinuance of the once popular Plaitford Races, that the village had been losing popularity.

We know the increase in the popularity of the railways in the late 1840's and the decline in coaching affected the importance of the Shoe Inn as a posting inn, thus making Plaitford a less accessible and less attractive venue for race meetings.

Throughout the Second World War, Jerry Russett and his family had lived and stored their fairground equipment in the old gravel pit behind Bridgefoot Cottages. For a few years after the war they brought their fair back to Plaitford where it was set up at the bottom of the old racecourse.

Chapter 8
The Green Man Pub

The "Green Man Pub" has been part of local folklore for generations and no one really knows of its existence.

Its location on Plaitford Green has been handed down and there is no doubt that two parcels of cleared land either side of the footpath from Plaitford Green through Plaitford Green to Melchet Court could be the site.

The larger left hand clearing, partly surrounded by a ditch, does give some indication that a dwelling[1] may have stood on the site.

The older residents, whose families have lived in the area for many years, favour the right hand piece of land where a large barn now stands.

The person who may have lived on this land could have brewed cider or ale and supplied it to the workers on their way to and from Plaitford and Melchet Park.

The name Green Man could be a derivative of "the man on Plaitford Green" shortened to the Green Man, who knows?

As the original village of Plaitford is recorded as being to the north of the River Blackwater, it is very likely that during eighteenth and nineteenth century, Plaitford Green consisted of quite a few mud wall cottages. There is a pit fairly close to the "Green Man" site that is thought to be a result of clay extraction.

The current landowner has mentioned the location of a well close by, alongside the footpath from Plaitford Green to Landford wood.

In theory, any of the cottages on Plaitford Green in the eighteenth and nineteenth century could have been an Ale House or Pub known as the Green Man that served the community.

---

[1]We know from the 1841 Census and the 1842 Tithe Survey for Plaitford that Matthew Bright his wife Elizabeth, six children and Mary Martin occupied a cottage and garden on this site.

Chapter 9
Victorian School to Village Hall
By Sheila Cuell (nee Storr)

Children are recorded as attending school as early as 1828 in Plaitford. House of Commons papers from 1835 include the '1833 Abstract of Education Returns', which states: *The Parish of Plaitford (Pop 263). One Daily School (commenced 1828) containing 13 males and 15 females, who are instructed at the expense of their parents'* A further mention of an earlier school was at the trial of two farm workers charged with riot and assault on William Gray, Farmer of Plaitford in November 1830.

Mary Ann Jarrett, stepdaughter of William Gray giving evidence against the accused claiming she witnessed the attack, said: '*I was at school on that day and the mistress let us out at the usual time of 12 noon'* It is not known where the lessons took place.

Victorian School

The land for the school was gifted to the village by Henry Stephen Fox-Strangeways, Third Earl of Ilchester in 1840. Plans were drawn up, submitted and approved in around 1845. The school was opened in1846 after being built with the help of a grant of £84 from the Committee of Council for Education and administered as a National School by the Church of England. The opening date was built into the north wall but was partially destroyed by the addition of an extra doorway in 1912.

The original building was of a single-skin red brick construction with a traditional high pitch slate roof (still in place today) a brick floor and consisted of one room and an adjoining house for the resident head teacher. The house consisted of a living room with a pantry on the ground floor and two bedrooms above, one no bigger than a box room. Outside there was a fuel store and a pump. In the early days the house had no running water, toilet or bathroom etc. The south and west facing façades of the original school and house remain today and must not be changed as Test Valley Borough Council have now implemented a preservation restriction.

The original Victorian School was much smaller than today's village hall, with a classroom measuring just 28x18 feet with a raised gallery in one corner (to the left of the entrance porch). This could have been either for the elder scholars or the head-teacher to keep a weary eye on all the 60 plus children this room was expected to accommodate.

It is reported that in the 1870's the room was made into two classrooms with a dividing curtain. This was to either separate the boys from the girls, or infants from older pupils. A curtain divider was still in place up to the 1950's when a teaching assistant helped the younger children. Originally, some of these children were as young as three years old. Was Plaitford a forerunner to Nursery Education?

The school was originally started by the Society for Promotion of Christian Knowledge (SPCK). Scholars had to take two exams a year – one religious and one general.

Benefactors of the school included Lady Ashburton of Melchet Court, Sidney Herbert of Wilton House, together with Captain Hugh Berners of Manor Farm, who also represented Plaitford on the Romsey Board of Guardians for the workhouse in the 1870's, without such Benefactors and the local clergy the school would not have existed.

There was a fuel store presumably to keep logs and coal dry for the two fires, one situated at each end of the room. Fires usually started in October using faggots of brushwood and coal. In very cold weather, desks were rearranged several times to enable heat to be radiated most effectively across the room- the infants closest to the heat. Apparently, the children's sense of humour came to the fore when faced with the cold weather as they laughed at the moaning noises the wind made as it came through the door. Sometimes, it was so bitterly cold that the children couldn't stop crying and one little girl in 1890 was refused admittance as she lived some way across Plaitford Common and the School Authorities thought it too far for her to walk in such conditions.

Heating was a problem. The original fireplace didn't seem to generate enough heat and in 1875, a stove was first suggested – in 1896, a new grate was installed and the fireplace temporarily restored. In 1903, a fireguard was requested and this was reiterated in the 1940's! In 1906, a 'Carron' fireplace was fitted, and in 1912, a 'Tortoise' stove. One teacher requested coke to burn as the coal supplied threw out no heat. By 1934, it was back to square one as a new grate replaced the coke stove.

Hot weather was also a problem. The windows were high up and diamond paned – as they still are at the front of the school house. In 1897, H.M Inspector states "room inconveniently overcrowded (60 plus children and 2 adults) very hot and oppressive. Ventilation to be improved and windows re-constructed to let in more air and light" During the very hot weather, lessons were taken outside – this still happened when I came to this school in the early 1950's, so nothing much had changed.

Unfortunately, with the adverse weather conditions and close proximity with each other, all round health was a problem. Diphtheria, scarlet fever and whooping cough were rampant. In 1866, diphtheria killed 5 children and in 1867, an outbreak of scarlet fever delayed Christmas present distribution until February. The school was closed completely on several occasions to stop these diseases (much the same as with Swine Flu in 2009). Very often the school closed so that friends could follow their schoolmate's coffin to church. One such occasion, in May 1907, was that of Ellen Lovell, who lived at Bridgefoot Cottages. "Tinny" as she was lovingly known was tragically drowned in the swollen Blackwater which ran along the bottom of the gardens at Bridgefoot. Her coffin was carried by children from the school, and a memorial stone was paid for by a collection from school friends and villagers and can still be seen in the church yard.

Head lice were another problem as in 1866, the Rev Barton promised to present a good pair of scissors to all girls who would keep their hair short for a year.

Cleanliness and hygiene were a continuous problem. In 1876, one boy was sent home to wash his face – obviously no facilities for this at the school. The "closets" or "offices" so-called had a common entrance with each closet having a double seat and a semi partition – who remembers Wellow's reading room double-holed loo? The older boys had the job of cleaning the pumps – some were apparently punished for making the water thick (presumably from washing) on the common where there was a spring. As there was no drinking water in the school and for people living on the common, this caused real problems, and all water had to be boiled. Though the water was tested regularly through the years, it was not until June 1941 that the school was informed that the well water no longer needed to be boiled.

Financial changes took place nationally in 1891, regarding grants and parental contribution. Payment of Government grants from 1858 to 1890 depended on how many children attended and how many passed exams, but, from 1891-5, these grants were replaced by a system of block grants. Plaitford received £58.6s 6d. In 1874, the school penny paid by parents had been doubled to two for children of farmers and trades people, whilst extra-parochial pupils paid three half-pennies. Poorer parents were excused altogether. As most of Plaitford's employment appears to have been farm labouring and the possibility of three children or more being of school age, one penny per day for each child would amount to quite a high percentage of a family income, so it would be quite safe, I think, to assume a farm labourer's family would be exempt from paying school fees. In 1891, all payments ceased.

During Harvest and other seasonal tasks, some of the children were required by their parents to stay home, either to look after younger siblings to enable mum to work on the land, or to do the work themselves. Haymaking was usually a family occasion, also fruit and vegetable gathering, acorn gathering and collecting turf and peat.

During the latter half of the 19th century the attendance of children continued to stay at around 60, although Plaitford's population had almost halved between 1855 to 1901 (330 to 175). The school room being so small in 1901, the managers decided not to admit any more children from Wellow or Landford without consent. However, they still attended. I can remember Freda Geary from Rover Hill in the 1950's with Christopher Moody, Gerald and Anne Vinnal from Partridge Hill, Landford, in our later photographs.

Between 1878 and 1881, the Reverend Gay encouraged the children to study and pass exams by generously giving them a monetary reward of nine old pence for three subjects, six old pence for two subjects and three old pence for one subject.

Previously, in 1873, Capt Berners gave money for mental arithmetic and together with his wife, who helped with needlework lessons, gave calico and flannel for sewing. At Christmas, bonnets, capes and dresses were awarded to the girls, with caps and shirts to the boys, but only if they attended and behaved well. When Capt and Mrs. Berners daughter married, some of her trousseau, including nightdresses, was made by the pupils.

Needlework played a big part in the education of the girls at the school, right from the early days until the 1930's, ranging from hankies, shirts, nightdresses and cushion covers. See diary of events 1930.

Diary of Events and Children's Escapades

1863: School writing slates gradually being replaced. Pencils and quills were introduced for older children

1867: Fanny Bungay was expelled for being obstructive and disobedient.

1869: Seven girls and two boys were given half hour detention for laughing during prayers.

1870: January. Seasonal party. Each child received an orange and a bag of sweets from the Rev Barton. Those of the scholars most regularly attending school received a pair of boots from the Rev Barton. An expensive day for the number of children to receive boots was 54.

1876: Two girls were fined one shilling each after entering the school by a window and breaking the harmonium. H.M Inspectors report of 1909 (33 years later) states that "the harmonium now used is a wrecked instrument and a new one is needed" Both Mr. Griffin and Mrs. Travis Holmes were church organists, so it is safe to assume that music played a part in the school curriculum in the late 1890's and early 1900's.

1877: A burglar broke several panes of glass to gain entrance and opened the missionary box – several shillings were stolen – no one was ever caught.

1879: Ellen Moore punished for repeated disobedience. Mrs. Moore "fetched her away from school with great violence"

January 13 1879: Ernest Bowles accidentally shot whilst coming to school but wound not very serious.

March 7 1879: Ernest Bowles away through shooting himself (again!)

Ernest Bowles was fourteen on the 1881 Census. He was born at Gunsfield Cottage and was still there as Head Woodman in 1911. He married Sarah J. Hatch in 1898.

1883: The roof was struck by lightning, "but needed repair anyway"

January 1896: Mrs. Turner, head teacher and her husband, who assisted, received a leaving bonus of two guineas between them.

April 1896: Mr. Griffin joined the school as headmaster at a monthly salary of five pounds sixteen shillings and eight pence.

1899: A cricket team was formed by Mr. Griffin. In July, Plaitford School played a match against Landford at the Rectory, Plaitford won by eighteen runs.

Education Bill 1902: In the early part of the nineteenth century, the growth of charitable educational institutions and the formation of voluntary schools led to the Elementary Education Act of 1870. Too many compromises were alleged to have been made, leading to the new Education Bill of 1902.

At a meeting held at Braishfield in November 1902, the speaker, Mr. Smith of Romsey, said:-

"At present, since 1870, there were Board schools, voluntary schools, technical schools, secondary, science and art schools, all existing in a haphazard and unconnected manner. The new bill was introduced to co-ordinate these varying educational factors. Mr. Smith did not think this would happen, as it would establish new education

authorities that were not elected for their work. They would have a nominal control only over the various schools in their areas, especially voluntary schools where the authority would only have one third representatives amongst the managers. The areas for secondary education purposes differed from elementary education and it was thought that such a system would produce an unsatisfactory and unworkable state of affairs'.

Mr. Smith then pointed out that the financial part of the bill gave one body the power of levying the rate and another the spending of the money, whilst the poor rate-payers who paid the piper would be unable to call the tune.

April 1906: Education Bill- The trustees of Plaitford School are not going to decide anything finally until the Education Bill is before the House of Commons and then, unless justice is done according to the Trust Deed, the school will close. The Trustees can never accept the bill as it is now.

1903: Mr. Griffin was presented with a "splendid standard floor lamp" on his retirement in February 1903.

The new Head Mr. Travis-Holmes introduced gardening during his stint as headmaster. The boys also formed a cricket team.

In August the H.M Inspector reported *'The school under new leadership is in good order and promises well under new teachers, Mr. and Mrs. Travis-Holmes. Written Work and reading are generally good and arithmetic is intelligent. In some oral subjects the children are backward but this is not the fault of the present teachers'.*

A further report in September states *'Religious instruction under the new teachers caused the syllabus to suffer with quantity but the quality was promising for the year ahead'.*

1904: The H.M Inspector stated that the school, under the leadership of Mr. Travis Holmes, had the highest percentage of attendance in the Romsey Division.

1905: H.M Inspectors report in August. *'Mixed department school under Mr. and Mrs. Travis-Holmes is in a creditable condition, children well cared for, sensibly taught and profit by instruction. Attendance good. The infants' class is sharp, busy and well advanced'.*

July 1906: Attendance prizes were awarded by the Education Committee of the County Council. Two medals, eight bronze shields, twenty certificates and eight leaving certificates. The medals were won by Annie Hood and Maud Harrison

1908: The children are trained in habits of industry and tidiness and take great interest in their work – written part very neat and tidy.
September 1910: Army Airship was hovering near the school. The airship made a forced landing in the area of Wellow Wood attracting a large crowd.

The school gardens c1913, where the village hall green is today. You can just make out the old brick toilet block in the background behind John Travis Holmes who was Head teacher from 1903 until his death in April 1914.

1917/1918: The pupils collected a great many eggs for wounded Soldiers and these were packed in cartons and forwarded by Mr. Cook. They also collected £3.6s.0p for Red Cross Flag Day.
September 23 1918: An aeroplane came down on the common and in consequence only 23 pupils attended school in the afternoon
1924: The older children went to the British Exhibition at Wembley financed by Sir Alfred Mond of Melchet Court.
1925 The older children went to the I.O.W and the younger children to Milford-on-Sea; all financed my Lady Mond, Sir Fredrick Preston (Landford Manor) and Mr. Douglas Eyre (Lords Oak, Landford). October: Lady Mond gave a Lantern Lecture on her tour of Egypt and Palestine.
Mrs. Bungay retired as caretaker after 20 years. She was presented with a hot water bottle and a purse of money.
1929: 180 garments sent to H.M the Queen in connection with Queen Mary's London Needlework Guild to be distributed to homes,

hospitals and orphanages. All the material was provided by Lady Melchet.

In July, Mrs. Creeth noticed that a young lad of ten years of age was uncomfortable, when asked what was wrong, she discovered, after undressing him that the boy had extensive bruising on both arms and parts of the body. When taking his shirt off he nearly fainted. She put him to bed and reported the incident to the NSPCC and Police. The boy's guardian of Maury's Lane found herself in court, charged with cruelty towards her nephew, who had been staying with her for about a year. She was fined £5 with £1 costs. The boy went home to his family in Wales.

September 8 1930: During the summer holiday the school was decorated and a new green curtain used as a partition between the infants and the senior children was fitted. It cost eighteen shillings and nine pence.

Also, at a recent show held at Melchet Court, Plaitford school children were successful in obtaining all prizes for under eleven and under fourteen plain and fancy needlework. All prizes for knitting amounting to nearly three pounds. Lawrence Hood won first prize for raffia work. Peggy Moody, William Rickman and Lilian Rickman, won first, second and third prize for handwriting. The show was open to all villages in the area and all prizes were gained in open competition with other schools from Hampshire and Wiltshire.

1931: Again saw success at Melchet Court Show with Muriel Harrison and Rosalie Moody first and second for plain needlework. Two first prizes for socks. Lillian Rickman and Phyllis Robinson won first and second prize for handwriting. George Curtis and Ronald Curtis gained second and third for poster painting. This success continued at subsequent shows held at Melchet Court throughout the 1930's.

1930's: Mrs. Creeth was a very enthusiastic teacher. With the support of her assistant teachers, she arranged the pageants each May that involved the whole village (See Empire Day and May Queen Pageant).

The School-Armistice Day, 15 November 1935, was observed by teachers, pupils and a number of parents, followed by a ceremony of tree planting to commemorate the Silver Jubilee of King George V. Each child in the school planted a Silver Birch Tree and affixed a label bearing their name and date of planting. It was hoped in years to come the trees would form a little copse in the precinct of the school. Sadly, due to the common area around the school being left to grow wild over the last 40 years, the area is now covered in silver birch trees!

1935: A shed for the children to shelter in was purchased at a cost of thirteen pounds including guttering.

1936: Egg collecting again, this time for Romsey Hospital. The total collected over the year was 218 plus a sack of potatoes.

1940's: During the war years, children would come from Southampton to the school. As it was already crowded with village children and evacuees, alternate morning and afternoon sessions had to be arranged. Despite the war, the schoolchildren had many enjoyable parties due to the generosity of the people of the village.

1940: In June, pupils and parents sent 150 children's garments to a Belgian refugee depot in London. This was a very commendable effort for a small village.

1942: Mrs. Creeth died in February after almost twenty years as head teacher

1943: Head teacher Miss Turner founded the Girls' Club at the school. Later that year it was affiliated to the National Council of Girls' Clubs.

At the end of the 1940's, a tatty partition curtain was still in place.

1952: When Mrs. Bottrill arrived as head teacher, social events for the whole village were held again. We had a concert that went on tour to Wellow, and a great celebration for the Queen's Coronation.

At this time, Mrs. Bungay and Mrs. Lacey were dinner ladies.

Empire Day and May Queen Pageant

Throughout the first half of the twentieth century, it was often a custom for schools to celebrate Queen Victoria's Birthday, known officially as Empire Day.

Between 1932 and 1938, Empire Day celebrations including the crowning of a May Queen were held at Plaitford School, with the exception of 1937 when it was held at Manor Farm. Each year the May Queen was chosen by fellow pupils. Early in the morning, a lesson on the Empire was given by Mrs. Creeth who was Headmistress throughout this period.

1932: Empire day was celebrated, and for the first time Plaitford also held a May festival. Myrtle Harrison was crowned as May Queen. There were two maids-of-honour, Muriel Harrison and Betty Moore. The Coronation was performed by Rosalie Moody, a senior girl.

1933: The May Queen this year was Betty Moore and her two maids-of-honour were Phyllis Robinson and Lena Bungay. Old English, Scottish and Welsh songs were sung. Ambulance display was given by the six eldest girls with boys as patients. Tea was served in the orchard adjoining the school for parents and friends. The weather was excellent and drill display was given on the common followed by races and team games.

1934: The Queen chosen this year was Joyce Dibden and her maids-of-honour were Rosalie Moody, Betty Dibden and Jean Vinall. Mothers and friends were invited to the ceremony, which was followed by a concert in the school.

1935: Empire day and the crowning of the May Queen formed a major part of Plaitford's celebration of GeorgeV's Silver Jubilee. A pageant was performed under the apple trees in the orchard adjoining the school. Children dressed in costumes of countries throughout the Empire.

Betty Dibden was crowned as May Queen and her maids-of-honour were Rhoda Sharland and Gladys Rickman.

The ceremony was followed by a procession through the village to Manor Farm barn, where tea was provided for all parishioners. The barn, lent by Mr. Curtis, was decorated for the occasion.

After tea, Mr.George Cook, chairman of the Celebrations Committee, presented all babies and school children of Plaitford with Jubilee medals

The remainder of the evening was devoted to sports, a programme having been arranged by Mrs. Creeth and Mrs. Bungay for schoolchildren and adults.

1936: Plaitford School was one of few places in the area which maintained the old ceremony of crowning a May Queen which took place on Empire Day. The Queen this year was Dorothy Rickman and her maids-of-honour Peggy Kemish and Gladys Mead

1937: This was the Coronation year of King George VI and the Pageant of Empire and the crowning of the May Queen formed a chief part of the parish coronation celebrations. This year the pageant took place in the rickyard of Manor Farm, which was decorated for the occasion with flags and a flower decked throne for the May Queen. A huge thatched rick was a background to the stage. Schoolchildren dressed in the costumes of the countries that formed the British Empire. Gladys Rickman was crowned May Queen. The crowning was followed by a concert of songs and recitations by schoolchildren.

The whole parish was entertained to tea, which was prepared in the decorated barn. After tea came a full program of sport for children 8 to 80.

Music was provided throughout the day by radio. Speakers had been situated around the field. At eight o'clock, all the company heard His Majesty's speech.

The children received mugs, the gift of Mr. Simmons, oranges from Mr. G Cooke, Chairman of the Parish Council, packets of sweets from Mrs. Kemp and a Coronation Medal and new sixpence from the Parish Council.

The day's celebrations ended with the release of several huge rockets.

1937 Coronation Pageant held at Manor Farm with Gladys Rickman as May Queen

1938: This would appear to be the last recorded Empire day and May queen celebrations in Plaitford. This year the May Queen was Peggy Kemish and her maids-of-honour were Hazel Ireland and Brenda Challis. Mothers and friends were invited to the ceremony which was followed by a concert.

1953: A pageant of a different kind took place in the school grounds on Saturday 6 June 1953 to celebrate the coronation of Queen

Elizabeth II. Starting at 2.30pm, the afternoon consisted of a Fancy Dress Parade for children and adults, Children and adult's sports and culminating at 8.30pm with a bonfire and community singing. Sheila Storr was selected by the school to be Queen for the day, attended by her younger sister Pat and Freda Stone. Dresses were made by Mrs. Doris Vinall and crown by Mrs. Botterill, head teacher.

Memories of Plaitford School

The late Mrs. Marion Harding started at Plaitford School when she was three years old and left in 1910 at the age of fourteen, having passed the Labour Examination. To do this she walked from Plaitford to Romsey and took the exam in the old Boys' National School building (now the Romsey Library). She passed with a boy named Frank Mells.

Jim Bowles remembers a favorite activity at playtime was to try and ride any of the donkeys and ponies that roamed freely around the school (in those days the New Forest was not fenced as it is today). The late Roy Hayter recalled getting on a pony during a mid morning break. The animal was so frightened it bolted with Roy hanging on for dear life. The pony eventually stopped at Sturtmore Pond where it and Roy parted company. Roy arrived back to school some time later. Suffice to say, Mrs. Creeth the head teacher was not amused!

At the outbreak of the Second World War, Eileen Gander, nee Sullivan, moved from Southampton with her mother, Florence and brother, Vernon to live with her Grandma Hutchings at Brook Cottage, Plaitford. Her father, Richard, a member of Southampton Fire Brigade, advised his wife to leave Southampton before war was declared.

Eileen started in the infants' class at Plaitford School in 1940 and remembers: '*The cloakroom was down some steps and it was a bit dark and scary. We had to leave our coats and gas masks there. We all had gas masks and had to carry them to and from school each day. My teacher was Miss Dyke, she was very young and pretty and I remember she would hang her stockings on the fireguard to dry them. When Miss Dyke left to get married, my Aunt, Mrs. Walter Hutchings came to teach us. She was very strict. We all had to drink milk. It was in pint bottles and was put by the stove to warm it. I hated milk and still do. It was lukewarm and very rich (full cream). We each had our own cup that held about $1/3^{rd}$ of a pint. My cup which was blue and white, got broken, and mother told auntie we hadn't another of the correct size. Hurrah! I didn't have to have any more milk. There was a vegetable garden between the school and the toilets. Who ate what* *was grown, I don't know. Only the big ones gardened. During the war, the school was used for social events and fund raising days. I remember dressing up in fancy dress for the "Wings for Victory day". Also during the war years, the evacuees and poorer children had a spoonful of cod liver oil and malt. It looked delicious, all brown and sticky. I pestered my mum to get some. It was horrid- all fishy and nasty, but my brother, Vernon, ate it. The children who had it all had their own spoons.'*

Miss Annie Turner, headmistress from 1942 to 1946, wrote her memories in a letter to the late Frances Cale: *'From the outside, the school resembled Anne Hathaway's cottage with its diamond panes. The school had just one room with a tatty curtain to divide it between the infants and top school (until 1944 to the age of 14+). The school opened into a small compact cottage – one and a half rooms down and one and a half rooms up!! No modcons, you had to go down the path to a pump house (with your buckets or kettles) and across the path to toilets!! There was a small kitchen with a sink but no taps and I had an Aladdin cooker, oil lamps and candles.*

I was headmistress of the school during the war years and the school became a social centre with a thriving active girls' club, it was a library, a place for "Shilling Hops", National Savings Weeks and Social Events. The school thrived – I never knew how many children would arrive from town on a Monday morning and out would come my own chairs. We had school dinners bought from a centre in Romsey – good mothers came to wash up (hot water being bought by the dinner people). My caretaker, Mr. Bungay, lit the coal fires each morning, and his dear wife kept our school clean'

Anne Strong, nee McDiarmid started at Plaitford School when Mrs. Botterell was head teacher, later succeeded by Mrs. Stephenson. Anne recalls: *'How I liked Mrs. Silverio, a part time teacher at the school, who told us wonderful stories and taught us some Spanish! On one occasion we acted a play in which we did some dancing. I did a Spanish dancing with another girl, Ann Dias. We wore crepe paper frocks with crepe shawls which had been very carefully made by Mrs. Silverio. Mine was a red dress and white shawl that had a red rose on it. Ann's was completely opposite. Lyn Dawkins danced a parasol dance and she wore a short white ballet frock.*

I also remember the headmistress, Mrs. Stephenson, taking the four oldest children, including me, to see HMS Victory in Portsmouth'.

Carol Finch nee Curtis, attended Plaitford School from 1962 – 1965 and was among the last pupils and she left to go to Wellow School on the day Plaitford closed. She recalls some of her memories - *'I do not* remember Mum walking me to school, but I suppose that to begin with she must have. Gwen Collins, who lived at Plaitford Green, used to cycle with her daughter Joan in a child seat on the back. When Joan got her own bike, Gwen would stop at our gate and I would climb into the child seat and off we would go. We would cut through Botley's and across the common. There was one bit where there was a big dip and I loved it when we went down and up on the bike.

The common in those days was grazed by the cattle and ponies that at that time could cross the A36 at will. When the forest was fenced in, the common was left to go to rack and ruin. Where there was bowling-green grass and a few gorse bushes, there are now trees, brambles and rough grass. When the dew was heavy, the cobwebs on the gorse bushes looked like diamond necklaces. I thought they looked beautiful. We learnt a song at school, "Daisy's are our silver, buttercups our gold, these are all the treasures we can have to hold". Well, those cobwebs with their dew on were my diamonds!

The teacher was Mrs. Stephenson when I started. She was nice but had a few strange ideas as far as we country kids were concerned. Such as, when apples were in the small orchard at the back of the school, we had to take a penny to buy one instead of having crisps and chocolate biscuits. We did not think this was a very good idea. You can get fed up with apples day after day. One bright spark on learning that the proceeds were to go to the poor children in Africa, asked if we could pick all the apples and send them instead. This did not go down too well, but we were ever so inventive and after a while I think the penny dropped, so to speak. You can lead a child to the apple but you can't make it eat it!

One of the first things we were told on starting the school was that you "DO NOT GO DOWN THE FIELD TO THE OLD PRIVIES, AND DO NOT RUN UP AND DOWN THE ASH HEAP". Of course we couldn't wait to disobey these two rules. In my case I have always hated spiders, and a quick look into the old privies was all I needed not to repeat the experience.

The school was heated by one large tortoise stove with a large fireguard around it. We would hang our scarves and gloves on it in the winter.

It was not long after I started that Mrs. Stephenson left and was replaced by the lovely Mrs. Brook. I remember she had dark hair and wore bright red lipstick. She was a great fun teacher and we all loved her. She bought a present for every child on their birthday and at Christmas.

When it was Halloween, we did not have pumpkins but we used to hollow out and carve Swedes. How our little hands managed those hard vegetables I do not know. I have enough trouble chopping them for Sunday lunch!

We had two dinner ladies, Florence Sullivan and Peggy Moody. The dinners were delivered by van then finished off and dished up in the kitchen, which was down the far end of the building next to the children's toilets. There was a little lobby in between, if I remember rightly.

I didn't mind school dinners but one that I could not stand was veal stew with pearl barley in it. We seemed to have that meal quite a lot, which seems strange as now veal is quite expensive. I still do not eat it. One day I really was having a lot of trouble eating my stew, but one of the dinner ladies said "Carol Curtis, you will sit there and finish your dinner". Well, the afternoon lessons started and I was still stuck with this by now gluttonous stew, till I hit on an idea. I kept making faces in my dinner and made the other pupils laugh. So in the end the plate was removed. Quite a result I thought, till I realized that I had missed out on chocolate cracknel which was my favourite pud!

Mrs. Edwina Offer was the school secretary. She was always beautifully dressed without a hair out of place. She spoke quietly and was such a lovely lady. We used to queue up to buy saving stamps. I think they were two shillings each. I don't know what mum did with them.

In the corner of the room we had a little Wendy house. I remember a little blue welsh dresser and large sweet jars filled with rice, split peas, lentils etc and we had scales to weigh them. I loved going into the Wendy house.

To help with number work we had a box of little sticks of wood all different lengths and colours. For instance, number 1 was a little white cube, number 2 was twice the length of the cube etc etc. It was called "Quizinaire" I don't know if that's spelt right, but it was very useful and fun to play with.

I never looked forward to sports day. I have always been rubbish at running and jumping so was nearly always last or I would trip over etc.

One day a week on an afternoon, the Vicar, Mr. Freeman, would come to read us a bible story. A lot of us went to Sunday school, so it meant a double dose and in the summer, when it could get really warm in the classroom, some of us fell asleep.

At Christmas, balls of cotton wool would be stuck on the windows to look like snow, and we would take shoe boxes and make little Christmas scenes in them.

I have many happy memories of Plaitford School. I was the last of the Curtis family to serve my full time there, as it closed the day I left. I think my cousin Nick would have been the next to start there but had to start at Wellow instead.

The parents collected to give Mrs. Brooks a present, and I think my mum bought it. It was a dressing table set. I don't remember what else they gave her. All the children were given a cartridge pen with a real gold nib etc. Blue marble effect for the boys and red for the girls, all with our initials engraved on them.

There were little flower beds under a couple of the windows and "honesty" grew in them. I was intrigued by the pearly discs, and the plant always makes me think of the school.

On Mondays, mum would collect me from school and we would walk across the common to "Powells Farm" for tea. My grandparents lived there then. We always had boiled eggs from the free range hens, strawberry jelly with thick cream from the milk of the farm and granny Ellie made butter as well. Sometimes, I would make a little butter in a kilner jar, but it took an awful lot of shaking. Butter has never tasted as good as that homemade. I used to watch Basil Brush on television with my Uncle Morry. And there were always Maryland cookies in the biscuit tin, one of my favourites.

One day a week, a lady whose name was Mrs. Silverio came to teach us arts and crafts. I can just remember making paper flowers, I thought she was very clever, but she had an accent and sometimes we could not quite understand her. I think she lived Southampton way.

One of the boys was given a wind-up boat for his birthday and we all crowded into the school house bathroom and tried it out in the bath. Plaitford School was really like a large family, and it was quite a shock when I moved to Wellow, there were certainly no fun loving teachers there!

Some children from Wellow were at the school with me, Susan Reynolds, Sally Fothergill and Carol Babey.

Some of the Plaitford gang were Martin Flack, Terry Stone, Amanda Bowles, Sally McDiarmid, Jocelyn Matthews, Lorna Bowles, Joan Collins and Paul Moody'.

In 1944, children started to be transferred to Wellow School, and by 1950, the school was down to one class up to eight years old. Due to a fall in numbers, Plaitford School closed in 1965. The closure meant that all Plaitford children had to travel to Wellow School.

As official school records did not start until 1860, we do not have the names of head teachers between the opening of the school in 1846 and 1850 and between 1852 and 1856. From the first recorded head teacher in 1851 until the closure of the school in 1965 there were 25 head teachers, six temporary supply head teachers and over 50 teaching assistants.

Head Teachers

1846-1850: No record
March 1851: Harvey White
1852-1856: No Record
1857: Mr. T Irons
1859: Robert Worthington
March 1861: William Faulkner
1861-July 1868: Miss Mary Eliza Kidd
August 1868-May 1873: Miss Mary Wheeler
June 1873-December 1877: Miss Elizabeth Brewster
January 1878-December 1878: Martha or Matilda Collins
January 1879-December 1879: Miss Janet Johnson
January 1880-December 1883: Miss Agnes Prewitt
December 1883-December 1885: Miss Edith Fox
January 1886-December 1887: Miss Thirza Reynolds
January 1888-January 1889: Miss Rapson
January 1889-August 1890: Miss K W Whistler
September 1890-August 1891: Miss Hannah Uphill
September 1891-March 1896: Mrs. Edith Launder Turner
March 16-27 1896: Miss Thirza Reynolds (Supply Teacher)
April 1896-February 1903: Mr. Joseph Griffin
February 1903-April 1914: John Travis (Gaffer) Holmes. Died 26 April 1914
April 29-May 1 1914: Constance Lloyd (Supply Teacher)
May 4 – December 23 1914: Jessie G Clark (Supply Teacher)
January 1915-June 1921: Sarah Ann Brown
June 27-July 29 1921 V Thompson (Supply Teacher)
September 5-December 1921: Miss Florence Grivatt (Supply Teacher)
January 1922-February 1942: Mrs. Selina Creeth. Died 25 February 1942
February 26-June 1942: Mrs. Edith Hutchings (Supply Teacher)
June 1942-1946: Miss Annie Turner
1946-1952: Mrs. Purkiss
1952-1956: Mrs. Dillys Bottrill

1956-1962: Mrs. Edith Stephenson
1962-1965: Mrs. Brook

A school photograph from 1945. Miss Annie Turner, in the dark cardigan, was head teacher from 1942-1946 and was secretary of the original village hall committee set up in the 1940's.

Until 1970 Plaitford didn't have a village hall and the school room was used for many varying social occasions. Such as – Christmas parties, dances, whist drives, and girls' club and Parish Council meetings. Also, it was used for elections both local and national. One such election was the District Local Election in April 1904. Mr. G Curtis stood for re-election against Mr. W Hurst. *'Polling took place from 12 o'clock until 8 pm when during the first two hours 4 people voted, but after 6.30 the rate of polling was "a trifle quicker". The result was Mr. G Curtis 19, Mr. W Hurst 11. The figures being received with applause. The number of voters on the list was 36'.*

Sources:
LTVAS (Lower Test Valley Archaeological Study Group) Pots and Papers. Autmn 2005
Wellow History Society Chairman Micheal Sleigh for the late Frances Cale archive on Plaitford School containing typed and hand written extracts from Plaitford School Log Books.

The school house 1956, with Mrs. Dillys Botterill, Head teacher by the porch.

A village hall committee is formed

During the Second World War, a few villagers got together to form a committee with the aim of building a village hall. Miss Turner, headmistress of the school, was the first secretary. Miss Turner moved to a new position as headmistress at Copythorne School in 1946, The first meeting recorded in the available minute books took place on 13th November that year at Hillrise, Partridge Hill, Landford, (the home of Chairman Mr. Alf Jewell). Other members present were Treasurer Mr. L Holt, Mrs. T Biddlecombe, Mrs. H Bungay, Mrs. Hayter, Mrs.L Holt, Mrs. A Jewell,
Mr. Elrad Matthews, Mr. George Stone and Mr. E Whetron. Mr. Elrad Matthews agreed to fill the post of secretary. *Elrad Matthews retired from the village hall committee in March 2012 after almost 66 years' service.*
It was proposed that the minutes left by Miss Turner were accepted and preserved. *We have not been able to track down these minutes.*
A general meeting open to all parishioners was held on November 21 1946 at Plaitford School. The original committee were re-elected, and it was agreed to strengthen the committee and a further four floor members were elected, Mr. Alan Jewell, Miss Kath Gradidge, Mr. E Robinson and Miss Jean Scrivan. An entertainments sub-committee was also elected with members Mrs. T Biddlecombe, Mrs. Henry

Bungay, Miss Eva Curtis, Mrs Hayter, Mrs. L Holt and Mrs. A Jewell.

The treasurer, Mr. L Holt, presented the accounts with £331.19s. 9p brought forward from previous fund raising events.

At a committee meeting on March 26 1947, it was proposed that the church authorities should be approached concerning a piece of land (on the opposite side of the road from the current hall) regarded by the committee as being a suitable site for the village hall. A letter of approach was written to the Rev Walters.

It was discovered before the next meeting in April that the land in question did not belong to the church. It was in the ownership of the parish school board. An approach was made and it is recorded in the minutes of a meeting in September 1947 that the committee offered £350 for the whole block of land consisting of approximately fifteen acres.

In February 1948, a reply from the Rev. Walters, Chairman of the school board, offered the hall committee the first refusal on two acres of land for the sum of £160. In the event of the purchase the school board would refund £60 as a donation to the hall fund. The chairman of the school board made it clear that they had no intention of selling any land beyond the two acres. A parish meeting open to all interested was held later that month. After some concern that the position of the hall would be at a great disadvantage to the people living in the northern end of the village, it was proposed that the committee should accept the offer from the school board.

Three more meetings were held in 1948. The first in March was a joint meeting between the hall committee and the school board where an exchange of solicitors took place. The next meeting in April was given up to a talk from Capt, Cowley Miller a representative of the National Council of Social Services about the requirements of acquiring a village hall. The final meeting in August mentions proposed gymkhana to be held at Powells Farm in September. There is no more mention in the minute book of the land acquisition. Elrad Matthews, the last surviving member of the hall committee, was secretary at the time but, unfortunately, he cannot remember the reasons behind the decision not to go ahead with the purchase. He does, however, agree that the following theory may well have been the reason: As early as June 1946 a school managers meeting discussed the possible closure of Plaitford School. Children would be sent to Wellow School, which had by that time been extended. It is thought that the hall committee decided, or was advised by the school managers and the church, to hold fire and wait until the school eventually closed. The committee may have been told there was a good chance of buying the school and converting it to a village hall. As it was they had to wait seventeen years until it closed in 1965. Throughout this time the hall committee had been told that the school room could be used for social events.

The next meeting recorded in the minute book is eleven years later in May 1959. Three meetings were held between May 1959 and January 1961, all were mostly concerned as to where to store the hall chairs, tables and crockery. These items had been stored at the Shoe Inn for many years and transported to the school as and when required. As the Shoe could no longer be used for storage it was decided that the chairs and tables would go to Powells Farm and the crockery would be left at the school in the care of Mrs. Stevenson, head teacher, to be used as required for social events. No further meetings took place until March 1966.

The School becomes the Village Hall

Plaitford School closed in 1965 and the hall committee decided to see if they could obtain the school and turn it into a village hall. With this intention, the next meeting in the minute book took place March 10 1966 when a public meeting was convened. An election of the following committee members took place, Chairman, Les Curtis; Vice Chairman, Edmond Robinson; Secretary, Gwen Bowles and Treasurer, Elrad Matthews. The following floor members were elected - Ken Billen, Maurice and Audrey Bowles, Gwen Collins, Hylda Holt and Alan Jewell. Elected trustees were Henry Bungay and Clem Moore. The bank balance was recorded as £777.14s.1d.

Adrian McConnell, School Trustee, addressed the meeting and explaining the rightful ownership of Plaitford School. He said that regrettably the parish had no claim to the school premises because of a clause in the deeds indicating that 'While the school was provided by Lord Ilchester for the education of the children of the parish, the parish had no claim if the school ceased as such.' He went on to say *'the hall committee should go on using the school for committee meetings and fun raising events whilst the premises are available'.* The chairman proposed that Mr. McConnell approach the Diocesan Council with the full support of the committee.

Three meetings were held in April 1966 in which Adrian McConnell and Miss Annie Turner (original committee secretary) were co-opted on to the hall committee. Contact was made with Mr. Greenslade of The National Council of Social services and the Bishop of Salisbury representative the Rev. Warne.

At the first of three committee meetings held in May 1966, Alan Jewell advised that he, Adrian McConnell and Mr. Greenslade attended a meeting with Reverend Warne in Salisbury, and made it known to the church authorities that Plaitford Village wished to purchase the school building for a village hall. Reverend Warne advised those present that the building would be valued and the hall committee would be advised of the value as soon as possible. The other meetings held in May dealt with fund raising events such as beetle-drives, whist-drives, outdoor skittles and a village fete was discussed and a provisional date of July 16 was agreed.

Meetings continued through the summer of 1966 mostly dealing with arrangements for the fete and other fund raising events. By October the Village Hall Fund had risen to £1,038.

Mr. Greenslade attended the September meeting and gave the committee a talk on grants for village halls. He also advised the committee to make contact with Mr. F Gardener, Assistant Surveyor of Romsey and Stockbridge Rural District Council (RDC). Contact was made and Mr. Gardener agreed to attend the October meeting to discuss possible alterations to the school building in the event of a successful purchase taking place. Mr. Gardener agreed to draw up a plan of the school building incorporating some of the ideas suggested by the committee. He also suggested the committee apply for planning permission to convert the school into a village hall.

A further meeting was held in October to discuss the provisional plans produced by Mr. Gardener.

The January 1967 meeting brought some good news from Mr. Greenslade. Firstly: In the event of the school being sold, only the school trusties, Rev, Paul Bunday, Adrian McConnell and Jack Gradidge, can seek permission from the Department of Education and Science to sell the school. Secondly: Mr. Greenslade had received permission from the Department of Education and Science for Plaitford Village Hall Committee to go ahead with negotiations for obtaining a grant in the event of purchasing the school. Mr. Greenslade went on to advise the committee to have plans drawn up and obtain estimates for alterations to the school building.

Over the next six months, the committee applied for planning permission, insurance was taken out on the school building, various fund raising activities took place and a fete was arranged for Saturday 16 July. It was brought to the committee's attention that a meeting was to be held at the school on Wednesday 5 July. Those attending would be representatives from the Ministry of Transport, the North West Area Planning Board, Hampshire County Council and the

Romsey and Stockbridge RDC. At a committee meeting held on Monday 3 July, planning issues were discussed and Mr. Greenslade suggested a member of the hall committee should be present at the meeting the following Wednesday.

Two letters were read to the committee at their meeting in December. The first, from the North West Area Planning Board giving planning permission to use the school as a village hall subject to a new entrance on the west boundary. The second, from the Salisbury Diocesan Council of Education, stating that the purchase price for the school was £3,500. After discussing this letter it was proposed that three representatives from the committee with Mr. Greenslade should meet with Cannon Warne of the Salisbury Diocesan Council of Education and offer £3,000 for the school and discuss payment terms. Over the next two years fund raising activities continued and at the AGM held in March 1969, the treasured reported that over the previous three years the hall fund had risen from £777 to £1,971. Alongside fund raising activities, the purchase of the school was well underway. The £3,000 offer was accepted by the Salisbury Diocesan Council of Education. Contracts were signed and a £300 deposit paid with the balance of £1,200 to be paid upon completion. A grant for £1,500 was received from the Department for Education and Science to help purchase the school. Further discussions were held with Romsey and Stockbridge RDC and it was agreed the car park entrance be positioned on to the A36, as it is today. Quotations were received from utility companies. An initial outlay of £8,000 including the purchase of the school, alterations, car park, gas heating, fixtures and fittings and legal fees would be required. It was agreed to ask Mr. Greenslade to go ahead with the committee's application for a 50% grant. The committee applied to the Charities Commission for charity status.

On January 1 1970, after almost 30 years, Plaitford officially had a Village Hall. At the AGM in April 1970, the election of committee member shows how local interest in their community has changed over the last 40 years. The committee in 1970 consisted of: Chairman: Les Curtis. Vice Chairman: Edmond Robinson. Secretary: Gwen Bowles. Treasurer: Elrad Matthews. Fixtures Secretary: Ken Billen. Floor Members: Audrey Bowles, Jim Bowles, Maurice Bowles, Gwen Collins, Pat Curtis and Hylda Holt.

The following organizations also had representatives on the committee: George Curtis and Alan Jewell for Melchet Park and Plaitford Parish Council; Les Curtis and Mr. D Stephens for Wellow and Plaitford Cricket Club; Mrs. W Godwood and Mr. F Kenyon for

Wellow School; Ken Billen and Clement Offer for Plaitford Church Council; Dinah Batten and Edna Stoneham for Plaitford Young Wives.

A total of nineteen committee members a marked contrast to today's (2012) committee of nine members.

Plans were submitted to convert the ground floor of the school house to a kitchen and toilets. A building sub-committee was set up in 1971 and by July refurbishment plans had been approved and specifications sent out to Bartlett & Gilbert and Truckell & Barter. M. E Hurst and Oakley Bros declined the offer to quote. Committee member Jim Bowles resigned from the building sub-committee to enable him to submit a tender. By November, tenders had been submitted as follows: Bartlett & Gilbert £4,556.76, Truckell & Barter £4,481.00 and Jim Bowles £4,470. Project architect, Mr. Hill, was asked to review the tenders and make recommendations to the committee. At a further meeting in November it was agreed by the committee to award the refurbishment of the hall to the lowest tender submitted by Jim Bowles.

As the premises had been paid for largely by grants and fund raising, St Peter's Church agreed to a loan of £1,500 at four percent interest with a repayment plan of ten equal payments plus interest to be paid on the first day of February and the first day of August, commencing February 1973. The refurbishment work started in July 1972.

Fund raising, including sponsored walks, jumble sales and annual fetes, continued throughout the 1970's.

The old school room (28 feet x 18 feet) was far too small for most hall activities. In early 1978, plans were submitted and approved to extend the main hall to the rear of the building; these plans also included a small kitchen and store room. The work carried out by Jukes Builders was completed in October 1979 at a cost of £14,000, funded by grants, hall savings and fund raising.

A summer fete to raise funds was held in the hall grounds annually from1966 to1979. The committee minutes for the meeting held in May 1980, record the decision not to hold a fete that year due to difficulties with obtaining helpers. There has not been a fete in the village since.

The village hall has not changed since the late1970's and over the years, committee members have come and gone. There are two current members who have been on the committee for over 100 years between them, Elrad Matthews 66 and Jim Bowles over 40.

The village hall now needs to be brought into the twenty-first century and the hall committee are currently raising funds to redecorate the building and upgrade the heating boiler, kitchen and toilets and install a toilet for the disabled.

In 2013, in order to aid the fundraising, it was decided to hold the first fete since 1979 (34 years) in the hall grounds. A fete sub-committee made up of volunteers was formed, lead by Sarah Peace, hall committee chairman. The date for the fete was set for Saturday 13 July and was to be opened by Elrad Matthews, Plaitford's oldest resident. The day turned out to be the hottest so far that year. The weather, attendance and money raised, (£1,817) far exceeded the expectations of the organizers. As we write, a decision has been made that "Plaitford Village Fete is back" and is to become an annual event.

Source: Plaitford Village Hall Minute books 1946-1974 and 1974-1989

Fancy dress parade at the first fete held in 1966 to raise funds to purchase the school and turn it into the village hall.

Chapter 10
Plaitford Farms
Including Gunsfield Lodge/Cottage

As with most rural communities, Plaitford is a village cast from agriculture and for its size had its fair share of farms. Records from the second half of the nineteenth century indicate there were fifteen farms in Plaitford. They were Bowers, Bowles, Bridgefoot, Fielders, Gardners, Gauntletts, Hutchens's (Yew Tree), Manor (previously Plaitford), New Lodge, Pickernals, Plaitford Wood, Powells, Redhouse, Savages and The Drove. Hazelwood Farm first appeared in the early 1900's. Most were active in agriculture until the 1960s. We have also included Bracken Farm which started business in the 1960's.

At the time of the 1844 Tithe Survey for Plaitford there were 420 acres of arable, 565 acres of meadow and pasture and 163 acres of woodland.

With the help of the Fox/Strangeways/Ilchester archive, we have been able to date some of the original people who may have put their name to farms still in existence today, such as John Bower 1715 (Bowers Farm), John Bowles 1741 (Bowles Farm), John Fielder 1750 (Fielders Farm), Thomas Gardner 1726 (Gardners Farm), Richard Gauntlett[1] 1710 (Gauntletts Farm), Robert Pickernell 1679 (Pickernals Farm) and John Savage 1682 (Savages Farm). From the Harcourt-Powell archive we have traced the Powell name back to a Thomas Powell (Powells Farm) 1713. In fact, the Powell connection with Plaitford can be traced back to 1664 with William and Rice Powell. We don't know when the Powell and Harcourt families merged, but the first mention of a Harcourt Powell in Plaitford is 1776.

An accurate survey, including a detailed map and schedule of Plaitford Manor carried out in 1729 for The Hon. Stephen Fox[2], later to become the 1st Earl of Ilchester, records all leaseholders within the manor. There are a total of thirty two persons named on the survey with a majority leasing quite large acreages of land. This survey included what is now Hobbs Copse Farm, Ten Acre Farm, Giles Lane and Giles Lane Industrial Estate (Coates Sandpit) now all in Landford. We have managed to pinpoint many of the existing farms and for the remainder of this chapter, where applicable, this survey will be referred to as the "1729 manor survey".

The earliest record of occupancy of other farms in Plaitford comes from the 1841 Census Return and the 1844 Tithe Survey.

When Giles Stephen Holland Fox-Strangeways, 6th Earl of Ilchester split up and sold Plaitford Manor in 1911 (from hereon referred to as the "1911 manor sale") the following farms were indicated in the sale catalogue as sold to sitting tenants: Bowers Farm (23.30 acres) sold to Frank, Walter and Henry Michael Curtis, Bowles Farm (32.74 acres) sold to William and Alfred Bowles, Gardeners Farm (31.29 acres) sold to Charles E Brooke, Gauntlets Farm (34.62 acres) sold to Charles J Dovey and Powells Farm (52.51 acres), Savages Farm (42.21 acres) and a 'Snug Little Arable Farm' now Hobbs Copse just over the border in Landford (36.62 acres) sold to George Curtis. Bowles Farm is the only complete farm listed in the sale catalogue, to be continuously farmed by the same family. Today it is run by Maurice Bowles, the grandson of Alfred Bowles. Gauntletts Farm, though rented over the years is still owned by the Dovey family. Powells Farmhouse and 30 acres of land are still in the hands of the great-grandsons of George Curtis, Keith and Nicholas Curtis. Plaitford Wood Cottage later to become Plaitford Wood Farm was purchased by James or his son Harvey Bowles at the sale in 1911 and is still run today by Harvey's grandson, Harvey.

Research into the farms of Plaitford has not been made easy due to the lack of information entered on the manor records in the Ilchester archive. Most rent rolls and annual manor surveys only show the individual's name and the rent collected and do not include a name or location of the property being rented. Also the first three census surveys for Plaitford, taken every ten years from 1841 to 1861, do not include addresses, and as most properties in Plaitford were occupied by farmers and agricultural labourers, pinpointing a particular farm has been difficult. However, we have managed to find some information on most of the farms and the people who lived and worked them.

[1]A headstone dated 1710 at Plaitford Church to Jane Gauntlett aged 73, wife of Richard Gauntlett. From Jane Gauntlett's age it is possible that the Gauntlett family were resident in Plaitford from the late 1600s.

[2]Held at Dorset History Centre Ref: D/FSI (Fox/Strangeways/Ilchester) Box 8V/198

Bowers Farm

The Bronze Age hoard discovered in a sandpit at Bowers Farm in 1928, (see chapter 1 -The Beginning) is only one of a few sites in the parish with evidence of Bronze Age occupation dating back to the period 2,200 to 801BC (2,800 to 4,200 years). Bowers farm happened to be built on one of these sites. We have mentioned the discovery as something unique to the history of the area of Bowers Farm. So far it is the only known Bronze Age site in the village within the boundary of a residential property.

John Bower appears on the manor rent rolls as early as 1715, William Bower in 1720 and another John Bower on the 1729 manor survey as leasing a house and 22 acres of land at Bowers Farm. After which we have been unable to find further record of occupation of the farm until the 1840s. The 1844 tithe survey records the property as owned by the Earl of Ilchester and was leased to John Fielder as a lifeholder[1]. We don't know who John Fielder was as he does not appear in any of the nineteenth century census surveys for Plaitford. The farm was 22 acres comprising fifteen acres of arable and the rest was meadow. As far as the people who occupied Bowers Farm, this has been a difficult task. Due to no addresses shown on the first census in 1841, we had to start with the 1851 census which records James and Elizabeth Dunn in occupation of Bowers and work backwards to the 1841 census to find James and Elizabeth and make an educated guess that they were living in the same property. The 1861 census records an area in Pound Lane beyond Gauntletts Farm as Bowers, containing ten properties including Gardeners Farm occupied by Oliver Brooke. The only other farmer in this area is Henry Green. Taking another educated guess and also considering the occupation of the farm in subsequent census returns we have placed Henry and Sarah Green at Bowers Farm. Unfortunately, the 1871 census is more confusing as Andrew and Mary Hutchings are recorded at Bowers Farm and Henry and Sarah Green are recorded as occupying a "farmhouse". Henry Green died in January 1872. The next three censuses, from 1881 to 1901, clearly show Henry Green's son, Alfred, and his wife, Sarah, as the occupiers of the farm with their daughter, Ida Kate, who went on to marry Walter Curtis at Manor Farm.

Alfred Green died in 1903, and Sarah moved to Savages Farm to live with her mother, Elizabeth Hutchings.

The next occupiers were Frank and Ruth Curtis, Frank and his brothers, Walter and Henry Michael, had leased the farm, and as sitting tenants when the manor was sold in 1911, they purchased the farm, then 23 acres. Prior to the sale the annual rent, agreed on 20 April 1905, was £30. Frank and Ruth continued to live at the farm until 1938. The following auction notice appeared in the Western Gazette, 3 February 1939:

"BOWERS FARM, PLAITFORD - Sale of Live and Dead - farming stock. Mr. Frank Jenvey (Auctioneer) *having sold the farm has been*

instructed by Mr. Frank Curtis to sell the above at auction on Monday 6 February 1939".

This could account for the farm not being mentioned on he electoral roll for 1939/40 (it was probably unoccupied). As there were no electoral rolls during the Second World War, we don't know who lived at the farm. George and Alice Roberts are recorded at the property from May 1945 to 1955, followed in the 1960s by David and Joan Hankey then Robert and Sarah Coles from 1965 to1975/6 and from1976/7 to the early 1980s, Michael and Pamela Hemens. In 1981 a family by the name of Waddington are recorded and in 1986, Arthur (Tim) and Dorothy Torlesse purchased Bowers Farm.

It is reputed that early in the twentieth century Bowers Farmhouse was damaged by fire as a result of sparks from a traction engine's smoke stack setting fire to the thatch.

The earliest local record of the name Bower comes from the Wellow register, that of the baptism of William Bower, 4 November 1708.

[1]A lifeholder or life lease means that the lease is for the life of the tenant.
A three-life lease means a lease on a property until the deaths have occurred of three named people (with an upper limit of 99 years).

Bowles Farm

The original Bowles Farmhouse, now Meadow Cottage, is a listed building and dates from the seventeenth century and was altered in the nineteenth century. A peat shed in the cottage grounds has a listed roof that dates from the early nineteenth century.

The earliest and only mention of a property where Bowles farm now stands, prior to the 1840s, comes from the 1729 manor survey in which it is recorded that Giles Gantlet (Gauntlett) leases 55 acres of land including, as written, a House, Homestall (Homestead or Farmyard) and Pleck (obsolete word for a plot of land of no particular size).

As mentioned earlier in this chapter, the Bowles family, have been in Plaitford since the mid 1700s. Unfortunately, we can only trace their connection with Bowles Farm from 1841.

On the Tithe Survey of 1844, the Earl of Ilchester owned the property that was leased to Rebecca Bowles, second wife of William, son of John Bowles who had arrived in Plaitford in the early 1740s.

In 1844, Rebecca leased a total of 67 acres, consisting of 39 acres in the area of Bowles Farm made up of 36 acres of arable, two acres of meadow and a one acre plot containing a cottage and orchard. The remainder of her lease was made up of land and a cottage in the corner of Sherfield English Lane and Flowers Lane and in the area of New Lodge Farm and Gauntletts Farm. She also leased, as a lifeholder, three acres with a cottage opposite Yew Tree Farm. From the time of the first census in 1841, Rebecca rented Bowles Farm house to William Martin, whose occupation is recorded as a farm labourer, probably one of many working the land held by Rebecca. At this point we must stress that until the 1891 census the property had no name and was recorded as an agricultural labourer's cottage. William Martin continued to live in the cottage until his death in March 1880. He was unmarried and employed his niece, Charlotte Pope, as Housekeeper. The first mention of Charlotte is given on the 1861 census, and on 25 March 1869 she married William Bowles, grandson of the aforementioned William Bowles and his first wife, Martha. Their son, Alfred, was baptized at Plaitford on 13 June 1869. William Bowles originally came from Plaitford Wood Farm and is recorded on the 1881 census as a Farm Servant. Charlotte died in August 1886, and on the 1891 census William is recorded as a farmer living with his son, Alfred. The first mention of the name Bowles Farm comes from the Hampshire Advertiser, 1 October 1887 in which is advertised a live and dead stock sale to be held at Bowles Farm. This may give a clue as to when William Bowles took over the lease of the farm.

Stepping back in time, Rebecca Bowles died in November 1850, and we have no record to indicate if either of her daughters, Sophia Bowles or Eliza Futcher, took over her leases. From what we have discovered, both had land in Plaitford that could have included Bowles Farm. Sophia died in 1873 and Eliza in1891.

At the time of the 1911 manor sale, William and Alfred Bowles, as sitting tenants, purchased the farm consisting of 33 acres. Prior to the sale the annual rent, agreed on the 12 April 1904, was £49. The farm has remained in the Bowles Family and has been run by Alfred's grandson, Maurice, and his wife, Audrey, since 1959 and is now 32 acres made up of grass and woodland.

Maurice and Audrey sold the original Bowles Farmhouse in the 1990s and moved into a new property they had built on farm land next door.

Bracken Farm (Originally Gunsfield Piggeries)
Gunsfield Piggeries/Bracken Farm is a relatively new farm compared to other farms in Plaitford. The farm was established in 1964 in a wooded area on the border with Melchet Park next to Gunsfield House and was run as a partnership between Tony Porter and James Hill, MP for Southampton Test (later to become Sir James).

A herd of Pure Bred Large White pigs was established from the outset and the breed line continues today.

Originally the farm was mostly woodland, and the first pigs were kept in sties amongst the trees. Over the years most of the woodland has given way to open grass land, and the farm now covers approx forty acres.

In the 1970s, Tony Porter built a house on the site, and a range of concrete block and wooden pig sties, built by Jim Bowles, followed. In the 1980s, Tony and his wife, Reene, decided to try their hand at keeping sheep, which continues to this day.

The partnership with Sir James Hill was dissolved in the late 1990s, and Tony and Reene took on sole ownership of the farm. Sir James Hill died in 1999 and soon after the name of the farm was changed to Bracken Farm.

Tony now serves as a Parish Councillor, with responsibility for the Melchet Park area.

Bridgefoot Farm

Bridgefoot Farmhouse is a listed building and dates from the eighteenth century, possibly earlier.

The earliest mention of a property at what is now Bridgefoot Farm, comes from the 1729 manor survey in which a house and land amounting to nineteen acres and leased by Matthias Woodyear is recorded. There appears to be no further record of Bridgefoot Farm until the following notice in the Salisbury & Winchester Journal, 4 August 1823:

"To be SOLD by PRIVATE CONTRACT, - A small LEASEHOLD ESTATE, called BRIDGE FOOT, in the parish of Plaitford, in the county of Wilts; consisting of a good Farm-House, barn, stables, cow shed, granary and turf-house, cart-house, &c.; and about 20 acres of Pasture and Arable Land, with unlimited Right of Pasture in the common, and to cut Turf and Heath.- This is a most eligible concern for a person wishing for a little business and comfortable home, as it is adjoining the Salisbury turnpike, where a constant carriage work might be done in taking coal from Southampton to Sarum.- Particulars as to terms might be known on application to Mr. Wm. H. Attwood, Stockbridge, Hants; and to view the premises apply to Mr. Moor, at Manor Farm, Plaitford".

Unfortunately, we don't know if William Attwood was the vender, vender's solicitor or the auctioneer. An auction notice in the same newspaper in May 1829 may give a clue as to who may have purchased the lease. It states that Mr. W Gray who *"under stress from rent"* is selling by auction all live and dead farming stock and household furniture at Bridgefoot Farm.

The earliest record of occupation comes from the 1844 Tithe Survey for Plaitford. The survey records the farm as just over sixteen acres, made up of thirteen acres of arable and three of meadow. The farm was owned by the Earl of Ilchester and leased to Thomas Henry Smith as a *lifeholder* (Leased for the life of the lease holder). We found a mention of a later *three-life lease* (Leased until the deaths have occurred of three named people with an upper limit of 99 years) dated 1849 to Thomas Henry Smith aged 35 and his son, Alfred, aged eight, and Arthur ? aged fourteen. This lease mentions the tenement at Bridgefoot as *"late Bakers"* indicating the name of a previous lease holder.

According to the census returns, Thomas Henry Smith rented the farm to James and Mary Fielder from 1841 to 1861, and on the 1851 census James Fielder is recorded as farming 24 acres. A notice in the Salisbury & Winchester Journal of an auction of farm stock and household furniture, to be held on 24 April 1861, advises that *"Mr. J Fielder is quitting the farm"*.

Thomas and Sarah Futcher occupied the farm on the 1871 and 1881 censuses. They must have left the farm in September 1881 as a newspaper cutting in the Hampshire Advertised dated 17 September gives notice of a sale of stock etc. at Bridgefoot Farm.

The farm was occupied by Charles and Elizabeth Bungay on the censuses from 1891 to 1901.

When Plaitford Manor was sold in 1911 the sale catalogue records Bridgefoot Farm as seventeen acres on the life of Alfred Smith aged about 70 at a rent of twelve shillings per annum, agreed on 13 February 1849. It also states that George Cook, who was occupying and farming the property, was paying Alfred Smith £25 per annum! It would appear that the Smith family rented the farm to the various occupiers from before 1841 to 1911. At the manor sale in 1911, Henry Cornish Knapman purchased Bridgefoot Farm and seventeen acres of land.

The Knapman family owned the property for the next 50 years and throughout that period the house was rented to various families, George and Alice Cook 1911-1922 (Alice died in 1917), Harry and Gladys Rogers 1925-1927, Henry and Mabel Biddlecombe 1930-1940, Walter and Edmond Robinson 1940?-1946 and William and Edith Barnes 1946-1950. The electoral rolls 1930-1939/40 record

George Cook and his second wife Rose, who were living at Hobbs Copse Farm, Landford, as farming the land at Bridgefoot.

In September 1948, Stanley Curtis rented the farmhouse and seventeen acres of land from Henry Cornish Knapman. After they married in 1951, Stanley's son, Leslie, and his wife, Patricia, moved to Bridgefoot Farm. For the next twelve years Les worked the farm for his father. Stanley Curtis died in 1963, and in1964 Les and Pat purchased the farmhouse from the Knapman family for £1,100. They continued to rent the land around the farm that comprised almost the same area and acreage as it was on the 1844 tithe survey.

On one occasion, after spending a long day cutting and packing cabbages at the farm, Pat discovered she had lost her wedding ring and only after a frantic search through about 100 boxes of cabbages the ring was found. Pat died in 2001 and Les in 2003 and the farmhouse became the property of their sons, Keith and Nicholas. The house was sold to Zack and Paula Cogan in 2004 they also purchased the field behind the farm from George Knapman, grandson of Henry Cornish. Two or three years later George Knapman sold the fields behind and to the east of the church to Hugh and Hilary Harper, Manor Farm.

Bridgefoot Farmhouse 1890's with Charles and Elizabeth Bungay and George Dovey sitting on the fence.

Fielders Farm (Known as Bacons pre 1819)
and Yew Tree Farm (Known as Hutchens's in 1844)

We decided to cover Fielders Farm and Yew Tree Farm together because their history from 1841 to the 1870s appears to be closely linked. The ten year census surveys from 1841 to 1871 do not include addresses, and in the case of these two farms all properties north of Bowles Farm are lumped together in one area, either Plaitford Green or Plaitford Wood. The first mention of Fielders Farm is in the 1881 census, and Yew Tree Farm is not mentioned until the 1911 census. The link between the two farms comes from the 1844 Tithe Survey where we find both properties in the ownership of the Earl of Ilchester and leased by John Fielder as a lifeholder. There is no record of John Fielder living in Plaitford so it is likely that the properties were occupied by agricultural laboures.

From maps of both farms printed in the twentieth century we have been able to match the property and land with the 1844 tithe survey map. In 1844, the area we know as Fielders had thirteen and a half acres consisting of a house, barn, garden and orchard and thirteen acres of arable land. The area we know as Yew Tree was recorded on the tithe survey as *"Hutchens's"* and was seventeen acres consisting of a house, outhouses, garden, orchard, two an a half acres of meadow and thirteen and a half acres of arable land. As part of this lease John Fielder also laid claim to the area where the Castle family now live. We don't know how long John Fielder held the lease to both farms but think it quite possible that he ran both farms together.

Fielders Farm: There is no property shown on the 1729 manor survey map in the position of what we know today as Fielders Farm. A later map of the area produced in 1773 does show a property close to where the farmhouse stands today.

An auction notice in the Salisbury and Winchester Journal, November 1819, informs us that a valuable *freehold estate* called *"Bacons",* late in the occupation of Mr. John Fielder was to be auctioned on 9 December 1819. The notice also mentions that the farm is one mile from The Shoe Inn and covers thirteen acres. These two points coincide with the position of Fielders Farm today and the acreage shown on the 1844 tithe survey. With the added bonus of John Fielder we are sure that this property known as Bacons[1] became known as Fielders from this period. John Fielder was 93 when he died on 13 October 1819 and having been born in 1726 it is possible that he could have been responsible for building a house in the mid 1700's where Fielders Farm stands today. We can only make an educated guess that Bacons was a rented freehold[2] property owned by the Earl of Ilchester. At the time of the 1844 Tithe survey another John Fielder, possibly related, held lease to the property.

The name Fielders Farm does not appear until the 1881 census that records Walter and Fanny Hart still farming thirteen and a half acres. From the 1891 to the 1911 census, William and Sarah Hurst rented the farm, and we are sure that it was sold to William Hurst when the manor was sold in 1911. William Hurst continued to live at the farm until the late 1920s. As far as we know, Fielders farm has had five owners since William Hurst. From the late 1920s to 1939/40 - Louis and Jessie Smith, early 1940's to 1975/6 - Stanley and Brenda Wing, 1975/6 to c1990 - Adrian and Jennifer Lightfoot and early1990's - Tim and Anna Mynot. The current owners Ben and Polly Savage bought the property with four and a half acres of land in 1996.

The earliest local record of the name Fielder comes from the Wellow register, that of the marriage of Joane Fielder and Walter Cardy, 21 April 1592. The earliest recorded from the Plaitford register is the baptism of 'Son' Fielder of James and Jane, 5 April 1729.

[1]The Dorset History Centre hold a Plaitford Manor rent roll for 1720 where in a Thomas Baccon is recorded as holding freehold property in Plaitford ref: D/FSI (Fox/Strangeways/Ilchester) Archive, Box 9c. The Wiltshire & Swindon History Centre hold the will of Thomas Bacon, Yeoman of Plaitford dated 1717 ref: P2/B/1353 and an Administration Bond of Elizabeth Copper formerly Bacon, Shopkeepers wife of Plaitford dated 1755 ref: P2/C/1287.

[2]Freehold: tenure in fee simple, i.e. absolute and unlimited, though possibly paying a fixed rent.

Yew Tree Farm: The earliest record of a house in the position of Yew Tree Farmhouse comes from the 1729 manor survey. The survey records a house and fourteen acres of land leased to Nicholas Baugh. The first recorded mention of Yew Tree Farm is recorded on the 1911 census in the occupation of Harry Dibden. Harry Dibden was living in Wellow at the time of the 1901 census and did not start renting the farm until August 1902. In September 1911 he purchased the farm and the same land mentioned on the 1844 tithe survey, including the plot now belonging to the Castle family. Harry died in 1933 and it would appear that his wife, Susan Rosanna, sold the farm to Henry 2nd Baron Melchet as it formed part of lot twelve in the Melchet Court sale catalogue dated 1935, excluding the Castle family plot. It is thought that Lewis Smith of Fielders Farm purchased what is now the Castle family plot from Susan Dibden and later sold it to William Castle in 1934.

The Melchet sale catalogue records Harvey Bowles as tenant of the land at Yew Tree Farm and Mrs. Susan Dibden renting the house.

Yew Tree Farm, Plaitford Wood and part of Boulder Wood, a total of seventy seven acres were purchased by Hammerfield Estates Limited and Albert Edward Bechely Bechely-Crundall on the 11 July 1935. On 20 September that year, they sold Yew Tree Farm and the rest of the aforementioned land to Hugh Quigley for £1,175 - the same figure the property had sold for at the auction. The electoral rolls records Hugh Quigley living at the farm from 1936 to1938, Reginald Pugh from the early 1940's to 1946 and Mervin and Eleanor Denty 1946 to 1948/9. When the farm was sold to the Denty's in 1946, its acreage had reduced to nine and a half acres. George and Florence Adams took on the property after the Denty's left and stayed until 1952. The farm, totaling eight and a half acres, was sold by auction in June 1952 to Hallam and Betty McDiarmid. The farm is still in the hands of the McDiarmid family. Hallam died in April 1989 and Betty in 2008.

Gardeners Farm

Gardeners[1] Farmhouse (now known as Sweet Briar Cottage) is one of the oldest surviving domestic buildings in Plaitford. The cottage, a listed building, is about 400 years old and dates from the Tudor period around 1590-1625 and was built for a yeoman farmer.

From old rent rolls and annual manor surveys, we have traced the name Gardner (as spelt) in Plaitford back to 1720, in fact there were two: Charles at Manor Farm (1720-1729) and Thomas, who is recorded in the manor rent rolls from 1726 until 1775. Could Thomas be the Gardner the farm was named after? The 1729 manor survey records the area of Gardeners Farm as leased by Mr. Perier (this could be Edward Perier recorded on an earlier survey in 1727). Along with a house, he leased 25 acres of land. Gardners were the only family not just to have given their name to a farm but also the lane on which it stood. Sadly, Gardeners Lane no longer exists, the name was changed to Flowers Lane some years ago.

Like most other properties, we have to move forward to the 1844 tithe survey, where we again find the farm is owned by the Earl of Ilchester and leased to Richard Webb as a lifeholder. The farm was fourteen acres with a house, barn, yard and garden, nine acres of arable land and four acres of meadow.

As there are no Webb's recorded on any Plaitford census of the 1800s, we are sure Richard Webb is a member of the Webb[2] family who lived at Melchet Park from 1824/5 to 1844. The original Richard Webb, a land agent, died in 1837. His son, Richard, also a land agent, is recorded on the 1841 census for Melchet Park, as living in the mansion with his mother, Selina. Richard Webb died in April 1844, aged 28. His mother vacated the mansion in October the same year. The 1841 and 1851 census give us no information as to who was living at Gardeners Farm, the former has no addresses and the later lumps every property in the area as Bowers.

We do know that somewhen between the 1851 and 1861 census, Oliver Brooke, his wife, Sarah (nee Hutchings), and their daughter, Sarah Jane, moved from Gauntletts Farm to Gardeners Farm. Oliver and Sarah had ten children: seven girls and three boys. Their first son, Thomas Alexander, died in infancy in 1851/52 and their second son, William Oliver, died in December 1866, aged nine, one of five children who attended Plaitford School to die of diphtheria that winter. Oliver Brooke died six months later in May 1867, aged 44. Sarah continued to run the farm and a shop, and by the 1901 census her only surviving son, Charles Ernest, is recorded as farmer. Sarah died in July 1906, aged 79. When the manor was sold in 1911, Charles Brooks as sitting tenant purchased the farm, then 31 acres. Prior to the sale Charles Brooke was paying two amounts of annual rent: fifteen pounds under an agreement dated 23 December 1890 and £21.15shillings under an agreement dated 11 April 1893.

A tragedy struck the farm in April 1923 when Frederick Bowles, aged nineteen, in the employ of Charles Brooke was killed by a lightning strike whilst sheltering under a tree. (For the full story see chapter 12 -Twentieth Century)

Charles Brooke continued to run the farm until his death in February 1936, aged 72. From 1911-1931, Ernest Brooke was collector of the King's taxes for Plaitford, West Wellow, Nomansland, Landford, Melchet Park and Bramshaw. He was also a church warden at Plaitford for fifty years and his gravestone is inscribed "A Faithful Church Warden for over 50 years".

In June 1936, Gardeners Farm was sold by auction to Alfred Jewell. It was agreed that Charles Brooke's youngest sister, Hope Ella, should continue to live in the farmhouse for as long as she wished. In March 1942, Alfred Jewell sold the farm to his brother, Alan. Hope Brooke died in June 1952, and the Jewell family decided to sell Gardeners Farmhouse, then known as Sweet Briar Cottage. It was sold in September 1953 to Miss Rosemary Barrett who later that year changed her name to Wood by deed pole. Miss Wood sold the cottage in June 1959 to Miss Nellie Bailey (later to become Mrs. Charles Wall). Charles and Nelly Wall sold Sweet Briar Cottage to William (Terry) and Margaret Drabble in August 1981.

Today, the Jewell family still retains some of land they purchased in 1936.

Access to documents by kind permission of William Drabble.

The earliest local record of the name Gardiner (as spelt) comes from the Wellow register, that of the marriage of Susanna Gardiner and Thomas Wilton, 20 December 1662.

[1]For continuity we have spelt the name Gardener in this way. We have also used the spelling Gardner as it is recorded on documents from the 1700's.

[2]At this point, we go back 30 years to an indenture dated 6 July 1816, between the Earl of Ilchester and John Noble of Broughton. The document mentions previous tenants in reverse order: John Hinton, Thomas Gardner and William Botley. Another indenture dated 25 March 1833 between Ilchester and Richard Webb of Melchet Court, mentions previous tenants as Mark Noble (John Nobles son), John Noble, John Hinton and William Botley. There is no mention of Thomas Gardner in this document. Unfortunately, neither indenture mentions the name of the property but the description and acreage is identical to the 1844 tithe survey. If we are correct and these documents do refer to Gardeners Farm and William Botley did lease the farm, our lease hold history would go back to the early 1700s before Edward Perier. Records show that no Botley has leased or rented property in Plaitford since 1727. The other lease holders named will helps fill some of the gap between Thomas Gardner and Richard Webb.

Gauntletts Farm

Richard Gauntlett and later brothers Giles and Henry put their name to Gauntletts Farm sometime between pre [1]1626 until 1741. We have no record of when the Gauntlett family was at Gauntletts. We have found from the 1729 manor survey a Mr. Williams was leasing the house and fifteen acres of land in the area of Gauntletts Farm. The survey map also shows a second property in the area of Gaultletts Farm consisting of a house and eight acres of land leased by Mr. Coward. He may be Edward Coward mentioned on a 1720 rent roll. John Bowles and his sister, Ruth, took over the lease after Giles Gauntlett in 1741.

In the annual survey of 1748, the farm, still leased by John Bowles, consisted of a house, barn, stable and cowshed, about four acres of meadow and 36 acres of arable.

The 1844 tithe survey records the farm having 24 acres including two cottages, nineteen acres of arable and three acres of pasture. The ten year census surveys from 1841 to 1871 record Thomas Hutchings as tenant, Thomas died in October 1873 and his son, Charles, a widower, became tenant until his death in November 1878. Charles Hutchings second wife, Anne (formerly Mabbett), held the tenancy until October 1883. After 1883, William and Anne Barns were tenants and in 1901, George and Hester Roud. We know that Charles J Dovey had taken over the tenancy between 1901 and 1905 from a newspaper article dated December 1905 about a serious fire at Gauntlets Farm that destroyed the cottage of Mr. J Davey foreman to

Mr. Charles Dovey. (The full newspaper report can be seen in chapter 12 - Twentieth Century) At the time of the 1911 manor sale, Charles J Dovey as sitting tenant purchased the farm, then 35 acres. Prior to the sale the annual rent, under an agreement dated 12 April 1904, was £52.10shillings. From 1923 to 1927, Felix Cook and his son, George, who had been married to Charles Dovey's sister, Alice, until her death in February 1917, rented the farm. In 1928, George and his second wife, Rose, moved to Hobbs Copse Farm, Landford but continued to farm the land at Gauntletts until 1934. Felix Cook continued to live in Gauntletts Farm house until 1934.

Frederick Stone started work for George Cook in 1923 at the age of fourteen. On Michaelmas day, 29 September 1934, he took over as tenant of Gauntletts where he stayed until his death in April 1992. Frederick had been connected with the farm for 69 years. His wife Bertha continued to live in the farmhouse until her death in 1997.

It is has always been believed that Fred Stone took delivery of the first Ferguson Tractor in this area. The following transcript of a notice from Harry Ferguson Ltd of Huddersfield in The Western Gazette dated Friday 10 September 1937 gives some support to this claim:

"By kind permission of Mr. F J Stone
**A DEMONSTRATION OF PLOUGHING,
CULTIVATING, AND ROW CROP WORK
WITH THE
FERGUSON
TRACTOR AND IMPLEMENTS**
will be held at GAUNTLETTS FARM
PLAITFORD, NEAR ROMSEY on
Thursday Next, September 16th, at 11 a.m.
Harry Ferguson Ltd.
Huddersfield"

Gauntletts Farm is still owned by the Dovey family, and Chris Lovell, related by marriage, has lived at and run an engineering business from the farm since 1997. The farm land is currently rented out for the growing of fruit.

A timber framed barn on a brick plinth at Gauntletts Farm is a listed building and dates from the eighteenth century.

The earliest local record of the name Gauntlet comes from the Wellow register, that of the burial of Elenor Gauntlet, 4 December 1570.

[1]Plaitford parish register records the marriage of Joan Gantlett and the burial of Margaret Gantlett both in 1626. There is also a head stone in Plaitford Churchyard to Jane Gantlet wife of Richard, who died in November 1710 aged 73,

Hazelwood (Hazeldown) Farm

We don't know much about Hazelwood farm prior to the early years of the twentieth century. On the 1844 tithe survey map there are no buildings shown in the area of the existing Hazelwood Farm. The map shows a two acre piece of arable land known then as "Little Cally Downs" owned by the Earl of Ilchester and leased by William Petty and thought to be farmed as part of New Lodge farm.

The census returns of 1891, 1901 record Charles and Elizabeth Bungay as tenants at Bridgefoot Farm. By the 1907 they had purchased land and built a house in Flowers Lane that was to become Hazelwood Farm. According to the Plaitford Manor sale catalogue and map, dated 1911, Hazelwood (as it is named on the map) was not included as part of the manor. This would indicate that Charles Bungay purchased the land prior to the 1911 manor sale. The electoral rolls from 1915 to 1930 record the farm as Hazeldown and from 1932 it is recorded as Hazelwood. Charles died in June 1927 and Elizabeth in April 1940. However, their son, Philip, and daughter, Olive continued to live at the farm. Olive died in February 1957 and Philip in December 1971. Philip's brother, Charles Ebenezer (Ebby), continued to run the farm until it was sold along with fourteen and a half acres to its current owner in 1974. Ebby died in December 1980.

Manor Farm (Formerly The Farm, 1700s & Plaitford Farm, 1800s)

Manor Farmhouse is a listed building dating from the late seventeenth century. The property was altered in the nineteenth century with an extension added in the 1970s.

Opposite the farmhouse is a moated area, possibly the site of a medieval hunting lodge, protected by English Heritage as a Scheduled Monument. More on this can be found in chapter 2 – Domesday to 1800.

According to the 1729 manor survey and rent rolls of the 1720s, Manor Farm was known as "The Farm" and later Plaitford Farm. Manor papers record that Charles Gardner leased: *"The Capital Messuage Farm, Barns, Stables, Cowhouses, 130 acres of arable, 25½ acres of meadow, 32 acres of pasture, six acres of coppice and 55 acres of woodland,* a total of 258½ acres. The manor rent roll for 1720 records him paying an annual rent of £62.10shillings. We don't know exactly how long Charles Gardner leased "The Farm", but we do know he was there from 1720 to 1729.

An indenture dated 29 September 1759 records John Hinton as taking over the lease of Plaitford Farm. The indenture also records that the farm was late in the tenure of (previously rented by) John Whitlock. Manor rent rolls record John Hinton as tenant until 1784.

The timber and thatched granary on staddle stones opposite the farmhouse is a listed building and dates from this period.

We now move forward almost 40 years and "The Farm" had become Plaitford Farm or Manor Farm and was still the property of the Earl of Ilchester and in the occupation of Samuel Moore. A sale notice for Bridgefoot Farm in the Salisbury and Winchester Journal dated 4 August 1823 refers to a Mr. Moor[e] at Manor Farm as the contact for anyone wishing to view Bridgefoot. We are sure this is the same Mr. Samuel Moore, aged 75, who is recorded at Plaitford Farm on the 1841 census and the 1844 tithe survey. At the time of the tithe survey, the overall size of the farm had reduced to 170 acres, comprising 126 acres arable, 24 acres pasture, seventeen acres meadow and three acres coppice. The tithe survey map shows the farmhouse with most of the farm buildings on the opposite side of the road opposite the entrance to Compton Drive. It has been impossible to trace an exact date, but it is thought that the quadrangle of brick farm buildings and wooden barn were built in the 1860s.

Samuel Moore died in February 1849 aged 83 and his son John took over the lease, and the 1851 census survey shows him still farming 170 acres with five labourers.

An auction notice in the Salisbury & Winchester Journal, 25 September 1858, mentions that John Moore was quitting Manor Farm.

In 1858/9, Captain Hugh Berners RN[1] took on the lease to Plaitford Farm and the 1861 census records the occupier as Henry Feltham, Bailiff[1]. The first appearance of the name Manor Farm to appear on a census return is in 1871, and Samuel Andrews was the new Bailiff to Captain Berners.

The Reading Mercury, 15 August 1874, records a stock, hay and implement sale at Manor Farm to be held on 28 August 1874, the property of Captain Berners RN who is quitting the farm at Michaelmas next. During his time in Plaitford, Captain Berners was a governor and sponsor of Plaitford School.

A notice in The Hampshire Advertiser dated 4 October 1880 reports that Mr. A S Elliott gave up the farm at Michaelmas (29 September) and an auction of livestock and contents would take place later in October. This would indicate that Mr. Elliott may have taken on the lease after Captain Berners.

Charles Curtis the first of the Curtis family to settle in Plaitford arrived from Martin with his wife, Mary, in 1874. It is possible he worked for Mr. Elliott until 1880 when he took over the lease which he held until his death in 1887, aged 38.

After Charles' death, his father, Walter, moved from Martin and took on the lease of the Farm, and the 1891 census records him, his common-law wife, Fanny Eldridge, and sons, Frank and Walter, living at the farm.

We have been unable to trace the name of Walter Curtis's first wife, the mother of Charles. The story goes that whilst on her death bed she made Walter promise that he would never remarry. He kept this promise and spent the rest of his life with his common law wife, Fanny Eldridge, and between them they had nine children. Although there is no record of them ever having married, Fanny was always known as Mrs. Curtis. It is reputed that Walter Curtis allowed his farm labourers to sow potatoes in the headland on Good Friday. The headland is at the top and bottom of a ploughed field to allow the plough to be turned. Cultivating and growing potatoes helped keep weeds away from the main crop in the field.

Walter Curtis died in September 1898, aged 76 and on the 1901 census, Fanny, his son, Walter, aged 24, farmer and another son, Harry (Henry Michael), aged 26, farmer are running the farm. Fanny Curtis died in July 1901, aged 68.

By the time of the 1911 Census, Walter Curtis and his wife, Ida Kate, held the lease. Walter continued to live at in the farmhouse until c1940. The electoral rolls for 1925 to 1930 record Walter's brother, Michael Henry, as farming the land whilst living at Fir Copse, Landford. From the early 1930s, Stanley Curtis, Walter's cousin living at Redhouse Farm, held the lease to the farm. Ida died in May 1935 and Walter married Doris Annie Matthews in 1937. Walter died in 1956, aged 80 and Doris in 2002, aged 102.

During Walter Curtis's time at Manor Farm there were a few changes in ownership of the property, which we will try to explain as follows: At the time of the 1911 manor sale, the farm consisted of 190 acres and was leased to Frank, Walter and Henry Michael Curtis under an agreement dated 7 May 1900.[2]

The sale catalogue records an annual rent of £191.5 shillings agreed on 23 May 1904.

It now becomes slightly confusing! As far as we can tell, part of the farm, about fifteen acres, was conveyed to Arthur Hugh Clough on 4 October 1912. This piece of land was sold by A H Clough to Sir Alfred Mond of Melchet Park on 18 January 1923.

It would appear that the remaining 175 acres had been purchased in 1911 by S H Spry Esq. Seven years later, Mr. Spry sold the farm along with a further 15 acres by auction in April 1918 for £7,500. We are sure the purchaser was Sir Alfred Mond because Manor Farm formed part of the Melchet Court Estate sale in 1935.

Sir Alfred Mond now 1st Baron Melchet died in 1930, and in 1935 his son, Henry, 2nd Baron Melchet, split and sold Melchet Park Estate including the property known as Woodfalls. Woodfalls[3] was purchased along with three farms: Woodfalls Farm[3], Melchet Court Farm[3] and Manor Farm, by this time 102 acres, with Stanley Curtis as tenant at a rent of £85.12s.0p. Collectively they became known as Woodfalls Estate (546 acres). The purchaser was Major Denys Angus Lambert Dwyer who paid £3,225 for Manor Farm. Stanley Curtis continued as tenant until around the outbreak of the Second World War at the same time that Walter and Doris Curtis moved to Wellow. Unfortunately, there were no electoral rolls produced between 1940 and 1944. However, the discovery of an advertisement in The Times newspaper dated February 1943, in which a Mr. Smith required two Land Girls to work at the farm, does shed some light on the matter. With the help of the electoral rolls for 1945 and 1946 we think that Mr. Smith was Geoffrey Smith, who with his wife, Hazel, and Frederick Wyndham Hewitt was living at Manor Farm. The advertisement for the Land Girls stated that the farm was 300 acres and this probably included Melchet Court Farm as part of the Woodfalls Estate. It was during or just after the Second World War that the old dairy behind the house was converted to a cottage.

From 1947 to 1950, Francis and Clare Edwards are recorded as living at the farm.

In February 1951, Major Dwyer sold Woodfalls Estate by auction, and Manor Farm, now 154 acres, was purchased by Commander John Charles Horatio Nelson RN, great, great, great nephew of Admiral Horatio Lord Nelson.

Adrian and Penelope (Penny) McConnell purchased Manor Farm from Commander Nelson on Trafalgar day – 21 October 1958. At the same time the McConnell's purchased ten acres of woodland taking the farm to 164 acres. During the 1970s a single story attachment was replaced by a two story extension to the west end of the farm. After a lightning strike in 1994 this extension had to be rebuilt. Adrian and Penny were well known for their prize winning herd of rare breed English Long Horn cattle. Adrian served as one of the last school trustees before the school closed in 1965 and was a parish councilor for many years. Penny died in July 2003 and Adrian sold Manor Farm to Hugh and Hilary Harper in 2006. Manor Farm now consists of 49.90 hectares (123 acres) and is an all grass farm with woodland as it has been since the 1960's.

In the early 1930's, Gilbert Matthews (elder brother of Elrad) married Walter Curtis's daughter Ida. In 1937, his sister, Doris Annie, married widower Walter Curtis and became Gilbert's step-mother-in-law!

[1]Captain Berners RN lived for a short while at Landford Manor and also had properties in Midanbury, Southampton and Eaton Square, London. Upon the death of his brother in 1886, he inherited the family seat at Woolverstone Park, Suffolk. He died there in 1891. During his time in Plaitford, Captain Berners was a Governor of Plaitford School. We know from the 1867 Kellys Directory that Henry Feltham was Bailiff to Captain Berners.

[2]The Curtis Brothers also leased the property known today as The Drove which stands on the other side of the River Blackwater from Manor farm in the direction of Bridgefoot. The property was then a double tenement known as Manor Farm Cottage's.

[3]At the auction held at Melchet Park in July 1935, Woodfalls House and Farm and Melchet Court Farm are marked as unsold. They were sold after the auction privately and along with Manor Farm they formed Woodfalls Estate by 1951.

New Lodge Farm

As we have mentioned previously there are no addresses shown on the 1841 census. The census for 1851 puts properties into areas such as Plaitford Common, Bowers and Plaitford Wood. New Lodge formed part of Plaitford Wood along with eleven other properties. Unlike some of the properties in the area, Mary Parker, who is recorded as occupier on the 1861, does not leave a trail back to 1851. The Tithe Survey of 1844 records the property was owned by the Earl of Ilchester and leased to William Petty as a lifeholder. The farm was eleven acres consisting of a house, barn, and orchard, two and a half acres of meadow and eight and a half acres of arable. There is no mention of William Petty on any of the Plaitford census records for the1800's. A sale catalogue for New Lodge dated 1907 caused some confusion with the following passage "*The title of the property shall commence with the will dated 11 January 1838 of William Petty who died 24 December 1841. The purchaser shall assume that the said William Petty was duly seized in fee simple of the property at the date of his death*". From this sale catalogue it would appear that William Petty died almost three years before the tithe survey was completed. A discovery of an auction notice from the Hampshire Advertiser dated 19 March 1892 cleared the confusion by stating that the trustees of the will of William Petty were to auction the freehold estate of New Lodge on 31 March 1892. It would appear that the property had remained with the Petty family after William's death.

New Lodge Farmhouse is a rather grand property of Victorian design, slightly out of place when compared to other farmhouses in the area. The March 1892 auction notice refers to the property as *"A comfortable and substantially-erected residence with gardens"*. This would indicate that the original part of the house we see today was probably built during the 'Petty' era, pre 1838 to 1892.

Unfortunately, we have not found any documents to give a more precise date. However, a notice in the Hampshire Advertiser and Salisbury Guardian, March 1843, of an auction of farm stock and household furniture etc at New Lodge may give a clue of an early date. The quality and quantity of furniture listed would indicate a wealthy owner with a largish property. Unfortunately, we do not know who was vacating the property.

Mary Parker recorded as occupier on the 1861 census died in 1865, and the three subsequent census surveys record Eliza Futcher, widow and farmer living at New Lodge. Eliza nee Bowles was granddaughter of John Bowles who came to Gauntletts Farm in 1741.She died in November 1891.

We think that Mr. L C Marriott purchased the property at the aforementioned auction in March 1892. The first mention we have found of Mr. Marriott comes from the following auction notice from the Hampshire Advertiser, 11 November 1893:

"Monday, November 27, 1893
New Lodge Plaitford

MR. HANNEN is favoured with instructions from Mr. Marriott in consequence of contemplated erection of new buildings and letting a portion of the farm, to SELL by AUCTION the FARM STOCK, LARGE BARN, PIGSTIES, CARRIAGE HOUSE and COW PENS."

In February 1895, Mr. Marriott left Plaitford, and his livestock and farming equipment was sold by auction. A notice in the Hampshire Advertiser 9 Feb 1895 says; *"The residence, – New Lodge and newly erected outbuildings and a few acres of land to be let"*.

The lack of a mention of any work carried out on the house confirms our thoughts that New Lodge was a substantial property prior to 1892.

The 1901 census records David J Townsend, a retired author, and his wife, Rebecca, as living at the property. Their son, Percy, was a cycle maker and is also recorded on the census, and a sales advertisement for a ladies cycle (with pneumatic tyres for two pound fifteen shillings) placed in the Western Gazette in November 1899 places him at New Lodge.

Following on from the Townsends, the only information we can find comes from the following – A brief mention of *Mr. H E Harris* of New Lodge, Plaitford in the Reading Mercury in June 1903 and an article in the Romsey Advertiser dated September 1904 reports on the death of John Vietch of Salisbury. He died whilst on a visit to *Mr. H E Harris* of New Lodge, Plaitford. The property was put up for auction in March 1906 and again in April and October 1907. It was advertised as a well fitted residence with modern first class brick built stabling for fourteen horses with carriage house, enclosed yard and men's-room – recently constructed.

We don't exactly know who purchased the property at any of the three auctions. It is possible that at the last auction it could have been Mr. T H Spry who is recorded as Mr. J H Spry in the 1911 and 1915 Kellys Directory as farmer at New Lodge. We think he is the same person as Mr. S H Spry (confused yet?) who purchased Manor Farm in 1911. We know that he did not live at New Lodge or Manor Farm. The 1911 census records Robertson Conaway and Annie Cohen in occupation, and from 1914 to 1918 the house was occupied by Arthur and Musidora Richards, and the 1915 electoral roll also mentions *Frank Horace Edward Harris*! Is this the same Mr. Harris who occupied the property in 1903, or a close relation?

In 1918, Mr. T H Spry sold New Lodge and having previously sold the property an auction of all household furniture, china and linen etc. was held on 21 June 1918.

As Mr. S H Spry he also sold Manor Farm in 1818 to Sir Alfred Mond of Melchet Park.

The electoral roll for 1920 makes no reference to New Lodge, indicating the property was probably empty. Joseph M MacCarthy is recorded in 1921 and a family by the name of Whiteside in 1923. Aleen Cust (1868-1937), Britain's first female veterinary surgeon lived at New Lodge from 1924 to March 1927. When she left Plaitford, she had intended to let the property for one year. In fact she never returned to Plaitford and died in Jamaica in 1937.

From October 1927 to 1939/40, William Benham and his wife, Edith, lived at New Lodge. William Benham was Bailiff to Muriel and Winifred Bowes-Lyon who were first cousins to Queen Elizabeth the Queen Mother. The Bowes-Lyon sisters acquired the farm to raise their herd of pedigree Jersey cattle. Plaitford's late centenarian Bill Robinson's father, Walter, and brother, Edmond, also worked for the Bowes-Lyons and lived in Thornycroft in Pound Lane, then part of New Lodge Farm (More on the Bowes-Lyons can be found in the chapter 12 - Twentieth Century)

Although there were no electoral rolls between 1940 and 1944, we have been informed by their son, Michael that his parents, Leonard and Winifred Caddy, moved into the property after the Benhams left in 1939/40. During their time at New Lodge, they continued to run a herd of pedigree Jersey cattle.

We found the following advertisement in the Western Gazette dated 21 May 1943: *"Pedigree Jersey Bull imported 5 years old for sale, tuberculin tested. Apply Caddy, Plaitford, Hants. West Wellow 313"*. In 1950/51 they moved with their son, Michael, and daughter, Mary, along the road to Hill Close, a bungalow they had built on the top of Pound Hill opposite Pound lane. They continued to farm a small herd of Jersey cattle on fifteen acres of land. Leonard died in 1980 and Winifred later moved to Wellow and died in 2000. A year later their son, Michael, and his wife, Norah sold Hill Close and moved to Sherfield English.

After the Caddys moved out, Denis and Daisy Clancy lived at New Lodge from 1952 – 1980, Ian and Maxine Vine in the 1980's and Richard and Judith Robson 1991 to present.

Pickernals Farm

We have managed to trace the Pickernal (spelt Pickernell) name in Plaitford back to an Administration Bond and Inventory of Robert Pickernell dated 1679. This would make it the oldest known confirmed name to be given to a farm in Plaitford.

Sir Stephen Fox, father of the first Earl of Ilchester, purchased the Manor of Plaitford from Richard Compton in 1679. Prior to 1679 Plaitford formed part of the Manor of Minstead.

The 1729 manor survey records William Pavey as leasing a house and homestall (homestead or farmyard) and 63 acres of land in the area of Pickernals Farm. Some of the land was beyond the parish boundary in West Wellow.

By comparing the map of the sale of Pickernals Farm at the time of the 1911 manor sale with the 1844 tithe survey record and map, we have been able to come up with who was living at the farm in 1844 and most probably at the time of the 1841 census. The farm was in the ownership of the Earl of Ilchester and leased to James Bowles as a lifeholder and in the occupation of William (Bowles) Noble Jnr and his wife, Mary. The farm was 26 acres consisting of a house, barn and part of garden, part of well plot, eighteen and a half acres of arable, five acres of meadow and two and a half acres of coppice. In 1851, the acreage had increased to 33 acres, and in 1881, it stood at 35 acres. The 1861 census was the first to address the farm as

Pickernals. Mary died in August 1881 and William in April 1890. At the time of the 1891 census James Russell and his wife, Emily, were tenants, and by 1901 Emily was a widow and her son, Thomas, was farming the land. In May 1901, a serious fire badly damaged one of the cottages at the farm. (For the full report on the fire see the chapter 12 - twentieth century.) At the time of the 1911 manor sale, Thomas Russell was still renting the farm of just under 33 acres at £52.10 shillings per annum, under an agreement dated 29 June 1899. We have no record of him buying the farm, but according to the 1915 electoral roll he was still in occupation. Over the years, Pickernals Farm has changed hands a few times, and from the electoral rolls we can name some: 1918, Thomas and Elizabeth Powell; 1919-1947/8, John and Ellen Scurlock followed by William and Evelyn Scurlock; 1949-1952 Colin and Joyce Kneller and 1953-1990 Henry and Caroline Barns and later Douglas and Signe Barnes.

The earliest local record of the name Pickernell comes from the Wellow register, that of the baptism of Luke, son of Robert, 4 May 1572.

Plaitford Wood Farm (Occupied by the Bowles family since before 1841)

On the 1844 tithe survey, Plaitford Wood Cottage was owned by the Earl of Ilchester and leased to John Fielder as a lifeholder. John Fielder also leased Fielders Farm and Yew Tree Farm close by. The 1841 census and tithe survey record Frederick Bowles, agricultural labourer, and his wife, Ann, as occupying Plaitford Wood Cottage. It is quite likely that Frederick Bowles worked for John Fielder. Frederick and Ann's descendants still live at Plaitford Wood Farm. However, this may not have been the case had things turned out differently in the 1870s - Frederick Bowles died in 1865. His widow, Ann, married Richard Harnett in October 1867. The 1871 census records Richard Harnett as head of the household at Plaitford Wood, living with his wife, Ann, stepson, James (Bowles), and daughter, Sarah (Harnett). Luckily, James Bowles and Sarah Harnett married in July 1877, thus continuing the Bowles line at Plaitford Wood.

We are not sure when Plaitford Wood Cottage became Plaitford Wood Farm. The census for 1891 records James as a farmer and dealer and the 1901 and 1911 censuses as a carpenter.

At the time of the 1911 manor sale, the sale catalogue records Plaitford Wood Cottage, in the occupation of Harvey and James Bowles at a rent of five pound ten shillings per annum. It is believed that Harvey or his father James purchased the cottage at the sale.

James was also tenant of The Cottage, Plaitford Green at five pound per annum, which he also purchased. They also rented two small pieces of land in Plaitford Wood on the boundary with Melchet Park. The 1911 census records Harvey and his wife, Beatrice, as living at Plaitford Wood and James and his wife, Sarah, living at Plaitford Green Cottage. This is confirmed on the 1918 and subsequent electoral rolls. Sarah died in December 1930 and James in December 1938.

James and Sarah Bowles outside Plaitford Green Cottage C1900

After service in WW1, Harvey and his wife, Beatrice, continued to live at Plaitford Wood and farmed land as tenants of Melchet Park Estate. The 1935 sale catalogue for Melchet Park records Harvey Bowles as tenant of almost 77 acres of farm land and woodland including Yew Tree Farm.

An auction notice in the Western Gazette dated 8 September 1939 would indicate that Harvey Bowles gave up the tenancy of the land at Yew Tree Farm. Over the next few years the tenancy of the remainder of the land, now owned by Hugh Quigley, was given up. Harvey died in September 1940 and Beatrice, along with her son, Harvey James, his wife, Edith, and their daughter, Gwen, and son, Harvey, continued to live at Plaitford Wood. The farm then consisted of twenty-nine acres and ran in a northerly direction towards Steplake. Beatrice died in February 1963, Harvey James in February 1982 and Edith in March 1984. Their son, Harvey, and his wife, Jean, moved into Plaitford Wood in 1982 and they still run the farm, now 39 acres. *The farmhouse at Plaitford Wood can claim to be the only property in the village to have been occupied continuously by the same family since our records began in 1841.*

After James died in 1938, various people rented The Cottage, Plaitford Green, and in the late 1950s, after a short spell living at The Frenches, Harvey's sister, Gwen, and her husband, Clem Collins, moved in. Clem died in September 1973 and Gwen in February 2008. Their daughter, Joan, still lives in the cottage.

The existing cottages replace the original and were built a year apart, Plaitford Wood in 1867[1] and Plaitford Green in 1868[1]. Timber used in their construction came from Plaitford Wood.

[1]We were originally told that these two cottages were rebuilt one year apart in 1862 and 1863. The date built into the wall of Plaitford Green Cottage has been confirmed as 1868, so we have dated Plaitford Wood as 1867.

Powells Farm
& Bridgefoot Cottages

We can trace the Powell (later Harcourt Powell) family connection with Plaitford as far back as 1664, and we know from the 1729 manor survey that land in the area of Powells Farm is clearly shown as Mr. Powells freehold. There is also sixteen acres of land that appear to include buildings that may be in the position of Powells Farmyard. This land was leased from the manor by William Newall, who is also mentioned on a rent roll from 1720. As well as his freehold land at Powells Farm, Thomas Powell also leased Redhouse Farm from 1752 – 1766.

We have no further record of Powells Farm until the mid 1840s. On the tithe survey for Plaitford in 1844, John Harcourt Powell owned Powells Farm - that consisting of about 20 acres. From 1815 to his death in 1862, James Cocks, Farmer and Landlord of the Shoe Inn, leased Powells Farm. During this period it is not known who occupied the farm house. After James Cocks died, Richard Nightingale took over the lease and on the 1871 census he was living at Powells Farm. In 1873, Thomas Harcourt Powell sold his estate in Plaitford and Landford and Powells Farm was purchased by the Earl of Ilchester. It would appear that soon after the Earl purchased the farm, new brick buildings were built. One of the buildings still has the date 1879 built into the brickwork.

George Curtis, half brother of Charles Curtis of Manor Farm and the eldest son of Walter and Fanny Eldridge moved from Martin to Powells Farm in 1880. By 1887 George Curtis was renting 101 acres of land from the Earl of Ilchester in Plaitford and Landford for a yearly rent of £100. The land consisted of a house and barn and 69 acres of arable with the rest made up of pasture and meadow. Between 1898 and 1899 Bridgefoot Cottages (previously known as Gravel Pit cottages) were built by the Earl of Ilchester on Powells Farm land.

At the time of the 1911 manor sale, George Curtis as sitting tenant purchased Powells, Savages (see Redhouse Farm and Savages Farm) and part of what is now Hobbs Copse Farm, a total of 131 acres. Prior to the sale the annual rent for Powells Farm, under an agreement dated 11 May 1897, was £66. George Curtis did not buy Bridgefoot Cottages as they were purchased by Sir Alfred Mond of Melchet Park. George or Stanley Curtis later purchased the cottages when Melchet Park was divided up and auctioned in July 1935, for £210. Under an agreement between the Earl and George Curtis, the existing Powells Farm house was built in 1910. In October 1919, George Curtis sold 50 acres of land to William Dibden, who was starting a new farm on the other side of Sherfield English Road from Powells Farm, now known as Hobbs Copse.

George Curtis is reputed to have been less of a farmer than a public man. He left his son to run Powells Farm whilst he served as a Methodist local preacher, a member of the Board of Guardians for the Romsey Union and as a member of Romsey Rural District Council and later Romsey and Stockbridge R.D.C.

In the Melchet Park sale catalogue of 1935 Stanley Curtis is also recorded as tenant of Manor Farm, then 102 acres. He continued as tenant of Manor Farm until around the outbreak of the Second World War. By this time he was running Powells Farm and by April 1941 he had increased the acreage back up to around 130 acres. Stanley Curtis died in 1963 and the farm was split between his sons Walter, Maurice and Leslie. In 1964, Leslie and his wife, Patricia, purchased Bridgefoot Farm where they had been living since the early 1950s and continued to help work Powells Farm. Sadly, Maurice took his own life in 1973, and Walter died a few years later in a motor accident in the Fordingbridge area. Their share of the farm totalling about 50 acres was sold in 1981 to David and Tina Pyebus, along with the farm buildings that were to become Pyesmead Farm. Powells farm house was then purchased by Leslie's two sons, Keith and Nicholas, in 1982. On Leslie's death in 2003 his third of Powells

Farm was settled on his two sons, Keith and Nicholas. Keith, Nicholas and their families now occupy the old Powells Farmhouse and between them still own 30 acres of land.

For six years between 1945 and 1950, the Wellow and District Gymkhana were held at Powells Farm. They took place in the field behind the farm house which is now the venue of the New Forest Folk Festival. Put on as a successful one day test event in 2012 it increased to three day annual event in 2013. The event attracted over twenty acts from the UK, Ireland and the USA.

Over the years, farmers who have leased or owned Powells Farm have also worked the land at Manor farm in the 1930's and Hobbs Copse Farm as far back as the 1840's. This tradition continues today with David and Tina Pyebus and their son Robert of Pyesmead Farm (previously part of Powells Farm), who in recent years have rented and farmed the land on both farms.

Bridgefoot Cottages were built in 1898/9 and being next to a large Gravel Pit, the terrace of three was originally known as Gravel Pit Cottages. The land they were built on formed part of Powells Farm leased by George Curtis. Records show that the first cottage to be occupied was number three by Henry and Fanny Lovell. Tragedy struck the Lovell's in April 1907 when their daughter, Ellen (Tinny), was drowned in the River Blackwater that runs close to the cottages; she was only five years old. (For the full story see chapter 12 – Twentieth Century)

The 1911 manor sale catalogue records George Curtis, Charles Dovey of Gauntletts Farm and Henry Lovell as tenants. We know that Henry Lovell was paying rent of six pound per annum. George Curtis and Charles Dovey probably rented their cottages to their farm labourers. At the time of the 1911 manor sale the cottages were purchased by Sir Alfred Mond and became part of Melchet Park Estate. Sir Alfred Mond (now 1st Baron Melchet of Landford) died in 1930 and his son, Henry 2nd Baron Melchet, sold Melchet Park including Bridgefoot Cottages by auction in 1935.George Curtis purchased the cottages for £210 and after his death in 1938 his son, Stanley, became the owner. Stanley died in 1963 and the cottages were passed to his son, Walter, who put them up for sale in the 1970s.

In 1940, Dennis and Lily Stone moved into number two, and after paying rent for some years to the Curtis family, they decided to buy their cottage. Dennis died in 1988 and Lily in 2012. Their youngest son, Terry, and his wife, Jean, still live in the cottage after 73 years of continuous occupation by one family. The other two cottages fall well behind number two in long time occupation. The Rickman family liver at number one for 50 years, from 1913 to c1963 and the longest at number three are relative newcomers, Adrian and Vivian Pratt who have lived there from 1991.

In preparation for this book, we have compiled a spread sheet of the occupation of Bridgefoot Cottages and as there are too many to include here, we will be happy to make the list available up on request.

Powells Farm in the 1890's with the old farmhouse behind the three ladies. The current farmhouse built in 1910 stands to the left of this photograph.

Redhouse Farm and Savages Farm

Researching these farms has been the most difficult, because as you will see their history becomes intertwined at the beginning of the twentieth century.

Redhouse Farm: The property we know today as Redhouse Farm is one of the oldest, if not the oldest dwelling in Plaitford. The previous owners of Redhouse submitted to us in writing what they knew about the property. We have put together their comments as follows:

During their time at the property from 2006 and 2013 they asked various experts in historical buildings to look at the house and it was agreed that the original property was undoubtedly an *open-hall* house. An *open-hall* house has a central hall open to the roof measuring one pole x two poles (16ftx32ft). There is also evidence of smoke-stained roof thatch and rafters that indicate the existence of a central open fire. One of the main trusses has the date 1528 carved into it. *Open-hall* houses date from the 1480's to the 1530's and was usually owned by the most prosperous yeomen (farmers); this is consistent with the 1528 beam date. Four Tudor groat coins were discovered in 2007 whilst renovating the chimney. Two were from the reign of King Henry VIII and two from the reign of Queen Elizabeth I, dating them from 1509-1603. The current layout is typical of an Elizabethan farmstead and this would indicate that it was adapted or rebuilt in the late 1500's.

We have no reason to doubt these findings, but because the property is not listed we are unable to verify them. Verification, if required, will be left to the current or future owners.

It is reputed that a Roman drain was discovered by Salisbury Museum under the kitchen at Redhouse during renovations in 1968. In June 2013, the author contacted the director of Salisbury Museum who checked the museum's annual reports for around 1968 and could find no reference to a Roman drain at Redhouse Farm. The standard procedure with any archaeological finds is they are reported to the applicable county council to be recorded. The author obtained a copy of the Hampshire County Council Archaeology and Historic Buildings Record and no Roman finds are recorded as being discovered in Plaitford.

It is a pity the story of the Roman drain cannot be substantiated because if one had been found it would be the only Roman find recorded in the village.

The 1729 manor survey records Thomas Heighter leasing a house and homestall (homestead or farmyard) and eighteen acres of land in the area of Redhouse Farm. At this time Thomas Powell had freehold land next to Redhouse Farm, in the area of what is now Powells Farm. It is recorded in the 1752 to 1766 rent rolls that Thomas Powell leased Redhouse Farm then recorded as formerly Hayters.

Old Savages Farm: An Administration bond and Inventory for John Savage, Yeoman, dated 1682, held by the Wiltshire and Swindon History Centre is the oldest record of the name Savage in Plaitford. The 1729 manor survey records John Keymarsh as leasing a house and seventeen acres of land in the area of Savages Farm. John Keymarsh is probably the same person as John Kemish mentioned in the 1720 rent roll.

We know from a rent roll dated 1741 that John Savage, his wife, Rebecca, and son, John, rented a house, barn and fourteen acres of arable land from the Horourable Stephen Fox. From the Plaitford burial records, William Bowles and his wife, Susanna, were living at

Savages at the time of William's death in 1798. An auction notice in the Salisbury and Winchester Journal in May 1808 mentions that the farm was occupied by a James Bowles. The notice also says that the farm comprised of a farmhouse, two orchards, garden, barn, stables, cow houses, granary, two cart houses, rick house and large yard. Through further research and a bit of luck we have found the location of the original Savages Farm. The 1844 tithe survey map shows what looks like a farm alongside the south west corner of Gore Copse (Grid Ref SU284195) now part of Pyesmead Farm. A later discovery of a mention of Savages Farm on a map dated 1876 confirms the farm's location with the tithe survey map. The tithe survey records that the farm was owned by the Earl of Ilchester and leased to William Noble Snr and his wife, Mary nee Bowles. The farm was eighteen acres and consisted of a house, barn, garden and seventeen acres of arable land. An advertisement to let Pickernals Farm in the Salisbury and Winchester Journal, January 1834, requests that to view the farm apply to Mr. William Noble at the adjoining farm. So we can place William and Mary at Savages on the 1841 and 1851 censuses. A rate book from 1853 records William Noble occupying a house and land at Savages. William Noble died in 1858 and his widow, Mary, aged 78, is recorded on the 1861 census as living at Savages Farm. Mary died in 1863 and from this date there is no further mention of Savages Farm until 1911. William Noble's son, William Bowles Noble, farmed at Pickernals Farm from 1841 until 188. Over the years the land belonging to Savages was probably swallowed up by Pickernals, Powells and Redhouse Farms, and the buildings fell into disrepair. The last map to show Savages Farm was produced between 1878 and 1881, and maps produced from 1896 shows no sign whatsoever of any building in the area of the old Savages Farm.

Redhouse to Savages to Redhouse: The 1891 census was the only census from the second half of the nineteenth century to mention Redhouse Farm. Previous censuses recorded the address as Plaitford Common or Farm House. The property was occupied in 1891 by Elizabeth and Lewis Hutchings. Elizabeth was the daughter of William and Sarah Tutt, who on the 1844 Tithe Survey are recorded as leasing a house, barn, garden and land amounting to 21 acres in the area of what is now Redhouse Farm. From this information, we think it safe to assume they were in the same property three years earlier at the time of the 1841 census. By the 1851 census, Elizabeth had married Lewis Hutchings and with their three children including Sarah, aged one (more of her later) they continued to live with

Elizabeth's parents, William and Sarah Tutt. The same goes for the 1861 census. William Tutt died in December 1870 and the 1871 and 1881 census records Sarah Tutt, widow, still living with Lewis and Elizabeth Hutchings. Sarah Tutt died in December 1881.

We are back to the 1891 census and Redhouse farm. We now move on to 1901 and the property still occupied by Lewis and Elizabeth Hutchings is recorded as *Tutts Farm*! Moving on to the 1911 census, Sarah Hutchings who was one year old in 1851 had gone on to marry Alfred Green and lived at Bowers Farm. After Alfred died in 1903, Sarah went to live with her mother, Elizabeth Hutchings, now a widow (Lewis died in December 1909), at *Savages Farm*!

At the time of the 1911 manor sale, George Curtis as sitting tenant purchased Savages Farm along with Powells Farm next door. The sale catalogue and map (HRO[1] Ref: 4M92/N44/2, Plan Three, Lot 23) for Savages Farm clearly show the farm house and buildings in the position of Redhouse Farm as we know it today. Prior to the sale the annual rent, under an agreement dated 4 December 1897, was £45. From the 1911 census and the electoral rolls from 1915 to 1928, there is no mention of Redhouse Farm on any documentation. There is, however, mention of Savages Farm, occupied by a Lewis Hutchings in 1915 with William Charles Curtis framing the land, Stanley Curtis and his first wife Hilda 1918-1926, and with his second wife Aurelia, 1927 and 1928. There was no electoral roll for 1929, and by 1930 Stanley and Aurelia were living in Redhouse Farm, the first mention since 1891. We have discovered only one mention of Savages Farm since 1928 from an auction document, dated July 1980 for the sale of 50 acres referred to as: *"A large block of agricultural land forming part of Redhouse Farm and Savages Farm"*. This land is now owned and farmed by David and Tina Pyebus as Pyesmead Farm. The name Redhouse has continued up to today with a spell during the second half of the twentieth century as Redhouse Cottage, Powells Farm.

We know that George Curtis purchased Savages Farm in 1911 and it remained with the Curtis family until August 1968 when, as Redhouse Farm, it was sold by Walter, Leslie and Maurice Curtis, grandsons of George, to James H D Wade. James Wade and his partner, Leonard Valentine, lived at Redhouse farm until 2006. From 2006 to January 2013 the property was occupied by Colin and Sally Shaw-Downie.

[1]HRO: Hampshire Record Office, Winchester

The Drove
(Also known as Manor Farm Cottages pre 1900 to 1911)

The Drove dates from the sixteenth century and was once two cottages, one facing north towards the River Blackwater and the church and the other facing south, over looking a large gravel pit where Bridge House, Cedar House and Gaymeade now stand.

The 1729 manor survey records widow Pavey as leasing 35 acres of land including a house and homestall (homestead or farmyard). The location of the land is similar to the following description from the 1844 tithe survey but also included the land where Giles Lane Industrial Estate and Frank Male's Ten Acre Farm, both just over the border in Landford, are now located.

The 1844 tithe survey records the area known today as The Drove was owned by the Earl of Ilchester and leased by Mark and John Noble. The farm consisted of a house, garden, barn and 23 acres of land made up of sixteen acres of arable and five acres of meadow and pasture. The land belonging to the farm formed a long narrow strip running from Bridgefoot to Giles Lane, between the River Blackwater on its northern boundary and the parish boundary of Plaitford and Landford to the south.

Both Mark and John Noble are recorded on the 1841 census for Plaitford but as no addresses are shown so we cannot be sure where they were living. As The Drove was originally a pair of cottages, they could have had a cottage each. On the census John and his son are listed immediately after Mark and his family.

John Noble is recorded on the 1840 tithe survey for Landford as leasing land in that parish. That land now belongs to Frank Male's Ten Acre Farm and Giles Lane Industrial Estate.

John died in May 1845, and his son, Frederick, is recorded on the 1851 census as lodging at the Shoe Inn. Mark died before the 1851 census that records his wife, Clemence, a widow and shopkeeper, living on Bridgefoot Road which may have been The Drove. Unfortunately, The Drove is not mentioned as an address before 1911.

In 1897, most of the farmland belonging to the farm formed part of a lease between the Earl of Ilchester and George Curtis of Powells Farm. This lease also included the land in Landford previously leased by John Noble.

Plaitford parish register records the wedding of James Musslewhite and Alice Dunn on 3 August 1907, and both are listed as living at Manor Farm Cottage. An electoral roll from 1907 records Rosa Moore as living at one of the cottages. On the 1911 census the cottages were known as Manor Farm Cottages[1] and record John Simmonds, his wife, Eliza[2], and their son, Joseph, in occupation of the south facing cottage, known as number one.

When the 1911 manor sale took place, the cottages were leased to Frank, Walter and Henry William Curtis under an agreement dated 7 May 1900 at £200 per annum. The Curtis brothers also leased Manor Farm, so it is likely that John and or Joseph worked for them.

A Draft Conveyance and Mortgage document held at the Hampshire Record office indicates that John Simmonds probably purchased the cottages when Plaitford Manor was sold in 1911. The conveyance dated 5 November 1923 makes reference to the will of John Simmonds dated 5 July 1920 in which he makes a request *that his son Joseph purchase the freehold property for the sum of £142-10shillings, being the price the testate paid for same"*. A mortgage was set up on 28 March 1924 between John Simmonds and Henry Cornish Knapman who was the executor of the aforementioned will.

Eliza died in September 1912, and by the 1918 electoral roll John and Joseph are joined by Joseph's wife, Lydia. John died in January 1923, and Joseph and Lydia continued to live in the cottage until the early 1960s. Joseph died in March 1963, and soon after Lydia moved to Canada Road, Wellow. She died in April 1971. The drove is not mentioned on the electoral rolls from 1964/65 to 1979/80.

The first recorded occupation of cottage number two comes from the 1911 census with Sidney and Rebecca Ware. There is no further mention until the 1920 electoral roll that records Frank Bowles who was also living there in 1921. Clement and Evelyn Moore 1923 to 1927, Percy and Eva Watts 1930 to 1934/35, Edward and Ada May Dibden 1935/36, George and Marjorie Gritt 1936 to 1937/38.

Reginald and Dora Hawkins occupied the cottage from 1937/8 to 1963/64. As with number one there is no further record of occupation.

The Drove was eventually sold and converted into the single dwelling it is today.

Records show that from c1982 until 1985/6 Thomas and Gwendolyn Humphreys lived at the property. The next occupier was pioneering cameraman John "Slim" MacDonnell lived at The Drove until his death in May 2012. Slim was one of the first cameramen to realize how mini-cams could be exploited for filming in difficult and dangerous situations on land, underwater and in the sky. He put cameras in the helmets of Formula 1 drivers, in footballs, and in divers' headgear.

Slim also worked in films and television, specializing in underwater scenes which were filmed in a special underwater facility at The Drove. His screen credits included Tarka the Otter and the Bond film Octopussy.

[1]Direct access to Manor Farm was by way of a footbridge over the River Blackwater and a footpath that crossed the field (where the lake is now situated) and came out opposite Manor Farm yard. Source: 1909 OS map of Plaitford.
[2] John and Eliza were the parents of John and James Simmonds who lost their lives in the Great War.

Woodland Management
& Gunsfield Cottage (Lodge) & Lodge (Cottage)

As with other estates and manors around the country, timber was big business during the eighteenth and nineteenth centuries. We have found numerous newspaper advertisements for tree and timber auctions held at the Shoe Inn during the late 1700s and early 1800s. Four in particular stood out:

Salisbury & Winchester Journal, 24 April 1775 – Auction 24 April of 446 Oak Trees standing in the parish of Plaitford in four lots of 162, 174, 40 & 70. For particulars contact John Compton.

Hampshire Chronicle, 18 March 1776 – Auction 29 March of 574 Oak Trees standing in the parish of Plaitford in 4 lots of 101, 108, 220 & 145. For particulars contact John Compton.

Salisbury & Winchester Journal 18 January 1779 – Now marked and to be sold 247 Ash Trees and their tops, standing on Plaitford Farm. For particulars contact John Compton.

Salisbury and Winchester Journal 24 April 1803 – Auction 5 May of Navy Timber – 222 Oak trees and knees all hewn and containing 7,548 feet. For particulars contact Mr. Newell at the Shoe Inn.

In the 28 years from 1775 to 1803, 1242 oak trees were cut down and sold from this small village!

The 1729 manor survey records the predominately wooded area in the north and north-west of the manor as Plaitford Wood, Boulder Wood, Hackers Coppice, Bushee Leys Coppice and Birch Acre Coppice consisting of 162 acres. The 1844 tithe survey records the area as Plaitford Wood and Plaitford Coppice (incorporating Boulder Wood and Hackers, Bushee Ley and Birch Acre Coppices) an area of 157 acres. By 1909 the area is known as Plaitford Wood, Boulder Wood, Hackers Copse and Lower Gypsy Copse - a total of 136 acres. Today, Plaitford Wood, Boulder Wood and Plaitford Copse total approx 118 acres.

Hacker and Plaitford Coppice contained large areas of hazel trees for coppicing for various uses such as hurdle making etc. Evidence of charcoal making in the same area was found in the late 1960s / early

1970s when woodland was being cleared at Bracken Farm. Three large black circular patches of burnt earth were discovered.

We don't know much about the John Compton referred to in three of the advertisements previously mentioned. Parish records show he and his wife, Mary, lived in Plaitford from before 1774 (Mary was buried at Plaitford on 4 May 1789 aged 57) until John's death in 1810. The registers record the baptism of their daughter, Hannah, on 3 April 1774 and her marriage to Roger Moody at Plaitford on 20 January 1795. There was also a son, John[1], who was buried at Plaitford on 4 April 1802, aged 42 and two other daughters, Mary and Sarah. We do not know if John Compton was related to the Compton family who sold Plaitford Manor to Sir Stephen Fox in 1679. From the advertisements, it would appear he was the Head Woodman and may have lived at Gunsfield Cottage. If this was the case, Compton Drive may be named after him, although it is more likely to have been named after the previous owners of the manor. John was buried at Plaitford on 23 January 1810, aged 76. From the parish records the family appears to have been the last Compton's to have lived in Plaitford.

Gunsfield Cottage: The 1729 manor survey map clearly shows a property in the area of Gunsfield Cottage then known as Hackers Coppice. Unfortunately, the accompanying schedule makes no reference to a lease holder and along with all other woodland in the immediate area it is referred to as *"in hand"*.

Moving forward to the 1844 tithe survey, the property known today as Gunsfield Cottage was owned by the Earl of Ilchester and leased to Edward Bowles[2]. The lease consisted of a house and garden with two closes of arable land and one meadow, a total of just over four acres. It is quite possible that Edward Bowles was leasing this property three years earlier at the time of 1841 census, which does not contain any addresses. The census records Edward Bowles, aged 50, described as a woodman and his wife, Jane, aged 40. Edward married Jane Batten in March 1821 and it is quite possible they had been living in the same property for some years prior to 1841. They are recorded on the next census in 1851 as living in Plaitford Coppice. Edward Bowles died in September 1852 and the 1861 census records Jane and her son, Charles, also a woodman, living at Garfield Lodge. The address becomes Gunvill Lodge on the 1871 census where we find Jane and Charles with his wife, Emily. Jane died in January 1880, aged 83. Charles continues as woodman and game keeper until his death in 1884, aged 48. His gravestone paid for by the Earl of Ilchester is inscribed *"In memory of a valued and faithful servant"*.

128

Charles and Emily's son, Ernest, took over his father's position as woodman and he and Emily continued to live at the property and were joined by Ernest's wife, Sarah (nee Hatch), in 1898. The 1911 census records Ernest, Sarah, their two daughters, Muriel and Florence, and Emily as living at Gunsfield Lodge. The sale catalogue for the auction of Plaitford Manor in 1911, records Gunsfield Lodge as a brick and thatched cottage. The property had six rooms, a dairy, a garden and five and a half acres of land. Ernest Bowles was recorded as tenant paying an annual rent of eight pound three shillings. Gunsfield Lodge was purchased by Sir Alfred Mond and became part of Melchet Park Estate. From the following advertisement that appeared regularly in the Western Gazette between May 1912 and November 1914 it would appear that Ernest Bowles stayed on as woodman:

"PLAITFORD WOOD SAWMILL
OAK, LARCH and FIR FENCING MATERIALS, GATE POSTS,
PILES, SLABS &c. - for prices apply E C BOWLES, Gunsfield
Lodge, Plaitford, Near Romsey".

Ernest is recorded on the 1915 male only electoral roll. Emily was buried in Plaitford on 4 December 1915, aged 78. After 1915 there is no further mention of Ernest, Sarah or their daughters.

We don't know why the property was referred to as a lodge from 1871 to 1914. It may have been because it acted as a lodge gate on the boundary between Plaitford Manor and Melchet Park. It continued to be known as Gunsfield Lodge or Gunsfield Cottage up until 1963 when it became Gunsfield cottage as it is today. In the early 1940s the cottage was badly damaged by fire, and in 1946 the owner Mrs. Ethel Joiner applied for planning permission to reinstate the building. Work started on 26 July 1946 and was carried out by G H Vinall Builders. The thatched roof was replaced with red clay tiles. In 1913, Mr. A H Clough of Burley applied for planning permission to build a cottage in Plaitford Copse, in the position where Gunsfield Lodge stands today. Planning permission was granted on 17 February 1913. We cannot be sure when this property was built; it is first recorded on the electoral roll for 1918. From that time it becomes confusing as to which was the cottage and which was the lodge[3]. We know that the cottage built between 1913 and 1918 is today known as Gunsfield Lodge. The other property known as Gunsfield Lodge from the mid 19th century is known today as Gunsfield Cottage.

Melchet Court was put up for auction in by Henry 2nd Baron Melchet on 5 July 1935. Both properties with land and woodland were purchased by Arthur Edward Betchley Betchley-Crundle for £1,525.

He later sold to Cyril Henry Gribble who then sold to Mr. Harry H Joiner on 4 November 1935 for £1,775. The total area purchased by Harry Joiner was just under 33 acres. An example of part of the confusion is that Harry and Ethel Joiner owned both properties from 1935 to 1963. In 1949, they were joined by their daughter and her husband, Kathleen and Arthur Phillips. It would appear the Joiners lived in what we know today as Gunsfield Lodge and the Phillips in the cottage but are recorded on the electoral rolls for that period as both living in the lodge.

On 26 October 1963, both properties with adjoining land were auctioned by the Joiner family and purchased by James and Ruby Hill for £15,500. They made the lodge their residence and rented out the cottage. In the 1970s, the cottage was sold for somewhere in the region of £14,000. James Hill, later to be Sir James, was the Conservative Member of Parliament for Southampton Test for 24 years. He was also a partner in Gunsfield Piggeries, now Bracken Farm, mentioned earlier in this chapter. Sir James died in 1999 and Lady Ruby, who was a CBE (Companion of the British Empire), sold Gunsfield Lodge c2000, she died in 2008. Both are buried at Plaitford.

[1]We are sure this John was a son of John & Mary who would have been 29 when he was born in c1760. This would make Mary 43 when Hannah was born. We have no baptism records for Mary and Sarah.

[2]Elder brother of Frederick Bowles see Plaitford Wood Cottage/Farm

[3]The author has tried to sort out who lived where and have come up with what we believe maybe the answer to the confusion between lodge and cottage. As there are quite a few gaps and some inconsistencies in what we have been told, we have decided not to print here what might be incorrect information. We are happy to make this information available to interested parties.

Chapter 11
Cottages & Houses
Including Furze Farm and Hobbs Copse

The chapter on Plaitford Farms covered most of the older properties in the village. In this chapter we look at six more cottages and we have included some information on the houses at Forest View and Purley Way. Some of the older cottages appear on a manor survey carried out for the Honourable Stephen Fox, later to become the 1st Earl of Ilchester, from now on referred to as the '1729 manor survey'. We also make reference to the split up and auction of the Manor of Plaitford in 1911 by Giles Stephen Holland Fox-Strangeways, 6th Earl of Ilchester, this will be referred to as the '1911 manor sale'.

For personal reasons, at the end of this chapter, we have taken the liberty of including Furze Farm and Hobbs Copse; although they are both just over the border in Landford, they have strong Plaitford connections.

Appledoor and Orchard Cottage

We start with the 1844 tithe survey that records a house and garden of about half an acre. The property is owned by the Earl of Ilchester and leased by James Petty a life holder and rented to George Pearce and Stephen Humby.

Three years earlier on the 1841 census a George Pearce, Blacksmith, aged 25 and Martha, his wife, aged 25, were living at one address and Stephen Humby, aged 70, living at another property. George Pearce died before 1851, and Stephen Humby was buried in Plaitford on 3 April 1850. (For further information of George Pearce's widow see Blacksmiths in chapter 5 – Nineteenth Century)

Today two semi-detached cottages stand on the site. The original single cottage was altered and a story added in 1873, and today is known as Appledore Cottage. In 1881, another cottage was added, now known as Orchard Cottage.

The sale catalogue for the 1911 manor sale records: "*A Brick built and slate double tenement, each containing three bedrooms on the first floor and two rooms on the ground floor together with a piece of fruit growing ground, an area of 1.775 acres.*
One is let to Curtis Brothers [1] *on a weekly tenancy (subject to two weeks notice) under an agreement dated 30 April 1900 at a weekly rent amounting to five pound three shillings per annum.* (On the 1911 census this property was rented by the Curtis Brothers to Joseph and Mary Jane Bowles) *The other with the ground to Mr. Henry Fanstone on a similar tenancy under an agreement dated 23 April 1895, at a*

weekly rent amounting to five pound per annum". (The 1911 census also records Henry and Annie Fanstone at this property)

Henry Fanstone, a wheelwright, born in Downton, is first mentioned on the 1851 census with his wife, Sophia. Their son, William Henry (also known as Henry), was born in 1859. From the 1861 census, Henry Snr is recorded as a carpenter - a profession his son would later take up. Throughout their time in Plaitford the address shown on the census records was Plaitford Common or Common Side. Is it possible the Fanstone's may have lived in one of the cottages and the previous single cottage from 1851-1911?

The double tenement was purchased at the 1911 manor sale by Alexander Alfred Green of Chapmans Farm, West Wellow for one hundred and ninety pounds. The purchase included the piece of fruit growing ground.

The cottages changed hands in February 1943 when Alexander Green sold the property to Harold John Harding, a baker from West Wellow, for the sum of seven hundred pounds. The conveyance mentions that the cottages were in the occupation of two families, Rothnie and Whetren.

The 1911 census records a double tenement and numbers the cottages as number one (Appledoor Cottage) occupied by Joseph Bowles and number two (Orchard Cottage) by Henry Fanstone.

Number 1: The 1915 electoral roll records Joseph and Mary Jane Bowles still living on the common, probably at number one. By 1918 they are living at number three Bridgefoot Cottages. We cannot be certain but with a process of elimination we think Henry and Charlotte Bowles were living at number one. Charlotte was buried at Plaitford on 2 January 1919, aged 64, and Henry with Ada (we don't know their relationship) continued to live in the cottage until 1925. Henry was buried at Plaitford on 30 May 1925, aged 74. We now have a nine year gap where we have been unable to place anyone at number one. From 1934/5-1947/8 Fred and Florence Whetren were living in the property followed by Laurie and Jean Finmore 1948/9-1995. The electoral roll effective October 1995 records Nigel Ramsey; the following year, 1996, Sharon Finmore-Wooldridge, daughter of Laurie and Jean Finmore, was in residence.

After Laurie and Jean Finmore took up the tenancy of number one in 1948/9 they named the cottage Appledoor. In 1973, they purchased the cottage for £5,500 from Harold Harding. They continued to live there until their deaths in January 1995, Jean on the first and Laurie on the nineteenth. Their daughter, Sharon, sold the cottage to Nigel and Sarah Pearce in 1998. The spelling of the name of the cottage was changed to Appledore.

Number 2: The Fanstone's continued to rent number two until 1936 and were followed by Peter and Elizabeth Rothnie who named the cottage Torren, Peter died in the early 1980's and Elizabeth continued to live in the cottage until c1990. Since Elizabeth Rothnie, the following people have lived at number two: c1990-1996, Laura Fellingham; 1997/98, Robert and Nichola Farley; 1999-early 2000's, Malcolm and Marlene Crosby; After the Crosbys left in the early 2000's they were followed by Tracey Dovey, and she was followed by an unnamed couple who left when the cottage was put up for sale by Beryl Quick, the daughter of Harold Harding, in 2005. The cottage was purchased by Amanda Gover who changed the name to Orchard Cottage. Amanda Cover sold the cottage in 2007 to the current owners Augustine and Genevieve Reynolds.

[1]Frank, Walter and Henry Michael Curtis as sitting tenants purchased Bowers Farm when the manor was split up and sold in 1911. Frank lived at Bowers Farm, Walter at Manor Farm and Henry Michael at Fir Copse, Landford.

Access to documents dated from 1911 to 1943 for both properties and 1943-1998 for number one by kind permission of Nigel & Sarah Pearce.

Evelyn & Sidney Cottages

In the late 1800s the population of Plaitford was on the decline with people moving away to find work. As an attempt to stem the decline and encourage more people into the village, the Reverend Alfred Gay, rector of Plaitford (1871-1899), bought up land and derelict cottages for renovation. The cottage with a piece of land would then be offered for rent. Evelyn and Sidney Cottages were part of this plan and were commissioned by Alfred Gay to be built on a piece of land he owned alongside the Southampton Road. The cottages were built in 1891/2 and advertised to rent in the Western Gazette on the 30 September 1892:

"COTTAGES, &c – To be let in Plaitford, to Church People, two new five-roomed COTTAGES, each with 1¼ acre of LAND. Rent £10 each – Apply THE RECTOR, PLAITFORD, ROMSEY"

The cottages were named after the Alfred Gay's eldest daughter, Charlotte Evelyn, and his eldest son, Sidney. On a visit to the United States, Sidney had died on 18 January 1887 near Orlando, Florida. He was twenty one years of age.

Alfred Gay left Plaitford in 1899 and left the cottages in trust to St Peter's Church. Evelyn Cottage is still owned by the church, Sidney Cottage was sold in1980.

The 1901 census shows George and Leonora Harrison at Evelyn Cottage and George and Hannah Billen at Sidney Cottage. From their ages recorded on the census, George Harrison, 45, and George Billen, 36, both men could have answered the advertisement in 1892.

The Harrisons moved from Evelyn Cottage to Dolce Domun (now The Milestone) on the other side of the road in 1924/25. Hubert and Margaret Bungay were the next to move in and stayed until 1950. A tragedy struck the Bungays in 1926 when their daughter, Hazel, was struck by a car and killed. (The full story can be found in chapter 12 - twentieth century). In 1951, Desmond and Joyce Pointer moved into the cottage. Joyce died 24 August 1980 and Desmond 22 August 2008, their son Keith still lives in the cottage.

The Billens lived at Sidney Cottage until 1934. Hanna died 17 June 1929, aged 72, and George 27 June1934. Hubert Bungay's brother, Henry, and his wife, Eva, took up residence in 1935. Eva died 1 May 1970, aged 86, and Henry 18 February 1979, aged 91. At the 1977 village fete to celebrate Queen Elizabeth II silver jubilee, Henry, then the oldest citizen, along with Victoria Palmer, the youngest, planted the copper beech tree that now stands on the village hall green.

Sidney cottage was sold to Bryan and Esme Trimmer in 1980. Esme sadly died in October 1998. Bryan joined the parish council in 1992 and from 1995 was ex-officio advisor on the New Forest; he became a parish councillor and vice chairman in 2004. Bryan continues to live in Sidney cottage with his second wife, Angela.

Here are a few snippits from the 1904-1968 Church Wardens accounts:

Easter 1904/05: Fire Insurance-Evelyn and Sidney Cottage, five shillings and nine pence. Easter 1907/08: Receipts - half year rent of four pound ten shillings from George Harrison (Evelyn) and George Billin (Sidney); payments – five shillings to Vinall Builders, for whitewashing dairy at Billin's cottage and three shillings to George Billin as an allowance for pig sty repairs.

Easter 1926: Receipts - half year rent of six pound from Hubert Bungay (Evelyn)) and four pound ten shillings from George Billin (Sidney).

Forest View, Church Lane

Church Lane Cottages as they were first named were built in the early 1920s on land given to Romsey Rural District Council by Sir Alfred Mond of Melchet Court.

Lady Violet Mond DBE laid the foundation stone in October 1920. Built by Frederick Vinall, the houses were completed in 1922. The three pairs of semi-detached houses were the very first to be erected by Romsey Rural District Council under their new housing scheme. The houses had no electricity or running water, but there was one well in the garden of the centre block that served all six properties. More information on these houses can be found in the chapter on the twentieth century in the piece entitled Plaitford in the 1930s. The electoral rolls for the 1920s addressed the houses as one to six Church Lane Cottages; from 1930 they were either Church Lane Cottages or Council Houses. Forest View first appeared in 1945, though only for properties one to four. Houses five and six were still addressed as Council Houses until 1953/54. From 1954 all six properties had become Forest View.

Over the years some of the houses have had many tenants and owners - there were also some periods where no tenants are recorded making it difficult to formulate a full list. However, we have selected the residents who lived for the longest period in each house over the last 91 years. Number 1 – William & Violet/Michael & Linda Turner 1964-2013 (49 years); number 2 – Arthur (Jim) & Edith (Edna) Grayer 1939-1992 (53 years); number 3 – Bert & Ivy Gritt/Fred & Ivy Cook[1] 1934-1997 (63years); number 4 – William & Ruby Angell 1939-1998 (59 years); number 5 – Leonard (George) & Elizabeth Stone 1932-1994 (62 years) and number 6 – George & Emily/Elrad & Rosemary Matthews 1933-2013 (80 years), making a combined total of 366 years. Only two other families have lived in the houses for twenty years or more: Number 1 – William & Hope Thornton pre 1945[2]-1964 (20 years +) and number 2 – Roger & Pauline Bysouth 1993-2013 (20 years).

[1]Ivy Gritt had lived at number three from 1934 and continued to live there after she was widowed in 1943. She married George Cook in 1947.
[2]There were no electoral rolls from 1940-1944 so we cannot say exactly when the Thornton's moved into number one.
In preparation for this book we prepared a spreadsheet of the occupation of Forest View. As there are too many to include here we will be happy to make the list available upon request.

Holly Cottage, Flowers Lane

A date stone above the front door of Holly Cottage bares the date June 1777. The 1986 Test Valley Borough Council grade two listing report dates the original cottage as circa eighteenth century, possibly earlier with nineteenth century additions.

Originally the property was a two-up two-down timber-framed, brick and thatch cottage. During the nineteenth century a one-up one-down extension was added to the right hand end, with what appears to be a separate entrance and no internal connecting doors, giving the appearance of a separate cottage.

Evidence from the 1729 manor survey map shows an earlier property standing on the site and the accompanying schedule records that it was leased by Richard Hembury and consisted of a house and eight acres of land. A Richard Embry is also mentioned on a1720 rent roll, it is probable that he is the same person at the same address. This information could date part of the cottage back to the seventeenth century. This would tie in with the beliefs of the current owner.

Moving forward to the1844 tithe survey, like most other property in the village it was owned by the Earl of Ilchester and leased to Rebecca Bowles. The property consisted of a house, barn and garden. At this time Rebecca Bowles leased over 60 acres of land and property in Plaitford, so it is likely that Holly Cottage was rented to an agricultural labourer.

We cannot trace the cottage or occupiers on the ten year census surveys from 1841 to 1871. We think it safe to say that Rebecca Bowles was leasing the property in 1841 and continued to do so until her death in 1850. After which the trail goes cold until 1881.

On the censuses of 1871 and 1881, William Trodd, a carpenter and his wife, Emma, were living in Plaitford in the area of Pound Lane and Bowers Farm. Their son, William, married Frances Hutchings on 1 September 1875. The 1881 census records William, also a carpenter, and Frances living at Plaitford Green where they continued to live for the rest of their lives. The catalogue for the 1911 manor sale names William Trodd as tenant at a rent of six pounds per annum under an agreement dated 9 March 1882. William Trodd purchased the property at the sale on the 4 October 1911 for the sum of £125. The cottage was listed in the sale catalogue as a red brick and thatched cottage with a yew porch. It had two bedrooms and a small room, kitchen or living room, wash-house and pantry and a garden at the front and rear with a wood and thatched piggery. Frances died in January 1926, aged 73, and William on 13 January 1930, aged 77.

The cottage was put up for sale by auction at the Shoe Inn on 27 June 1930. The description of the property on the sale document had not changed since the sale in 1911. The property was bought by Hylda Marjorie Holt for the sum of £410. Hylda and her husband, Leslie, took possession on 29 September 1930. From this time the property was known as Plaitford Green Cottage. When purchased in 1930 the total area was approx one-third of an acre. Additional land adjoining the cottage was purchased when Gardeners Farm next door was put up for auction in June 1936. A further purchase in1981 brought the total of land with the cottage to fourteen acres.

A bathroom extension was added in the 1950s with a one-up one-down extension to the left of the property in the early 1980s.

In 1972, Plaitford was within the New Forest boundary, and in July that year, Hylda Holt was granted forest and common rights under the New Forest Act 1964.

For the past 83 years the cottage has been occupied by a succession of the Holt Family. After Leslie and Hylda their son, Christopher, and his wife, Kathryn, lived in the property they renamed Holly Cottage. And from 2008 the cottage has been occupied by their daughter, Victoria.

Access to documents dating from 1911 to 1972 by kind permission of Victoria Holt

The Milestone c1920, the lady is Lavinia Harrison daughter of George and Leonora.

The Milestone, Southampton Road

We are unsure of the actual age of The Milestone. The earliest record we have again comes from the 1729 manor survey that records a cottage in the area of the Milestone, leased by Thomas Petty. We move forward to the 1844 tithe survey that records survey numbers 192a comprising a house and garden and 192b a close and 195 a house, garden and close of two acres, owned by the Earl of Ilchester and leased by William Hood, carpenter.

Back three years to the 1841 census we find two Hood families, William Hood aged 80, wheelwright, his wife, Martha[1], aged 70 and their son, Michael, also a wheelwright and his wife, Sarah, both living close by on Plaitford Common. It is probable they were living in the two cottages shown on the tithe survey.

By the 1851 census William and Mary are no longer recorded. Michael and Sarah are recorded as living at the property and continue to do so until their deaths in 1883, Michael 27 February and Sarah 19 March.

We need to mention two of their seven children: Olive, for her marriage to William Harrison, will become clear later and Ambrose who went on to marry Sarah Jane Dibden. They moved to Bramshaw in 1880 and in 1890 they had a son, also named Ambrose. Tragedy struck on 14 April 1912 when Ambrose and five others from the Bramshaw area were lost when the Whitestar Liner Titanic struck an iceberg.

The 1881 census again records two Hood families occupying both cottages; Michael and Sarah and their oldest son, George, also a wheelwright and his wife, Mary. The 1891 and 1901 census record George and Mary as still living at the property. Mary died 25 February 1907, aged 58.

The 1911 manor sale records Lot 17, a brick built and thatched cottage with sitting room, living room, three bedrooms with dairy and washhouse was sold to sitting tenant Mr. George Hood. The area of land amounted to a cottage and garden of 1.895 acres and 1.976 acres of pasture with a main road frontage of 414 feet. Almost the same land as held by the William Hood in 1844, minus one cottage (see the next paragraph). The annual rent paid before the sale was thirteen pound nine shillings. George lived at the property until his death on 12 January 1924, aged 80.

We now return to Michael and Sarah's daughter, Olive, who married William Harrison from Landford in about 1865. By the time of the 1871 census they had a son, George, aged six. The same George Harrison with his wife, Leonora, are recorded on the 1925 electoral roll as living at the property now known as Dolce Domun. In fact, at the time of the 1911 manor sale, George Harrison purchased the plot on the left of the entrance from the A36 to Powells and Pyesmead Farm, containing the second cottage leased for many years by the Hood family. He replaced the cottage with a bungalow which he later sold to a William Hood in 1925[2]. George Harrison died on 30 April 1929, aged 64; according to the electoral rolls Leonora continued to live in the cottage until 1932/33, she died in December 1945, aged 83.

In 1934/35, Thomas and Dorothy Davies (brother and sister) moved into the cottage they renamed the Milestone. Dorothy ran a tea shop from the premises until they left in 1938/39. With the help of the electoral rolls for Plaitford we can list the following occupiers: 1939/40, Anne Marsh and Jervase Monkman who continued to run the tea shop. There were no electoral rolls for 1940-1944; May 1945 - no mention; October 1945 - Clarence and Margaret Davis; 1946 - Kenneth and Isobel Hunt; 1947-1953 - Robert and Betty Bates (Betty was buried at Plaitford 4 June 1951 aged 42); 1954/5-1960/1 - Charles and Clair Downer; 1962/3-1968/9 - Richard and Maureen Saunders; 1969/70-1976 - Godfrey and Joan Jordon and finally 1977 to date Anthony and Victoria Hamilton.

[1]Martha Hood (nee Maury) was baptized in Wellow on 21 May 1771. Maurys Lane in West Wellow is named after her family.

[2]George and Leonora Harrison were renting Evelyn Cottage at the time of the 1911 census. The bungalow they sold in 1925 had just been completed and it is possible they intended to live there themselves. At the same time The Milestone became free and they probably decided to live there and sell the bungalow. William Hood paid £450 for the bungalow which he named Ferndale. He lived there with his wife, Florence Mary, until their deaths; Florence in May 1952, aged 75 and William in April 1963, aged 86. Their daughter, Florence May, continued to live there for some years. The bungalow was later converted to the house known today as Acorns.

Purley Way

The trusties of the Church-owned land, the Rev. William Walters, John Hurst Gradidge (Shoe Inn) and Alfred Jewell, Partridge hill, Landford, were authorized on 25 April 1947 to sell the parcel of land known as Purley Way within twelve months for not less than £86. By 28 April, Romsey and Stockbridge Rural District Council (R&SRDC) bought the 1.1 acres for £86 to build two pairs of semi-detached houses with an option to build a third at a later date. All six houses were completed and the first tenants moved in during 1951. Number six was the police house, and P C Edward Codd and his wife, Celia, were the first to live there followed by P C Dennis Moody and his wife, Dorothy. By the end of the 1950s its function as a police house ceased.

In the 62 years since the properties were built the longest occupation of each house is as follows: Number 1- Raymond & Peggy Dawkins 1959 to after 1990 (33 years plus); the first people to move into number 2 - Albert & Lilian Hayter 1951-1994 (43years); number 3 - Jose & Nancy Dias c1956-1996 (40 years); number 4 - Henry & Margaret Chant 1954 to 2001 (47years); number 5 - Ernest &

Kathleen Elkins 1954-1986 (32 years) and number 6 - Stephen & Veronica Greenham 1987-2013 (26 years). The flats at Purley Way were built in 1963.

Shoe Cottage

As with most of the other older property in the village we are unable to say when Shoe Cottage was originally built. The original thatched part of the cottage that stands to the left of The Shoe Inn is built of cob (thick mud and straw walls). During renovations in the 1990s, it was discovered that the original cob wall appeared to have been cut away and an inglenook fireplace had been inserted with a brick chimney. The addition of a brick chimney would date the original cottage to be earlier than the mid-sixteenth century when chimneys were introduced. During the renovations in the 1990s, the timber rafters (hazel poles) under the thatch were found to be clean and showed no evidence of smoke stain normally attributed to an earlier open fire in the centre of the floor. From this type of fire, smoke would have vented out through the roof staining the rafters and the underside of the thatch. The evidence would indicate that the roof may have been replaced at the time or after the fireplace and chimney was added. The existing tile hung extension to the cottage may have been built at the same time The Shoe Inn was extended in the third quarter of the eighteenth century (1766 to1775). The brickwork under the tile hanging matches The Shoe before it was rendered and is well-built with substantial oak timbers under the roof tiles. It is thought that a further addition to the rear of this extension was built in the mid-nineteenth century. The cottage was again added to in the nineteen fifties/sixties.

The 1729 manor survey records a cottage in the position of the existing Shoe Cottage as leased by John Martin. The 1841 census records Elizabeth Roberts, aged 40, and we are sure this is the same Betsy Roberts who is recorded on the 1844 tithe survey as a life holder. She was leasing the cottage with garden and three acres of land across the road from the cottage.

Unfortunately, as with other property in the village, there are no addresses shown on the ten year census from 1851 to 1891. Other than The Shoe Inn, properties in the area are addressed as the common, common side or Salisbury Road.

The next mention of the cottage is on the 1901 census that records the tenants as John and Eliza Simmonds. On the 1911 census Harry and Ella Dibden are renting the cottage. We have no further mention until 1918 where we find the first mention of Shoe Cottage since 1901. The 1918 electoral roll, records Frederick Peck and his mother,

Arabella, living in the cottage. By 1930 they are joined by Rosa, Frederick's wife. By 1932/33 Frederick and Rosa had moved out and Arabella continued to live in the cottage until her death in August 1934. The electoral rolls for 1934 to 1935 record May Murrey. There is no mention of Shoe Cottage on the electoral rolls from 1936/37 to 1939/40. No electoral rolls were produced between 1940 and 1944, but the May 1945 addition does record John Chambers. Again there is no mention of the property from 1946 until 1949 when Katherine and Katie Hedges are living in the cottage. Katie Hedges was on her own from 1952, and she continued to live in the cottage until her death on
8 August 1992, aged 96. Reginald and Julia Speare are recorded as occupying the cottage in 1993. Rodney and Dinah Batten bought Shoe Cottage in the winter of 1993/94. During the renovations which followed, a lot of the original features were discovered and sympathetically restored. Their son Nigel lived in the cottage until it was sold in 1999.

Thornycroft

Built around 1900, Thornycroft stands alone on the left hand side of Pound Lane. The cottage was built on land that belonged to New Lodge Farm. The 1901 census records John and Caroline Freemantle as living in the cottage. In 1911, it is recorded that Louise Harvey, a widow with four children, was living in the property. There is no mention on the 1915 or 1918 electoral roll. From later electoral rolls we find - 1921, Thornton and Louisa Green; 1922, no mention; 1923, Charles and Ellen Pack, they moved to Forest View, Church Lane in 1924/5; 1925, Elizabeth Rogers; 1927 to 1939/40 Walter, Jesse and Edmond Robinson. Walter and Edmond worked for the Muriel and Winifred Bowes-Lyon at New Lodge. In 1940 Walter and Edmond moved to Bridgefoot Farm. There were no electoral rolls between 1940 and 1944; May 1945 until 1947, Alfred, Edith and Vera Midlane; 1949 and 1950 no mention; 1951-1964/5, Alec and Alice Carter. In 1969 Thornycroft became the home of Philip (Bill) and Margaret Hart. Bill sadly died in 2008.

Hobbs to Furze Farm & Hobbs Copse Farm

Sometime back, as a family project, we decided to research the history and connections between these two Landford farms. We started with a fairly recent family connection between Sheila's maternal grandparents, George and Ruth Grayer, who purchased Furze Farm in 1913 and Silas (William) and Eva Dibden who purchased Hobbs Copse in 1912. Ruth Grayer and William Dibden were brother and sister. Our finding eventually took us back to the late 1500s. Because they stand right on the border with Plaitford and have over many years been known to, lived in and worked on by Plaitford people, we have, as a matter of interest, decided to include them in this book.

Although not technically in Plaitford, the area now known as Hobbs Copse Farm, Giles Lane Industrial estate and Ten Acre Farm are shown on the 1729 manor survey as being part of Plaitford Manor. Furze Farm borders Hobbs Copse to the south and prior to Hobbs Copse it was the only property on the left hand side of Sherfield English Road, between what is now the A36 and the River Blackwater.

Furze Farm was known as Hobbs up to the late 1800s and is referred to as such on the 1840 tithe survey for Landford. Hobbs Copse, originally a part of Hobbs, existed as a piece of woodland that later gave its name to a separate property. The first record of Furze Farm appears on the 1881 census for Landford. The occupation of Hobbs Copse began after 1912.

A survey of the original two up, two down Furze Farmhouse carried out in the 1990s dated visible brickwork to the 1720s. Though it was thought the building was of a much earlier construction. We now have evidence of a building on the site back to the second half of the 16th Century.

We have managed to trace a family named Hobbs, all of whom are recorded as colliers (charcoal makers), from 1591 to 1713. The earliest document we have is an Administration Bond and Inventory of Robert Hobbs[1] of Landford dated 26 May 1591; the will of his son, John, dated 24 February 1637; the will of his son, Giles, dated 17 March 1680. Next we have a lease document dated 25 March 1713 in which Giles Hobbs, grandson of John Hobbs, took lease of a tenement, garden and land known as Hobbs from Thomas Powell of London surrendering a lease dated 30 July 1675 made by Lewis March of Shambler, Isle of Wight to Giles Hobbs', father of the aforementioned. The new lease mentions Giles' wife, Mary, aged 30, and son, Giles, aged nine. This document is the last mention of Hobbs at this property,

It is probably around this period, early 1700s, that Hobbs tenement was re-built. This was confirmed during renovations in 2004, with the discovery of a brick imprinted with the date1716. Thomas Powell was from London, and some of the features mentioned in a survey carried out in the 1990s indicated a property belonged to or was influenced by a person of wealth. The large central chimney was fed by two back to back inglenook fireplaces, a bread oven and two open grates in the first floor rooms. The ceilings in the upstairs rooms were of a Jacobean style popular in London at the time.

From 1713 up to 1873 Hobbs remained in the hands of the Harcourt Powell family. We do not know the names of his lease holders until 1815 when James Cocks and his uncle, Samuel Cocks, took lease on the property. James Cocks was known to live at The Shoe Inn at the time until his death in 1862, so it is likely the property was occupied by one of his farm labourers.

On the 1840 Tithe Survey for Landford, a successor, John Harcourt Powell, still held title to Hobbs and some of the land that now forms part of Hobbs Copse Farm with the exception of Hobbs Copse Wood (held by John Nobel). The land was leased to James Cocks, farmer and landlord of The Shoe Inn.

The property in Plaitford and Landford now belonging to Thomas Harcourt Powell was sold by auction on 22 May 1873. The lease was held at the time by Richard Nightingale who lived at Powells Farm. The Hon. John Horatio Nelson purchased Hobbs tenement, farm buildings and land from the auction. The Eyre family and the Earl of Ilchester also made purchases of land at the auction.

The first mention of Furze Farm: As mentioned previously, James Cocks leased Hobbs from John Harcourt Powell. A farm labourer would have occupied the property and, as no addresses are shown on the 1841, 1851 and 1861 census returns, we have no way of knowing who actually occupied the house. James Cocks died in 1862, and the lease was taken up by Richard Nightingale again with a labourer in residence. It is not until the 1881 census return that we find the first mention of Furze Farm, in the occupation of Thomas Vinall, bricklayer and farmer of 18 acres and his wife, Mary. They are also mentioned in the 1891 census, but again no address is shown. We are unable to trace the farm on the 1901 census for the same reason.

We know that George and Ruth Grayer were renting Furze Farm from about 1906/7. From the census for 1911 their daughter, Gladys, aged 4, was the first of their children to be born in Landford. They eventually purchased the house, outbuildings and some land in September 1913 from the Honourable and Reverend John Horatio Nelson, and more land from Douglas Eyre in 1914 and 1919.

It is thought that the red brick extension to the original two up two down farmhouse was built around about 1920. George and Ruth Grayer's daughter, Hilda, married Stanley Curtis on 20 September 1916 they lived at Savages Farm (now Redhouse). Hilda bore Stanley six sons and sadly as a result of complications giving birth to their son Maurice she died in April 1926, aged 31. George Grayer died in December 1945, aged 80, and Ruth in May 1955, aged 86. They are buried at Plaitford Church. Their youngest daughter, Doris, and her husband, Silas Storr, purchased Furze Farm in September1955 from the estate of Ruth Grayer. Before moving to Furze Farm, Silas and Doris Storr had lived at number 3 Bridgefoot Cottages, Plaitford since 1936.

When Furze Farm was sold in 1956, besides the ten or so acres purchased by Silas Storr, the remainder of the land added by George Grayer since 1913 was sold for building plots. Today, all existing properties on the right of Sherfield English Road from Furze Farm to the A36 are built on what used to be Furze Farm land.

Silas Storr died in March 1969, aged 59, and Doris in January 2005, aged 92. They are buried at Plaitford Church. In 2004, Furze Farm was sold to Mark and Jenny Lucas.

The beginning of Hobbs Copse Farm: We know very little about who owned the land that makes up Hobbs Copse Farm as it is today. We do know that John Noble purchased Hobbs Coppice (woodland) in 1831/2. The 1840 tithe survey for Landford indicates that the land was split between John Harcourt Powell and John Noble, with a small parcel in the ownership of William Petty. We can only make an educated guess that when Thomas Harcourt Powell sold his estate in 1873, the Earl of Ilchester bought the land. The Ilchester Estate also purchased land from John Noble and William Penny or their successors, because by 1911 the Ilchester Estate held title to all land that later became Hobbs Copse Farm.

Silas (William) Dibden purchased Hobbs Copse and Great Field Copse, totalling 10.5 acres from the 1911 manor sale.

Seven years later, on 20 October 1919, William Dibden purchased a further 50 acres from George Curtis of Powells Farm.

The farm then covered an area of roughly 60 acres from its southern boundary with Furze Farm along the left hand side of Sherfield English road to the River Blackwater at Bridgefoot. Including the land where the properties Gaymeade, Cedar House (George Curtis's old scrap yard) and Bridge House (originally Gnome Nook) now stand. Excluding the property known as The Drove, the boundary followed the river to the ford in Giles Lane then left along Giles Lane, taking in what is now Giles Lane Industrial Estate (Coats Sandpit) and Frank Male's Ten Acre Farm. The boundary then turned left to follow the left hand side of the existing footpath from Giles Lane, through the Lavender Farm to Sherfield English Road.

Hobbs Copse Farmhouse: The first mention of William and Eva Dibden taking up residence at Hobbs Copse comes from the 1918 electoral register for Landford. The previous addition for 1915 makes no reference to any Dibden living in Landford. It would appear the house was built during the First World War. It is understood that timber taken from Hobbs Coppice was used in the construction. The bricks undoubtedly would have come from one of many brick works located in the area.

During September and October 1920, William Dibden sold all but fifteen acres. He retained Hobbs Copse and Great Field Copse along with one four and a half acre field from his 1919 purchase. Hobbs Copse remained at fifteen acres until it was sold in 1956 to Philip and Bertha Dovey.

In December 1927 or January 1928, William Dibden and his family moved to Lockerley, and Hobbs Copse was rented to George and Rose Cook who throughout the 1930s and 1940s farmed the land at Bridgefoot Farm. George Cook had in fact purchased thirteen acres of Hobbs Copse land from William Dibden in September 1920. George and Rose Cook were still tenants when Hobbs Copse was sold in June 1956. George Cook died in September that year, aged 88, and Rose, living in Eastleigh, died in December 1968, aged 92. Both are buried at Plaitford Church.

Philip Dovey set about increasing the land at Hobbs Copse by purchasing the thirteen acres from Rose Cook in May 1958. Nine years later, in 1967, he purchased the remaining land fronted to the east by Sherfield English Road to the border with Plaitford and to the west by Giles Lane Industrial. These purchases increased the farm to the 36.5 acres it is today. Bertha and Philip Dovey remained at Hobbs Copse farm until their deaths in 2000, aged 87, and 2002, aged 92 respectively.

Hobbs Copse farm was bought from the Dovey family by Doug and Penni Scott in December 2004.

[1] If Robert Hobbs was over 43 when he died, he would have been born in the reign of Henry VIII (1509-1547) and would have lived through the reigns of Edward VI (1547-1553), Mary I (1553-1558) and most of the reign of Elizabeth I (1558-1603).

Access to documents relating to Hobbs Copse Farm dating from 1911-1963 by kind permission of Doug & Penni Scott.

Chapter 12
Twentieth & Twenty-first Century

Throughout history, conflicts based on religion, power and greed have taken place through out the world. Though none, with such destructive power as would be seen in the twentieth century. The unnecessary carnage of the Great War 1914–1918 and twenty years later the fanatical attempts to control Europe, North Africa and the Far East brought on the Second World War 1939-1945.

Then came the Nuclear Age and the forty year Cold War, with the world living in fear of total destruction, whilst the two superpowers United States and the Soviet Union faced one another with fingers poised over their nuclear buttons.

As a result of conflict comes advancement- not only for the military, it also brought technology into our homes. During the second half of the century, the technical revolution of the twentieth century really took off.

Along with the rest of the country, the citizens of Plaitford took everything in their stride and carried on with all these events taking place around them.

Probably the biggest thing that changed the lives of residents of Plaitford was the decision in 1911 by Giles Stephen Holland Fox-Strangeways, 6th Earl of Ilchester (1874-1959), to divide up and sell the Manor of Plaitford. His family held title to Plaitford for 232 years since Sir Stephen Fox purchased the manor from Richard Compton in 1679. The sale of the manor gave lease holders a chance to buy and own their property.

The rural hardships and social life of the twentieth century are well documented. All but four of the chapters in this book cover the twentieth century. The four exceptions are Domesday to 1800, John Biddlecombe, Plaitford Races and the Green Man. In this chapter we have concentrated on living memories along with some interesting facts about Plaitford. Because of their importance, we have dedicated separate chapters to the First World War and the Second World War.

New Lodge, Bowes Lyon Connection

Miss Aleen Cust (1868-1937), Britain's first woman veterinary surgeon, lived at New Lodge from 1924 to 1927. In 1927, she decided to let the property for one year. In fact she never returned to Plaitford and died in Jamaica in 1937.

The electoral rolls for Plaitford from 1927 to 1939/40 indicate that William Benham was living at New Lodge. He is recorded as bailiff to Muriel and Winifred Bowes-Lyon, first cousins of Elizabeth Bowes Lyon later Queen Elizabeth the Queen Mother. The electoral roll states the Bowes-Lyon's abode as Ridley Hall, Barton Mill, Northumberland. As no electoral rolls were produced between 1940 and 1944, we are not sure when the Bowes-Lyons vacated the property. We know that the property was occupied by Leonard and Winifred Caddy from the early 1940s.

The late Bill Robinson, who lived at Purley Way, was working as a Chauffeur at Castle Malwood, Minstead in the 1920s. He recalled that at some time in the late 1920s The Hon. Francis Bowes-Lyon and his wife, Lady Ann, parents of Muriel and Winifred were, for health reasons, living at Malwood House, Minstead. The reason for their interest in New Lodge was on the recommendation of the Bailiff at Minstead, Mr. Furlong, as to its suitability to run their herd of prize winning Pedigree Jersey Cattle. Bill Robinson's father, Walter, and brother, Edmond, worked for the Bowes-Lyon at New Lodge and William Benham was Bill's uncle.

Bill Robinson always maintained the Bowes-Lyons rented New Lodge. If, as we believe, Aleen Cust owned the property, the Bowes-Lyons may well have rented early on. After Miss Cust decided not to return to Plaitford, she may have sold the property to the Bowes-Lyons. We have so far been unable to find any further information. We discovered a snippet of information about Miss Cust in the autobiography of the famous aviator, Amelia Earhart, by Doris L. Rich, in which she mentions that Aleen Cust was the sister of Sir Charles Leopold Cust RN (1861-1939), Equerry to King George V. He was in fact Equerry to the Prince of Wales in 1906 and was later gazetted as Equerry to George V in 1910 and still held the position in 1916.

The royal connection is too much of a coincidence. We think it possible that Miss Cust let the house and farm (and possibly sold later) to the Bowes-Lyons in 1927. At the time King George V was still on the throne, and the future George VI was married to Elizabeth Bowes-Lyon. Again it is possible that the Bowes-Lyons heard about the property becoming vacant through Sir Charles Cust and as a result a check on its suitability was then made by Mr. Furlong, the Bailiff of Minstead.

Muriel (1884-1968) and Winifred Bowes Lyon (1893-1968) never married.

Commemoration

To commemorate the Coronation of King George VI in 1937, six trees were planted in Plaitford as part of a nationwide tree planting celebration. Three copper beech trees *(Fagus Sylvatica Cuprea)* were planted on Bungays/Tutts Hill. One of these trees is still standing approx 50yards from the stile into the forest from the A36. The tree has a metal plaque at its base. Three scarlet oak trees *(Quercus Coccinea)* were planted on the school common. We know of one, now slightly leaning, by the post box on the A36 on the left hand corner of the track leading to Powells and Pyesmead Farms. Betty Sillence (nee Moore) remembered her father, Clement, and grandfather, Charles Moore, helping to plant these trees. The trees for the parishes in the Romsey and Stockbridge District were contributed by J Spedan Lewis of Leckford Abbas[1], the founder of the John Lewis and Waitrose stores.

Seventy five years later in January 2012, a joint committee made up of members of Melchet Park and Plaitford Parish Council, Plaitford History Society and Plaitford Village Hall Committee was formed to organize a tree planting and village party to celebrate the Diamond Jubilee of Queen Elizabeth II.

On 29 February, a sweet chestnut (*Castanea Sativa*) donated by the parish council was planted in the grounds of Plaitford Village Hall. Betty Sillence then Plaitford's most senior resident did the honour of planting the tree following a family tradition. A second tree, a red oak (*Quercus Rubra*) donated by Hampshire County Council, was also planted in the village hall grounds on 27 March.

Due to the need for both trees to be planted before the end of March, the committee arranged a village jubilee party around the unveiling of commemorative tree plaques, to be held on Sunday 10 June.

On a not so pleasant June afternoon, villagers assembled at the village hall for an American style finger buffet.

Unfortunately, due to ill health, Betty Sillence was unable to attend, so to continue the family tradition her son, David Babey, was invited to unveil the sweet chestnut plaque.

To mark their lifetime service to the community, Elrad Matthews and Jim Bowles were jointly invited to unveil the red oak plaque. Elrad retired from the village hall committee in March 2012 after 66 years. Jim has been a parish councillor for 64 years and a member of the village hall committee for over 40 years.

Parish Clerk, Jane Wright, had the honour of cutting the jubilee cake made by resident Marion Stacey.

The parish council organised commemorative mugs to be printed with the name of the parish; these were available to parishioners at a special price.

[1]The Royal Record of Tree Planting in honour of the coronation of His Majesty King George VI.

The annual fete held in July 1977 included a village celebration of the Queens Silver Jubilee. A copper beech *(Fagus Sylvatica Cupria)* tree was planted on the hall green by the oldest and youngest citizens, Henry Bungay and Victoria Palmer. A jubilee cake was cut by parish council chairman, George Curtis. Also to commemorate the silver jubilee a horse chestnut *(Aesculus Carnea)* tree was planted on the grass triangle at the top of Pound Hill by the late Bill Hart. Millennium celebrations took place at the village hall for Plaitford and Melchet Park residents and ex-residents on Saturday 1 July 2000. Organised by the parish council, the event featured an afternoon party for children and senior citizens, a fancy dress competition for all ages and an evening barn dance and barbecue. A unique millennium plate was presented to each household in the parish.

Memories of Marion Harding (nee Curtis)
Plaitford before the First World War

Marion Curtis, the daughter of Frank and Ruth, was born in Steplake Cottage, Wellow Wood in July 1896. By 1901 she was living in Plaitford in a cottage belonging to Manor Farm (possibly one of two cottages that later became The Drove) and attending Plaitford School. On the 1911 census the family was recorded as living at Bowers Farm where Marion lived until she was seventeen.

Marion recalled Sarah Bowles, the wife of Alfred, at Bowles Farm, keeping a parrot that would say 'There's someone at the door, Sarah' whenever a visitor arrived. Sarah Bowles grandson, Maurice, remembers a parrot when he was very young but cannot recall hearing it talk. As a young girl, Marion remembers a pinafore received as a birthday present from an aunt in London. Pinafores were worn by small girls until immediately after the First World War. The pinafore was unlike any owned by her fellow pupils, since it was trimmed with lace around the arms and around the neck, and embroidered. Caroline Roberts, the Rector's wife, died in May 1904 and Marion recalled being sent, with other pupils from Plaitford School, to collect spring flowers to line her grave. At the time the lining of graves with flowers was a widespread practice. In March 1910, Marion's younger sister, Blanche, died at the age of fourteen months. Her mother called in Sophie Bungay (who was the village

149

layer-out as well as a midwife) but was too distraught to be of assistance. Mrs. Bungay turned to Marion and said, 'You'll help me, my dear, won't you?' and the thirteen year old performed various small tasks as her sister was prepared for her coffin.

Florence Nightingale died in August 1910, and Marion remembered the long walk from Bowers Farm over muddy footpaths to attend the funeral at Wellow Church. She recalled, *"When we arrived, we could see the bright red coats of several Crimean War Veterans. Covering her coffin was the shawl or cape she used to wear in the hospital wards"*. At the age of seventeen, Marion moved to Nottingham to work at the Liberal club and then to London and Bognor before returning to the area to marry Harold Harding in 1922. She spent the rest of her life in Wellow where she died in 2003, a week after her 107th birthday.

Most of the memories of Marion Harding have been taken from 'Shot for a White-Faced Deer' by kind permission of the author Stephen Ings

Plaitford in the 1930s
Elrad Matthews' own words written in 2007

"The New Forest was unfenced in those days and the ponies wandered at will across the A36 – it wasn't known as the A36 then – it was the Salisbury or Southampton road depending on which way you were going – and they roamed the highways and byways and consequently the roadside verges were always kept neat by nibbling ponies and young growth on the hedges was also bitten off, if it was in reaching distance.

Heading north towards Plaitford the first dwelling on the left was Furze Farm followed by Hobbs Copse and the only dwelling on the right was a small cottage[1] occupied by the Hayter family and the property extended from the main road to where Terada now stands, providing enough grazing for a cow and sometimes a calf which kept them in milk.

The next dwelling was Gaymede which was built in the early thirties or late twenties at the side of a worked out gravel quarry. This eventually became George Curtis's scrap yard providing a useful source of bits and pieces for your car.

Bridgefoot cottages have not changed in profile. They may well have been built in the eighteen hundreds[2] – but have been extensively modernized.

Crossing the bridge – this was bounded on either side by white painted tubular railings with a ford at the side for horse drawn vehicles.

Bridgefoot Farm looks much the same as it has always done but has been considerably enhanced by new thatch.

As we start to go up the hill the road becomes a deep cutting, the land either side more than head height above the road surface and the turning to the church is a narrow lane – just the width of one vehicle and to continue down the hill past the church and on to Manor Farm with the occasional ancient oak growing out of the road side bank – the cutting continued up and over the hill and on towards Bowles Farm.

On top of the hill, Pound Hill, the triangle of grass featured the remains of a pound, a post and rail structure in which strayed animals were impounded pending being claimed by their owner.

To return to Church Lane – the cottages now called Forest View were constructed in 1922 ³ with concrete blocks believed to have been cast on site.

There was no main water supply, no electricity and no main drainage system. Water had to be wound up by windless – there was one well in the garden of the middle block and that supplied all six houses.

In the bathroom was a cast iron copper and if you wanted a bath you lit the fire in the copper and when hot enough you bailed water into the bath.

Cooking was done on a kitchen range with an oven at the side and this provided warmth as well as a cooking facility.

For lighting we had paraffin lamps and candles and we managed quite well without electricity, for what you've never had you don't miss.

In the days before WW2, housewives did not go on a weekly shopping trip as they do today, tradesmen called frequently and delivered to your door. The papers were delivered daily, as was the milk. The baker called two or three times a week, also the butcher, the baker was usually grocer as well. Also Herberts the hardware merchants in Romsey kept up a regular supply of paraffin oil and candles.

Plaitford Church was lit by large hanging paraffin lamps, the heating was provided by a large cast iron tortoise stove which stood where the organ now stands. Music in those days was supplied by a harmonium.

In the days before the war, the nights were darker than they are now, and on moonless nights with complete cloud cover the darkness was intense as there was little or no light pollution from the towns.

School days - we didn't have school dinners then – unless we lived near the school we took dinner with us. There was no school uniform – I went to Wellow School and the best I could manage was a cap with WS on it. We were a pretty scruffy lot really – with patches on our elbows and seats of our trousers- incidentally, everyone wore short trousers at school until leaving at fourteen – our best clothes were our Sunday clothes as lots of us went to Sunday school.

We left school at fourteen and started work – everyone found a job – some were apprenticed in the building trades – my first job was in a shop in Romsey where I earned ten shillings a week but you could buy ten cigarettes for four pennies.

Sundays were different before the war, shops were all closed with the exception of newsagents and tobacconists who opened Sunday mornings; Cricket and football matches were usually played on Saturday afternoons.

There was no five day week – everybody worked until twelve or one o'clock on Saturday."

[1]This cottage stood where the bungalow Lyndale now stands
[2]Bridgefoot Cottages were built in 1898/9
[3] Building started on Forest View Cottages in 1920

A scene from the top of Pound Lane towards Bowles Farm. Before the road was widened in 1968 it followed the pull-in now in front of the farmhouse.

Betty (Bet) Sillence (nee Moore) 1921-2013
Memories of a lifetime in Plaitford.

Betty "Bet" Sillence, Plaitford's most Senior Citizen was 91 when interviewed in April and May 2012. Her memories from these interviews and an interview she did for Plaitford History Society in 2007 have been collated as follows. Sadly Bet passed away on 9 March 2013.

Born in 1921, Bet was 18 months old when her father Clement "Clem" and mother Evelyn moved from Hamptworth to Plaitford. They lived at The Drove at Bridgefoot, (then a pair of dwellings), next door to Joseph and Lydia Simmonds. The cottage that Bet lived in looked out over the river and up towards the church, the other, where the Simmonds lived, looked over the gravel pit where Gaymeade, Cedar House and Bridge House now stand.

She remembers the fire in 1926 that destroyed her grandparents' cottage behind The Shoe Inn. She travelled on the back of her father Clem's bicycle from Bridgefoot to inspect the damage caused by a smouldering wooden chimney beam. Charles Moore, Bet's grandfather, had purchased the cottage from The Earl of Ilchester in October 1911 for the sum of £90. The cottage came with a strip of land behind The Shoe, from the stream on the left as far as the boundary with the milestone on the right.

Whilst their new house,'The Poplar' was being built, Betty's grandparents, Charles and Amy Moore, had temporary accommodation upstairs in the stable block at The Shoe.

In December 1927, Bet's father, Clem, purchased from his father, Charles, a piece of the land to the right of "The Poplar" where a local builder, Moodys of Landford, built the cottage Shalbourne Dean into which the family moved when Bet was about eight. The house was named after Shalbourne near Hungerford in Berkshire, where Bet's mother came from.

Bet started at Plaitford School on April 12, 1926, aged five, and stayed until she was fourteen. She remembers on one occasion the children were allowed to watch the local hunt set off into the forest through the old racecourse. This day she and a few others decided to follow. Knowing they would get into trouble didn't seem to worry them. When they decided to turn back, it was time for lunch so they went home. On returning to school in the afternoon, she recalls Mrs. Creeth, the head-teacher, caning each of the boy's hands and telling Bet to stand in the corner and hold her tongue. This she did and remembers her saliva running down her arm and dripping off her elbow.

On some occasions, as Bet was going home for lunch, Mrs. Creeth would ask her to bring her bicycle to school with her in the afternoon. This usually meant an afternoon cycling to the far reaches of the village with envelopes that she would deliver, wait for a reply and return to the school. Mrs. Creeth was very involved in arranging treats for the pupils, including outings. The letters were asking for financial support to help pay for these activities, and in most cases the replies that Bet took back to school contained money. Bet recalls the girls at the school entering the sewing competitions at the Melchet Court summer flower shows. The boys would enter the miniature garden competitions. Material was supplied by the Queen Mary Sewing Guild in London and the girls made first size baby clothes that were sent to London for the poor. On one occasion, Bet made the most and was presented with a thimble as a prize.

Looking back on her days at Plaitford School, she feels that Mrs. Creeth was a fair teacher, though at the time she didn't think so.

On Saturday's, whilst at school, Bet would accompany her father to the market at Kingsland Square in Southampton where they would buy meat for Sunday lunch and yellow haddock for Sunday breakfast. Loaded with bags they would then go to the Hippodrome to see the comedy variety acts such as Elsie and Doris Waters. They would sit in the six penny seats in the stalls.

Bet remembers the Walker family who sold petrol and odds and ends from a building where the BP garage and shop stands today. They eventually turned half the building into a shop. On one occasion Bet purchased 20 aniseed balls for a penny - they were wrapped in some paper from a sausage wrapper. When she opened the sweet wrapper, they were all stuck together with sausage fat! The Walkers lived in old railway carriages behind the shop.

Various traders made deliveries in Plaitford before the Second World War. Shone's bakers had a bakery in Canada Road. The family lived at Ower and on the evening of Saturday 22 June 1941, six members of the family were killed by a parachute mine dropped on the post office and adjoining cottage.

Milk was delivered by Jim Emms, who worked for Mr. Scurlock from Sherfield English, using a bicycle with a large can of milk. Coal was delivered by Billy Russell from Whinwistle and Drake Bros from Cadnam. Local shops were Babey's, later Palmerino's, in Wellow where the Nisa shop now stands and Hardings opposite the top of Slab Lane, Wellow.

Bet remembers visiting her great aunt Rose who lived in the original Moore family home of a two-up, two-down cottage with mud walls, thatched roof and an earth and clay floor. The cottage stood close to the border garage and when entering the door you would step down into the interior. Aunt Rose later had a cottage built next to the then school. The cottage was known as Rose Cottage and later became Martyns and is now Wisteria Cottage.

Bet left school on the Thursday before Good Friday 1935 and started work on the Easter Monday as a third chamber maid at Loperwood Manor near Tatchbury Mount. The property was sold a year later and she was laid off. After a month or so working at Copythorne, Betty worked for Miss Dorothy Davies at her tea room at the Milestone, the thatched property to the right of the Shoe Inn. The property had been owned by Bet's Great Uncle and Aunt, George and Leonora Harrison, who sold it to Miss Davies who changed the name of the property from Dulce Domum to the Milestone. In the morning, Bet made cakes and served them with tea in the afternoon. When the tea room first opened it was located in the lounge of the house. After a year or so an old cowshed that stood in the grounds to the right of the house was converted into a kitchen and tea room. This building later became Forest Acre, as it is still known today. Bet remembers she was paid ten shillings a week and a pot of tea was six pence and cakes two pence each. Another of her duties was to prepare Miss Davies two nephews for school each morning. The boys, Patrick and James, were the sons of Thomas Davies, the brother of Dorothy, who also lived at The Milestone.

The tea rooms were only open in the summer, and usually during the winter Miss Davies went away and Bet looked after the house.

Later, Bet went to work at Plaitford House for Sidney and the Misses Susie and Bella Simmonds. Whilst working at Plaitford House, Bet married her first husband, Leslie Babey, on October 7 1939. Sidney Simmonds drove her to the wedding at Plaitford church. Whilst at Plaitford House, Bet and other domestic staff had every Sunday off as the servants quarters were used for the Sunday school run by Miss Susie Simmonds.

During the war, Plaitford House was Plaitford's ARP (Air Raid Precaution) headquarters and Bet remembers the commotion one night in July 1940 when George Kemp was brought to the house after his cottage in Compton Drive had been bombed. She had crept to the top of the stairs and looked down into the hall and saw Mr. Kemp wrapped in a blanket. Sadly, his wife Helen had been killed.

Betty stayed at Plaitford House until she fell pregnant with her daughter, Lesley, who was born in 1941.

Throughout the war, no matter what, Bet's mother Evelyn, would catch the bus every Friday to Southampton to buy items she could not get in the local shops. She recalls her mother saying that she had out of curiosity joined long queues at food shops only to find she didn't want what was on sale.

Bet recalls during the war years most people in Plaitford owned a cow or two and chickens. Fresh eggs were readily available and Bet did not recall having the need to use powdered egg – she remembered preserving fresh eggs in isinglass. This came in a treacle type tin – emptied into a bucket and mixed with boiling water – when cool the eggs were placed in this semi-setting liquid and could be kept for up to a year. Eggs removed with a spoon had a crystal like coating and could be used in the normal way. Bet said she would always break the eggs into a cup to check they had not gone off! She also remembers sharing and exchanging rations and a great community spirit and that the blackout was always observed.

On one occasion, Bet was at her parents' house and went to the shed with a bowl to get some potatoes. A dogfight was taking place overhead at the time and shell cases were rattling on the tin roof of the shed, forcing her to empty the bowl and put it over her head and run back indoors.

For the rest of the war, Bet now with two children, (David was born in 1944), lived with her grandmother at "The Poplar". After her grandmother died in September 1944, Bet moved back in with her parents.

When her husband, Leslie, came home from the war, he and Betty rented one of the Sawpit Cottages at Melchet Park at ten shillings a week.

After two years or so, they moved to a property constructed from two ex army huts, purchased by Clem, Bet's father, on the site where the bungalow Cuffnells[1] now stands and next to what was then Martyns (now Wisteria Cottage).

During the late 1950s, Bet's first marriage failed and she and Lesley divorced. In 1963, Bet married William Ernest (Ernie) Sillence.

After aunt Rose Moore died in March 1949, aged 85, Clem and Evelyn sold Shalbourne Dean and moved into Martyns. Some time later, Bet and Ernie moved into a caravan on site whilst the ex-army huts are taken down and Clem built the bungalow Cuffnells. When it was finished, Clement and Evelyn moved in and Betty and Ernie moved into Martyns. Evelyn Moore died in May 1974, aged 76 and after Clem's death in September 1982, aged 86, Bet and Ernie moved into Cuffnells and Martyns was sold. Sadly Betty was widowed in

November 1983 when Ernie died, aged 53. Bet continued to live at Cuffnells until her death.

[1]The name Cuffnells comes from a house that stood in Lyndhurst occupied from 1880-1928 by Alice Pleasants Liddle who was destined to become the inspiration for Lewis Carroll's Alice in Wonderland, having first met the author in1856. For a brief period in the 1930s the house became a hotel before it was requisitioned in the Second World War for use by a Searchlight Battalion. Clement Moore purchased the army buildings from the military. Cuffnells was demolished early in the 1950s

The Castle family

The plot of land owned and settled by the Castle family in Plaitford Green, on the border with Wellow Wood, is recorded on the 1729 manor survey as woodland forming part of Plaitford Wood. By the time of the1844 tithe survey it had become a meadow belonging to the Earl of Ilchester and leased to John Fielder as a life holder. John Fielder also leased Fielders Farm and Yew Tree Farm, known then as Hutchens's, and this piece of land formed part of Hutchens's.

From August 1902, Harry and Susan Dibden rented Yew Tree Farm and in 1911when the Earl of Ilchester divided up and sold Plaitford Manor, Harry Dibden purchased the farm that still included the Castle plot.

Harry Dibden died in 1933 and his wife sold the piece of land to Lewis Smith at Fielders Farm, and in 1934 he sold it to William Castle. By the 1939/40 electoral roll, William and his wife, Matilda, had set up home on their land and their descendants still live there today.

William came from the London area where his family were flower sellers and belonged to a travelling family. During his travels he had come to this area where he met Matilda Cooper in the late 1800s. They stayed in the New Forest area and went on to have ten children. Up until the 1960s the family would travel all over the south of England during the summer months, carrying out seasonal work such as fruit and hop picking. Each winter they would return to Plaitford Green where they would work on local farms carrying out hedge cutting, ditching, and cutting and making fence posts. Over the last forty years the family has stopped travelling and is permanently settled in Plaitford. Although they live just within the Plaitford boundary, all the children attended Sherfield English School until its closure in the 1980s.

Since the 1930s, the family has continued to exercise their grazing rights on the common. William died on 27 May 1965, aged 87 and Matilda on 21 March 1967, aged 81, both are buried at Sherfield English.

Interview with Norman Castle 6 March 2013

Memories of Jim Bowles
Builder and Undertaker

After Jim's father, Charles "Charlie", left the army at the end of the First World War he went to work for Oliver Kendall, Undertaker in New Road, Landford. When Oliver died in 1935, his wife, Mary, asked Charlie if he would consider running the business. He agreed to do so eventually moving the business to his own property at Oaklands Plaitford Green. Charlie and his wife, Florence, had three sons, Cyril, Maurice and James "Jim", who was born in 1930. Jim went to Plaitford School and after leaving school he took on an apprenticeship as a wheelwright. In 1948, he was going to move to Canada to work at a lumber mill. His national service had been deferred because of his apprenticeship and because Jim was unable to take the job straight away he lost it.

Jim went in the army in 1950 and served in the Royal Artillery based in Germany and obtained the rank of sergeant. He left the army in 1953 and secured a contract with the MOD to dismantle huts from WW2 army camps around the area including at Tidworth, Salisbury Plain and Blandford. With a lorry and four men in his employ they would dismantle the huts and sell them on to farmers and other interested parties in twelve foot sections. Customers could by any length they wanted as long as it was divisible by twelve. In between times, Jim also assisted his father with the funeral business. Charlie died in July 1957, aged 60, and Jim took over as undertaker and would remain so until he retired in 1990. Jim would call on locals to assist as coffin bearers including, his brother, Maurice, father-in-law, Leo Pratt, Les Curtis, George Curtis and his son, Brian. Most of his help came from locals who worked from home, but with very few telephones Jim had to rush round the village to remind them that a funeral was taking place. Over the years the figure Jim paid his bearers rose from one pound ten shillings to five pounds per funeral. Jim used to dig each grave by hand which was quite easy in Landford, Plaitford and Wellow taking on average one and a half hours to dig to double grave depth. However, Sherfield English was not so easy and could take up to a day to complete. Coffins were supplied by Woodrow Building Supplies of Salisbury in kit form, two sides, base, lid and two ends. In one length that could be trimmed and widths of twenty one and twenty four inch. An early form of flat-pack! On one occasion, Jim was asked to take care of the funeral of a vicar of Sherfield English, a very tall, heavily built gentleman. Jim had to order a larger than normal coffin not held in stock by

Woodrows. They managed to organize one from their suppliers in the West Country to be put on a lorry bound for London. As the lorry had to be at its destination early in the morning it was arranged that Jim meet it in a lay-by on the A303 near Stonehenge at two o'clock in the morning. Luckily, everything went to plan. On another occasion a grave at Whiteparish collapsed due to wet weather. Jim advised the vicar of the problem and it was agreed an extra hymn, which Jim recalls was "Oh, God our help in ages past", would be sung to give time for the grave to be dug out.

Alongside his undertaking duties, Jim had moved on to build farm building and carrying out other building work including the refurbishment of Plaitford Village hall in the early 1970s. Jim recalls many occasions he would be working on a building and his wife, Gwen, would arrive to advise him there had been a death. He would have to down tools and rush home and change and take on his other roll of undertaker.

Taken from an interview with Jim Bowles 16 May 2013

Amenities

Plaitford has lacked the usual amenities still enjoyed today by its neighbours in Landford, Sherfield English and Wellow with their post office, shops and petrol station.

As we mention in the chapter on the nineteenth century, Plaitford was quite well off for general shopkeepers, bakers and grocers. By 1901, there was only one shop recorded in the village - that of Sarah Hurst at Fielders Farm. The 1911 census and the Kellys directories from 1903-1939, make no further mention of a shop or shopkeeper. It would appear that Sarah Hurst's was the last to be recorded in Plaitford.

There is no record of Plaitford having its own grocers/butchers/bakers shop or post office during the twentieth century. There was a petrol station from the 1930s to the 1960s run by Walter Hutchings alongside his blacksmith forge in the area of border garage on the A36, now Wellow Vehicle Sales. There were market gardens in the village with some selling their produce at the door.

Over the years, deliveries of the usual necessities, either daily, twice weekly or weekly were made by businesses from Romsey and the local area including:

Animal Feeds - Hickman's; Bread - Shones and Hardings from Wellow, Stainers later Dibdens from Landford and Riddet's from Nomansland; Butchers - Alf Moody and Frank Kemish from Wellow, customers went out to the van with their plates and the meat was cut to their requirements; Cakes and Pies - Mr. Beckley from New Road, Landford; Fish - Alf Saunders from Landford later Wellow; Candles and Paraffin oil - Herberts of Romsey; Ice Cream: Stop me and buy one - Mr. Crook on pedal cycle, later Carlo's from Wellow in his ice cream van; Milk - Sid Scurlock from Sherfield English and later by Eric and Lily Whitehorn from Nomansland; Papers - George Elkins from Wellow, delivered by Joyce Dibden from Whinwistle by bicycle; Shoe and boot repairs - King brothers formerly Plaitford, later Landford.

The closest grocery shop for the south of the village was just over the border on the other side of the A36 in Landford. Crusader Carpets on the right of the BP garage now occupy the premises. Residents in the north of the village were spoilt for choice, being probably equal distance from the A36 or Sherfield English.

Do you remember the Indian gentlemen in their turbans going from door-to door selling jewellery and towels? Betterwear and Kleen-e-z-e selling brushes, cleaning products and other household utensils door-to-door; the man from the *"Pru"* (Prudential Insurance Company) who called to collect your monthly insurance payments; dustbin man who collected your bin from back of your house, carried it out on his shoulder to the refuse cart, empties it and carried it back to where he got it from; the coalman, black as the ace of spades, with his special hood and back cloth, carrying heavy jute sacks containing one hundred weight of coal on his back to your coal shed; the local policeman with his bicycle, always available, he knew everything and everyone and always seemed to appear when you were up to mischief and the doctor doing his daily rounds visiting his patients at home…

Animal Pounds

A pound was a structure in which stray animals were impounded pending being claimed by their owners.

The 1844 tithe survey shows an animal pound on the Plaitford side of Botley's ford on the track that runs towards Powells and Pyesmead Farms from Sherfield English Road. Although no other pound is shown on the tithe survey, it is likely that another stood in the triangle at the top of Pound Hill at the junction of Pound Lane and Sherfield English Lane. A pound in this area is shown on the 1909 OS map and remains of its post and rail construction were removed when Sherfield English Road/Lane was widened from Bridgefoot to Plaitford Green in the late 1960s.

For many years a group of elm trees stood by the pound. As a result of the Dutch Elm disease that devastated the nation's elm trees in the early 1970s, they had to be cut down. When the elm trees were gone the top of Pound Hill looked bare, so to enhance the area and commemorate the Queen's Silver Jubilee, Margaret Hart's late husband, Bill, planted a horse chestnut tree on the triangle. Margaret, who lives in Pound Lane, remembers having to keep the tree watered through the hot summer of 1977. The tree still standing today was joined by a bench seat donated by the parish council to commemorate the millennium in 2000. In May 2013, Maurice Bowles of Bowles Farm retired from cutting the grass on the pound, a voluntary task he had carried out for twelve years.

River Fords

As mentioned at the beginning of chapter two, the name Plaitford probably means a ford where games were played. Well, Plaitford had plenty of fords in which to play. The village had six in total, two of which still exist today.

Our first ford was close to the border with West Wellow in the area of Monkeys Jump[1], where a stream now runs off Plaitford Common under the A36 and to the right of Border Garage (Wellow Vehicle Sales) and north to where it joins the River Blackwater.

Another stream that runs under the A36 on the Landford side of The Shoe Inn was originally crossed via a ford. The road would have originally run behind The Shoe, along the gravel track that exists today. The road was realigned to its current position in the late eighteenth century. This stream now acts as the Hants/Wilts border and following it north we come to Botley's ford[2] - one of two still active today. Heading north along Sherfield English Road to the River Blackwater at Bridgefoot, the road forded the river here. In the late 1800s, a wooden bridge was built to take light traffic only. Heavy horse drawn wagons and motor vehicles had to use the ford. The wooden bridge was replaced in the 1920s. The ford was still in use for heavy traffic until the late 1950s / early 1960s. Travelling west along the river we come to Dead Man's Ford[3], the second of our active fords. This ford dissects Church Lane, Plaitford and Giles Lane, Landford. Last but not least, we head north along Sherfield English Lane and into Steplake Lane to where the road dips approximately 200 metres just beyond the turning to Wellow Wood. This ford was replaced by a culvert under the road in the early 1970s.

[1]Monkeys Jump has nothing to do with apes. The name comes from medieval monks who would cross the stream by jumping the stepping stones.
[2]The origin of the name Botley can be found in chapter 2.
[3]It is not known where the name Dead Man's ford comes from; it is mentioned as *"Deadmans Fawrde"* in a description of the parish boundary in 1619.

Gravel Extraction

As well as other gravel pits in the area there were two situated in the area of Bridgefoot. The first shown on the 1909 OS map was behind and to the right of Bridgefoot Cottages. The recent widening of the entrance for the New Forest Folk Festival exposed a small seam of gravel in the bank. In the case of the other which was located on the opposite side of Sherfield English Road where Gaymeade and Cedar House now stand, we only have memory evidence. Locals remember gravel being extracted from this area, and the late Betty Sillence recalled when she lived in one of the two semi-detached cottages at The Drove in the 1920's that their cottage faced the river and church and next door faced the other way towards a gravel pit.

After the First War, the Tutt brothers, Alfred, William and Thomas, were self-employed gravel merchants and worked one or both of the pits.

Alfred, William and Thomas Tutt working one of the gravel pits at Bridgefoot just after the First War. All hard graft, no mechanical aids in those days!

For the duration of the Second World War, Jerry Russett stored his fairground equipment in the gravel pit behind Bridgefoot Cottages. He and his wife Florence lived on site throughout the war until 1946. The following newspaper reports are from the Romsey Advertiser unless otherwise indicated - some are amusing and some tragic. The full reports in *italics* are exact transcripts; others have been abridged and contain the main points. To run with the date sequence we have added some pieces from our own files.

1900: *"It has been reported that a private bridge on the Plaitford Farm Road at Plaitford, belonging to Lord Ilchester, is not safe and is in need of a new top on it. Mr. Curtis stated that when a traction engine went over it the other day it nearly went in the water".*

March 1900 Hampshire Advertiser: *"Susan Hannah Noyce of Plaitford pleaded guilty at Romsey County Bench to being drunk in Embley-lane on February 20. She said she was sorry it was true, but she left home without any breakfast, - P.C. Blunden said that on receiving information he went to Embley-lane, and found the defendant lying in a ditch wherein was some water. He got her up, as she was very drunk, he had to get a conveyance to take her home.- The chairman said he was sorry to see so respectable-looking a woman in such a position. He hoped she would not get into such a condition again. She was fined two shillings and six pence and six shillings and six pence costs. She paid part and had time to pay the rest".* Susan Hannah Noyce does not appear on the 1891 or 1901 census.

December 1900: *"Romsey Board of Guardians, Botleys Bridge, Plaitford. At the last meeting the surveyor put in a price from Mr. W Hood, of Wellow, for repairing the bridge, but the matter was deferred because someone suggested that Mr. Oliver, who lived near, should be asked to give a price. The latter offered to do the work for four pound ten shillings, Mr. Hood's price being five pound ten shillings. A member suggested that the press had made Mr. Hood's offer public, and that Mr. Oliver had then put in a lower tender, but this was denied; if the amount was made known it must have been by some member.-Eventually the motion of Mr. Clifton, seconded by Mr. Harris. Mr. Hood's tender was accepted".*

May 1901 Abridged: Picknells (Pickernals) Farm in Plaitford the property of Lord Ilchester and in the occupation of Mr. Russell suffered a serious fire. Earlier in the day the chimney had caught fire. This was put out, and everything was considered to be all right. This was not the case as the beam in the chimney was smouldering, and presently this burnt through to the thatch. A man with a horse and

163

cart was sent to fetch the fire brigade, five miles away in Romsey. It was stated at the time that a cyclist, if found would have accomplished the journey much quicker. The fire brigade received the call at four fifteen in the afternoon, the abbey bells giving the alarm. As the horses were not stabled at the time it took a while to fetch them and harness them to the engine. In the meantime the house roof was well alight and neighbours helped to get most of the furniture out. When the Fire Brigade eventually arrived the fire was practically burnt out. There was a pond nearby, and this supplied plenty of water, so attention was turned to houses in close proximity, to the large barn and cow pen and these were saved. The fire brigade, were helped by a strong north east wind blowing in the other direction. The brigade stayed on site for some hours, arriving back in Romsey at ten o'clock.

July 1905: *"THE MOTOR CAR NUISANCE: - The residents of Plaitford who live near the Shoe Inn are suffering much annoyance owing to the high speed at which motors travel along the road. Just on the border of Wiltshire and Hampshire, the road runs downhill and at this part of the road narrows for some distance, Despite this, motorists drive at an excessive rate, and only last week one road 'hog' ran over some fowls and killed them…Of course he never stopped and the dust prevented his number being taken. Instances of the callous and careless way in which motorists drive in this out of the way part of the world could be multiplied. Cannot the police set a trap in this neighbourhood or shall we have to wait until someone is killed?"*

October 1905: *"A Parish Council meeting held in the schoolroom. Mr. J.T Holmes in the chair and there was also present Messrs G Curtis, F Curtis, A Bowles, W Peck, C, Moore and S Sanson, A letter was read from the Postmaster General declining to give the lower part of Plaitford a second delivery of letters as asked for. Mr. Sanson, thereupon, gave notice that he would bring forward the subject of a second delivery for that portion of the parish at the March meeting. It is hoped that adjoining parishes will amalgamate with Plaitford in the endeavour to obtain better postal facilitie".*

December 1905: *"A serious fire destroyed a cottage at Gauntletts Farm. The very old cottage, part built of timber with a thatched roof, was occupied by Mr. Charles Dovey and his foreman George Davey with his wife and child. At the time of the fire, Mr. Dovey was in Salisbury. A fox terrier dog barking woke George Davey at 12.39 am. The flames were so fierce he had to force a window open and assist his wife and child out. He then went to a neighbouring farm for help.*

Efforts to extinguish the flames proved futile, and the property was burnt to the ground in a very short time. A very old fireplace was fitted in the kitchen, and some days previous was found to be on fire, but Davey thought the flames were out. In the chimney had been a big beam about 5 feet above the hearth and it is surmised that the beam had been smouldering ever since. Davey noticed that the fire was fiercest nearest the chimney. The night was very foggy, very few villagers knew of the tragedy until the next day. Mr. Davey and his family escaped in their nightclothes and lost all their possessions as did Mr. Dovey.

Mr. Davey's furniture was insured in the Union Fire Office but Mr. Dovey's was not insured. The furniture of both parties was valued at about £100 and the house £400.

Mr. Dovey moved to an empty house near Bridgefoot Farm and Mr. Davey and family were taken in by Mr. Curtis."

Charles & Eva Dovey moved to Gauntletts Farm sometime after the 1901 census.

May 1906: "*Postal Service Petition- A petition has been circulated round Lower Plaitford and largely signed, requesting postal authorities to grant a second delivery of letters in this part of the parish, a privilege which the inhabitants of Upper Plaitford already possess".*

July 1906*: "Mr. Sydney Sanson appointed "agent" to the Romsey Advertiser for Plaitford, E&W Wellow, Cadnam, Sherfield English and part of Landford".*

Sidney Sanson was born in Plaitford in 1874 to William a sawyer and his wife, Susan. The family appears on the 1881 and 1891 census for Plaitford, after which they left the village but stayed local as Sidney was a member of the Parish Council in 1905/6.

August 1906: *"Mr. A Dibden was returning to Canada from Whiteparish with a load of bricks when he was stopped by a man in Plaitford who noticed a lynch-pin on one wheel was loose. It was soon repaired by willing helpers and an accident was averted".*

May 1907 Abridged: Ellen Sarah (Tinny) Lovell, aged 5, daughter of Mr. Harry Frank Lovell of Bridgefoot Cottages, was drowned in the river by her house whilst playing with her elder sister. The child's mother ran to Powells Farm for Mr. George Curtis who returned with her to the scene where he found the child's body in the water. The sister told her mother that the deceased fell into the river, which was swollen from recent rains, and she held her hand as long as she could, but becoming exhausted she had to release her hold. She too fell into the water, but managed to get out by climbing the bank. An inquest held on Monday in Romsey returned a verdict of "accidental death". A funeral took place in St Peters churchyard on Wednesday afternoon. Her gravestone is inscribed "This stone was erected by the Sunday School teachers and Scholars of St Peters Church, Plaitford" Ellen was known to every one by her nickname Tinny - the story goes that she owed this name to her father who had a speech impediment. On seeing his youngest daughter for the first time, he is reputed to have said, 'Isn't she tinny?' a mispronunciation of the word tiny.

January 1908 Abridged: John Simmonds, Plaitford, was committed for trial at Winchester Assizes and pleaded guilty of night poaching on December 12th and sent to prison for four months hard labour.

May 1910: At Salisbury Petty Sessions, Mr. George Curtis, Powells Farm was summoned for allowing nine cows to stray on the highway at Landford on May 13th. Defendant pleaded not guilty. PC Long stated that he watched nine cows belonging to the defendant straying at Landford level on the Southampton Road for an hour from 2.30pm. Defendant said the policeman was referring to heifers not cows. He maintained he was not liable because he did not know he was committing an offence. PC long said he had received a complaint about cattle straying on the road and that they were a great nuisance. Defendant was fined ten shillings and six pence.

George Billen of Sidney Cottage, Plaitford was also summoned for allowing one cow to stray on the road at Landford on May 13th. Defendant did not appear and was given a fine- one shilling and costs in his absence.

September 1910: *"ASLEEP IN CHARGE – At Salisbury County Petty Sessions, John Dovey, a market gardener (Gauntletts Farm) was summoned for being asleep while in charge of a pony and trap on the highway at Alderbury on Aug. 16th. – P.C. Kite stated that on the day in question he saw defendant asleep whilst in charge of a trap. He woke him up and said "Don't you think it very dangerous to go asleep like this?" Defendant said "Well, I do, but I only dropped off at the top of the hill." which was a distance of 150 yards. – Defendant was fined seven shillings and six pence inclusive".*

1911/12 Authors Files: Plaitford Manor is divided up and sold by the 6th Earl of Ilchester after 232 years.

April 1911: *"At Southampton County Court, Messrs Andrews Bros., carriage builders, Above Bar, Southampton sued Robertson Conaway, gentleman of New House (Lodge) Plaitford to recover the sun of £30.1s., being £27 for the price of a dogcart sold to the defendant, and three pound one shilling for storing and cleaning it for 61 weeks at one shilling per week whilst waiting collection".*

July 1911: *"PLAITFORD LOCAL RECORD-On coronation day his Majesty's health (George V) was drunk from a William the fourth corn bushel. This was the fifth occasion on which this measure had been used for loyal purposes. Queen Victoria's Coronation Day saw it filled with beer for the first time. It was similarly replenished at the Jubilee's of 1887 and 1897, and then again in 1902 when King Edward VII was crowned. This surely constitutes an interesting local record".*

April 1912 Authors Files: Ambrose Hood jnr set sail on the Titanic with six friends from Bramshaw and Fritham. They were due to sail from Liverpool on the 6th April, but were offered an upgrade to second class on Titanic sailing six days later from Southampton. Although born in Bramshaw himself, some of Ambrose's siblings and his father were born in Plaitford. The Hood family of Plaitford can be traced back to the 1760s. His Great grandmother was Martha Maury, whose family lived in Maurys Lane, West Wellow. All six died when the Titanic sank, Ambrose Hood's body was never found.

1912 Abridged: George Bungay, rick thatcher, was working with Robert Blake on a rick at a farm in Landford when he fell backwards off the rick onto his back. He was put into a cart to be transported home to Plaitford Common but died on the way from a broken chest bone and a punctured lung.

January 1913 Abridged: Canadian papers report of a sad accident to Frank Loader (son of Mr. James Loader of Elm Cottage, Wellow Wood) who left the home of his parents on 10 September last year to work as a switchman for a Canadian Railway company. The accident occurred on 1 January, when Mr. Loader was hit by an engine and died on the way to hospital. The sad thing was he was due to marry on 18 January. His fiancée Miss Bungay of Plaitford had previously journeyed to Canada to be married.

We have been unable to find out who the Miss Bungay was?

January 1915: *"The effects of a recent storm are pretty plainly visible at Plaitford in the many fallen trees that can be noticed lying about; but only those who were in the thick of it at the time can form an idea of the danger in which life and property were placed whilst the storm lasted. Alongside Mr. Hutchins' garden at the smithy a stream runs which affords good drinking water in the winter, but the flood carried away the dipping place, and Mr. Hutchins, in order to get water, had to replace the gravel swept away. The fir trees near his house swayed backward and forward, nearly touching the house and one large hollow tree fell on the wash house, breaking the guttering down. As the wash house was built against the dwelling* *house the alarm caused to the inmates can be better imagined than described. Mr. and Mrs. Hutchins and family are to be congratulated on their escape".*

William Hutchings, blacksmith, his wife, Ellen, and their six children lived in Brook Cottage that stood behind their forge in the area of Border Garage

November 1915 Abridged: Harry White, dealer, of West Wellow and William Hutchins, Blacksmith, of Plaitford, were summoned at Salisbury and fined four pound and two pound respectively for excessive whipping of a horse, trying to make it gallop whilst pulling a light spring cart through Alderbury. Unbeknown to the defendants they were being pursued by an ex-sergeant of the metropolitan police on a bicycle.

October 1919 The Times: *"At Andover Petty Sessions, Charles John Dovey, farmer, of Plaitford, pleaded "Guilty" to a charge of assaulting Police-Sergeant Frampton while in the execution of his duty, and was fined £1. The charge arose out of a police case in which the defendant was fined £5 for permitting cruelty to a horse by allowing it to be worked in an unfit state. The defendant had to be ejected from the court, and he struck the police-sergeant who put him out".* Charles Dovey Lived at Gauntletts Farm

October 1920 Abridged: A first for Romsey District Council Housing Scheme, when in October 1920, the first foundation stone was laid by Lady Violet Mond for the first of three double cottages to be built in the district. The land in Church Lane, Plaitford, now known as Forest View, was given to the council by Sir Alfred Mond of Melchet Court.

February 1921: *"Philip Bungay, Hazelwood Farm, Plaitford, was in Salisbury when his horse injured its foot, and he could only proceed slowly home. Therefore, due to the delay, the lights on his trap went out. At 6.40pm on February 22nd he was stopped at Whiteparish, within five minutes from home and the result was that last week he appeared before Sarum County Sessions and was fined one pound two shilling".*

April 1923 Abridged: During a violent thunderstorm in the Romsey District on Monday a youth named Frederick Bowles, aged 19 of Bridgefoot Cottages, Plaitford, labourer, in the employ of Mr. Charles Ernest Brooke, Gardeners Farm, Plaitford, was killed by lightning. It appeared that Mr. Bowles had taken shelter under an oak tree where he had left his coat. He was subsequently found by his employer lying on the ground. Dr R. C Bartlett, of Romsey, was summoned, but could only pronounce life extinct. There were marks on the body as if he had been struck by lightning. An inquest was held in Plaitford Rectory by the County Coroner:

Charles Ebbie Bungay living at Hazelwood farm saw the deceased at 1.55 pm, working in a field belonging to Mr. Brooke. The storm had just commenced. He took shelter some 300yds from where the deceased was sheltering. He did not see the deceased struck but he saw the lightning and heard a very heavy clap of thunder. When the storm abated Mr. Bungay continued his work not knowing that anything untoward had happened.

Charles Ernest Brooke, the deceased's employer, said the storm was very severe with the lightning most vivid and it rained and hailed very heavily; in fact he had never seen any thing like it. As the youth had not come in with the horses he went to see where he was and found him under the oak tree. Mr. Brooke did not notice any mark on the deceased's face. His clothes were not burnt, but his left boot was torn open. Dr Ralph Bartlett's statement was that vivid marks on the left side of the neck and similar marks over a large portion of the body were due to a lightning stroke and death was instantaneous. Therefore, the Coroner returned a verdict of death by lightning stroke.

Frederick Bowles lived at number three Bridgefoot Cottages with his parents Joseph and Mary Jane.

April 1926 Abridged: The sad death on Mrs. Hilda Curtis (nee Grayer) aged 31. Wife of Mr. Stanley Curtis of Savages Farm died as a result of complications a few days after giving birth to their sixth son. Her funeral took place at Plaitford, her grave was lined with evergreens and flowers picked by the children of Plaitford School.

May 1926 Abridged: Mr. George Curtis of Powells Farm made a tragic discovery finding his married daughter, Mrs. Eva Stranger, dead in bed, having committed suicide by drinking Lysol. The deceased, who lived in Torquay with her husband, William, who ran an ironmongers business in partnership with his brother, had come to Powells Farm to look after the house while her mother was in Romsey Nursing Home.

July 1926 Abridged: A devastating fire occurred on the night of Thursday 15 July, at the Ally Bungalow (behind The Shoe Inn), the property of Mr. Moore of Plaitford. The building and contents were destroyed. The damage was estimated at £400 but the building was insured.

The bungalow was owned by Charles and Amy Moore. They later built a new house in the same grounds, now known as The Popler.

October 1926: *"A gloom has been cast over the village and a shadow cast over two families by an accident. Hazel Margaret and Lena Marion Bungay, sisters, aged 5 and 3 years, had gone out of doors to await their mother who was preparing a parcel to take to the post, and they crossed over the road and began playing on the waste-ground opposite their home. Hearing a motor horn, so it is surmised, they started to run back home hand in hand, but were knocked down by a car going from Landford to West Wellow, driven by Mr. E.H. Marshall of Lymington. Hazel was killed instantaneously but her baby sister was alive when picked up and was, on the advice if Dr G.H Johnson, removed later in the afternoon to Romsey Nursing Home, where the next day, despite her injuries, she rallied and will probably recover. Mr. Marshall was completely overcome by the accident and was practically prostrated by distress. Having little children of his own, he felt the unfortunate occurrence very keenly."*
The children were the daughters of Hubert and Margaret Bungay who lived at Evelyn Cottage from c1925 until 1950.

March 1932: *"Two cyclists who, riding in opposite directions, collided at Church Lane corner, were taken in the ambulance to Romsey and District Cottage Hospital where they were treated for the injuries they received. They were Alfred Tutt, Newtown, Romsey, and Ethel Fielder of Plaitford. Tutt received a nasty gash on the right temple, and the other cyclist was extensively bruised and received a badly cut mouth. After treatment, neither was detained".*
Ethel Fielder lived at number 6 Forest View with her husband James from 1931-1933.

March 11 1932 School Logbook: First Electricity Pylon erected in the village later to be replaced in the 1960s.

1935 Kellys Directories: First mention of telephone numbers recorded in Plaitford comes from the 1935 Kellys Directory. They were West Wellow numbers as follows: William Benham, New Lodge 11, Dorothy Davies, Tea Rooms at the Milestone, Southampton Road 53 and Walter Hutchings, Blacksmith and Petrol Station 56. By 1939 an extra digit had been added changing the numbers to 211, 353 and 356 respectively.

March 1935 Abridged: Mr. Thomas Harrison, 69, farm labourer at Powells Farm, was found dead after falling from a loft where he was accustomed to sleeping. The deceased was known for his bouts of heavy drinking that could last a fortnight at a time, on other occasions he would not touch alcohol for some considerable time. Mr. Stanley Curtis originally found the deceased at 9.30 pm on Monday, March 4th, lying on the ground under the loft door. Mr. Curtis asked him if he had fallen from the loft but could only get a few mumbling remarks. He appeared to be well under the influence of drink. As it was impossible to get him to his bed he put him in one of the empty stalls. He said he was alright and did not appear to be injured. It was a great surprise to find Mr. Harrison dead at 6 am the following morning. The Doctors report stated the deceased had a fractured skull and ribs and that injuries were consistent with a fall.

1936 Authors Files: Miss Hope Ella Brooke of Gardeners Farm sold a piece of embroidery to the Victoria and Albert Museum for £200. The embroidery, a burse - a purse-like pouch used to contain corporals, the linen cloths used in the celebration of the Christian Mass, dated from between 1310 and 1340. The surface of this example is embroidered, and is a fine example of Opus Anglicanum (Latin for 'English work'). Such high quality English embroidery was highly regarded throughout Europe. One side the burse shows Christ crucified with the Virgin and St. John, and on the other, the Coronation of the Virgin. Apparently Hope Brooke was under the mistaken impression that this piece of fourteenth-century needlework was the handiwork of her great-grandmother.

December 1937: At five pm on Tuesday 7 December, a violent snow storm with thunder and lightning began, and continued throughout the night. The snow fall was so bad that the weight of frozen snow on the telegraph wires was so heavy the poles snapped off like matchsticks. Reports state that wires were brought down over a four mile stretch of the road towards Salisbury. Many roads were impassible for days, and although post-office repair men came from all over the country, it was many weeks before telephone and telegraph services were completely restored. The most devastated area stretched from Landford to Shaftsbury. Plaitford was on the edge of the storm; though affected by the loss of communications, it was scarcely affected by the storm.

1939/40: A severe frost set in on December 17, 1939 and lasted with out intermission until February 18, 1940. The River Blackwater was completely frozen and a rare phenomenon of 'frozen rain' occurred on January 28 and lasted for three days. Everything was sheathed in a coating of ice. There were also several severe snowstorms in the course of the two months.

Christmas Eve 1942: *Mr. Kenneth William Tutt, blacksmith, of Forest View, Plaitford Common was in collision with a cyclist whilst driving to Salisbury through Alderbury. The cyclist, Ivy Emily Lucy Goldsworthy, a schoolgirl, aged 15, died shortly after in Salisbury Infirmary. A witness at the inquest told the coroner that he saw the* *cyclist come straight out of the side road and hit Mr. Tutt's van. The coroner recorded a verdict of "Accidental Death".*

December 1948: *"A lorry loaded with logs overturned on the Salisbury to Southampton Road, Plaitford, when the driver, Mr. W. C. Sherred of Plaitford Green, was attempting to avoid a vehicle driven by Mr. C.C. Wright of Cadnam. The lorry was badly damaged, but Mr. Sherred and his son, who was a passenger, crawled out unhurt. The road was partly blocked for some time".*

1949/1950 Authors Files: The houses in Purley Way were built. First occupation is shown on the November 1950 Electoral Roll for Plaitford.

July 1952 Abridged: A serious fire was brought under control at Landford service station by Romsey Fire Brigade. The service station is built above tanks containing 800 gallons of petrol and there was great concern at the time that they would explode and several families were removed for safety. By their efforts the firemen also saved the wooden bungalow where the proprietor, Mr. C.T Brinson, lived with his wife and one-year-child. It was Mrs. Brinson who stood in the garage with flames shooting through the roof, while the heat was exploding bottles of oil and dialed 999. The windows of the office, in which the telephone was, were cracking with the heat. Mrs. Brinson was dragged out by Mr. Leonard Ford, of Plaitford Lodge.

How many remember the burnt out car on the forecourt with a notice asking 'Is this your car'?

September 1952: It is expected that Wellow and Plaitford will be provided with full mains water supply before the end of the year.

March 1959: Amanda McConnel, aged 4, daughter of Adrian and Penny McConnel of Manor Farm, sadly drowned in the river Blackwater at Bridgefoot. Les Curtis of Bridgefoot farm found her body in the water.

October 1970 Abridged: Two small temporary flare stacks will come into operation during a five day period from October 25th at Plaitford near the Hants-Wilts border.

The stacks will burn off ethylene gas from a pipeline which has to be moved by the Esso Petroleum Company to allow works to start in the latter end of 1971 on the Cadnam section of the M27 South Coast Motorway.

July 1972 Abridged: The body of an unidentified elderly man was found in a pond on Plaitford Common at 7pm on Thursday. The discovery was made by Mr. John Hocking of Wateraven, Plaitford Common who found the body in Sturtmoor Pond. Mr. Hocking pulled the body from the water and telephoned the police. There was no identification on the man who was described as being between 60-70 years of age. **A later report states:** Drowned man named as Mr. Tom William Webb (68) of New Road, Landford. Mr. Webb suffered from epilepsy and the coroner said he died in circumstances unknown.

May 1973: *"Obviously troubled by his health" A Plaitford farmer committed suicide by drowning himself in a well. A verdict to this effect was recorded by Southampton County Coroner at the inquest of 47-year-old Mr. Maurice Ralph Curtis of Powells Farm at Romsey Court House on Monday. Evidence was given that Mr. Curtis, one of three farming brothers, had been ill with blood pressure and was taking tablets for the complaint, but had no financial worries running beef cattle on his part of the farm. On Wednesday evening of last week he went to the Shoe Inn for a while, but both there and at home he appeared his usual self. His stepmother Mrs. Aurelia White Curtis said she went to bed at 10.10pm leaving him in his armchair. Then at 7.30am on Thursday she got up to find a suicide note from him on the sitting room table, together with a sum of money amounting to £10. The note read:*

"Dear Mum-I shall not be seen in the morning, I have suffered enough mentally. Inwardly I blame no one. When you can no longer live half a normal life, you are dead. Anyway I will leave this money (found with the note) behind for you to carry on with until things are sorted. Tell Walter I shall be in the well behind the stable. Good bye, God bless- Maurice".

His brother, Walter, said he went to the disused well in question, saw the boards had been removed to one side and fount the body floating on the water. Maurice's door had been shut when he came in the night before, about 11.30, and he had assumed he was in bed.

PC W.J. Burrett said the body was recovered using ropes and Consultant Pathologist Dr. John Guthrie, who carried out the post mortem, gave cause of death as "Asphyxia by drowning".

February 1988 The following headline appeared in The Times newspaper: **Vicar beat wife to death over *Desert Island Discs*** *'I am mad, bad and I have murdered my wife who I loved dearly. She has gone to heaven ... and I will go to hell.*

A retired vicar beat his wife to death because he could not tune into his favourite radio programme, *Desert Island Discs*. The Rev. Shirley Freeman aged 74, was rector of Landford and Plaitford from 1953-1965. He killed his wife in a frenzied attack on 21 August 1988, he and his wife were being looked after by their son in Guildford. Judge Lymbery agreed to allow Freeman to spend the rest of his days at Alton Abbey, Hampshire, to be looked after by Benedictine monks. The judge said that in view of his age there was no point jailing him. Freeman admitted the manslaughter of his wife, Clarinda, aged 85 on the grounds of diminished responsibility. The Freeman's had been married for 46 years.

March 1994 Abridged: Villagers helped rescue furniture from the blazing Meadow Cottage part of Bowles Farm. School children spotted the fire shortly before 4pm, when the driver immediately stopped the bus. Rushing to the back of the farmhouse he rescued a dog from the porch while children dashed to a nearby house to raise the alarm. The fire that started in the thatch near the chimney was attended by appliances from Romsey, Totton and Redbridge. Firemen and villagers rushed to rescue furniture and furnishings from the water. The occupiers, Maurice and Audrey Bowles, were out when the fire was discovered, arriving home at about 4.45. Standing next to his rescued possessions on the lawn Mr. Bowles said, "If you are going to put something in the paper, please praise my neighbours. If it wasn't for them, I would have lost the lot''. The roof of the property was badly damaged and most of the thatch had to be removed,

July 27, 2012 Authors Files: To celebrate the opening of the third London Olympics a national bell ringing took place at 8.12am. For three minutes church bells rang out all over Great Britain including the single bell of Plaitford Church rung by Elrad Matthews.

Centenarian Bill Robinson 1910-2011

Bill was born at Birdham near Chichester on 22 August 1910, and soon after the family moved to Minstead. Bill started work as a telegraph boy at Minstead Post Office earning six shillings a week. His parents, brother and sister moved to Plaitford in the 1920s but Bill stayed in the Minstead area where he worked as a chauffeur for Lord Congleton at Minstead and Lord Hanbury at Castle Malwood. On one occasion, he drove Lord Hanbury to Alassio in Italy in his Rolls-Royce.

He married Freda, his wife of 55 years, a few months before the outbreak of war in 1939, but he was soon called up. He joined 571 Squadron, a Light Bomber unit of the Pathfinder Force and worked on the maintenance of Mosquito and Bleinheim aircraft throughout the war. Their daughter, Jean, was born during the war. After the war he worked with the Ministry of Defence at West Dean. In the mid 1970s Bill and Freda moved to Plaitford where Freda passed away in 1994. A long time member of the Royal British Legion, Bill joined the Wellow and District branch and continued to attend meetings well into his 90s. He also served on the village hall committee and regularly attended committee meetings into his 99th year.

To celebrate his centenary, a service of thanksgiving for his long life was held on his birthday at Plaitford Church. During the service tribute was paid to Bill's long service to the church and his outstanding work in looking after the churchyard. The service was followed in the afternoon by a party at the village hall attended by 100 family and friends. Bill sadly passed away on 20 March 2011.

Continuous occupation

The following seventeen properties have been occupied by the same family continuously for more than forty years, from the date shown until 2013:

Bowles - Plaitford Wood Farm, 1841 (172 years), Bowles - Bowles Farm, 1880 (133 years); Curtis - Powells Farm, 1880 (133 years); Bowles - Heathlands, Plaitford Green 1925[1] (88 years); Holt - Holly Cottage, Flowers Lane, 1930 (83 years), Matthews - Forest View, 1933 (80 years); Castle - Plaitford Green, 1934 (79 years); Stone - Bridgefoot Cottages 1940 (73 years); Moore/Babey/Sillence/Babey[2] - Cuffnells, Southampton Road, 1947 (66 years); Pointer - Evelyn Cottage, Southampton Road, 1951 (62 years); Collins - The Cottage, Plaitford Green, 1956 (57 years); Hocking- Water Avens, Plaitford Common, Porter - Bracken Farm and Turner - Forest View, 1964 (49 years each); Dovey - Sagres, Flowers Lane, 1968 (45 years); Hart - Thornycroft, Pound Lane and Owton - Maysfield, Compton Drive, 1969 (44 years each). A combined total of 1,306 years!

[1] Planning application date-Hampshire Record Office
[2]Betty Moore married Leslie Babey and later Ernie Sillence after her death in 2013 her son David Babey moved in to Cuffnells.

Continuous ownership

The following nine properties have been owned by the same family or the church continuously from the date shown until 2013

St Peter's Church - Evelyn Cottage[1], Southampton Road 1899 (114 years); Bowles – Plaitford Wood Cottage/Farm, Bowles/Collins - Plait ford Green Cottage, Bowles- Bowles Farm[2], Curtis - Powells Farm, Dovey - Gauntlets Farm and Knapman - land in Plaitford, 1911 (102 years each); Jewell, land at Gardeners Farm, 1936 (77 years) and McDiarmid - Yew Tree Farm, 1952 (61 years).A combined total of 924 years.

[1]Two semi detached cottages, Evelyn and Sidney, were built by Rev. Gay in 1892 on land owned by him. When he left Plaitford in 1899 he left the cottages to Plaitford Church. Sidney cottage was sold c1980. [2]Includes the property Heathlands, Plaitford Green

Bowles & Curtis

The Bowles and the Curtis families are the two longest standing in the village. The following is a potted history of the two families.

John Bowles with his wife, Elizabeth, and his sister, Ruth, first appeared at Gauntletts Farm in Plaitford in the 1740s. One of their children, William, married Susanna with whom he had six children. One of their sons, William, married Martha Roberts² and they had seven children. Their second eldest son, Edward, married Jane Batten in 1821 and lived in Gunsfield Cottage and worked as head woodman. His son, Charles, and grandson, Ernest, followed his profession and continued to live at Gunsfield Cottage until 1914. From this point there are no further local records of this line of the family. William and Martha's other son, Frederick, lived at Plaitford Wood Cottage (later Farm) and married Ann Arter and they had six children including two sons, William and James, and this is where the family in Plaitford divides into two.

William moved to what is now Bowles Farm where he worked for and lodged with William Martin and his niece, Charlotte Pope. William Bowles and Charlotte married in March 1869 and their son, Alfred, was born in June the same year. After William Martin's death in 1880, William Bowles took over the farm that later became known as Bowles Farm. When there time came Alfred and his wife, Sarah, took on the farm, they had three children, Charles, Robert and Eva. Robert, sadly a casualty of the First World War, died in 1918 at the age of eighteen. Eva went on to marry Charles Hood and continued to live in the village. Charles and his wife, Florence, had three sons - Cyril, Maurice and James, and lived at Oaklands on the northern edge of Bowles Farm. Maurice and his wife Audrey have lived at and farmed Bowles Farm since the late 1950s and James "Jim", a builder and undertaker has continued to live at Oaklands. The property has been split into three to accommodate Jim's sons, Shaun and Paul, and their families.

Going back to Frederick, his other son James stayed at Plaitford Wood Farm and married Sarah Harnett and their son, Harvey, is the grandfather of Harvey who lives at the farm today. In fact, Plaitford Wood Farmhouse is the only property in the village to have been occupied continuously by the same family since our records began in 1841

The family have been a major part of the community for many years. Four generations have served on the Parish Council; the first, Alfred, was a member in early 1900s followed by his son, Charles, and his son, Jim, who after 66 years service retired in 2013. Shaun, Jim's son is the fourth generation to serve as a parish councilor. Jim's late wife, Gwen, along with his brother, Maurice, and his wife, Audrey, served on the Village Hall Committee in the early 1960s and continued until the late 1970s and early 1980s. Jim joined the hall committee in the early 1970s and is still a committee member today.

Both of the Bowles families, at Bowles Farm and Oaklands and Plaitford Wood Farm have common ancestry that goes back 270 years, ten generations in Plaitford.

[1]Martha Bowles died in 1798 and William married Rebecca Scott and they had three children, Sophia, born 1803, Eliza, born 1807 and Vincent, born 1809. William died in 1839 and at the time of the 1841 census Rebecca, who it would appear was a wealthy woman, was leasing property and 60 acres of land from the Earl of Ilchester. Rebecca died in 1850. Her son, Vincent, had died at the age of twelve in 1821. Sophia died in 1873 and Eliza (later Pavey then Futcher (see New Lodge Farm chapter 10 - Plaitford Farms.) in 1891.
A plaque inside Plaitford Church on the south wall in memory of William, Rebecca, Sophia and Vincent Bowles was probably dedicated by Eliza.

Charles Curtis moved to Plaitford in 1873 from Martin to become tenant of the Earl of Ilchester at Manor Farm. Less than ten years later his younger brother, George, arrived as a tenant at Powells Farm. Charles died in June 1887, aged 38, at this time and certainly by the 1891 census his father, Walter, had moved from Martin and had taken over the tenancy of Manor Farm which he ran with the help of his other sons, Frank and Walter. Frank later went on to farm at Bowers Farm.

Through out his life at Powells Farm from the age of 22 until his death at 78 in 1938, George was an active member of local Government. In 1884, at the age of 25 he was elected Waywarden of the parish - a post that was to disappear when new rural district councils were formed under the Local Government Act of 1894. George was a candidate for the first election and with all 23 votes polled in the parish going to him he was elected as a member of the newly formed Romsey Rural District Council. In 1930, the Romsey and Stockbridge Rural District Council was formed to which George was elected. George held the post of vice-chairman for two years and continued to serve until his death. We are not sure whether George ever served on the Parish Council. His son, Stanley, was a parish councillor in the late 1940s followed by his sons – George, who served as a councillor from 1954 until his death in 1989 and was chairman at the time of the Queen's Silver Jubilee in 1977, and Leslie who served for many years as member and chairman on the Parish Council and Village Hall Committee where he was chairman at the time the village school became the village hall in 1970. After 140 years, the fifth generation of the Curtis family to live in Plaitford is

Leslie Curtis's two sons Keith and Nicholas who still live with their families at Powells Farm. Both are parish councillors and Keith has been council chairman for the past nine years. Both Keith and Nicholas have daughters. Sadly, Nicholas's son, Paul, died in a motor accident in 2002.

Chapter 13
The Great War 1914 – 1918

Nineteen young men from Plaitford took the King's shilling and joined the services to do their bit for King and Country in the 'war to end all wars'. By the end of 1916 two had lost their lives, and another was to die in May 1918. A list of Absent Naval and Military voters appears on the 1918 electoral roll[1] for Plaitford. There are sixteen names listed and they are as follows: Alfred Bowles (Bridgefoot Cottages), Charles Bowles, Harvey Bowles, Henry Bright, Hubert Bungay, William Dunn, Alfred Fanstone, Henry Leuis Fanstone, William Loader, Clement Moore, Frederick Peck, Kempton Shepherd, Fred Shepherd, George William Sherwood, Edmond Tutt and William Tutt. As far as we know, all survived the war. As a result of a bombing raid on the War Office in 1940, 60 percent of 6.5 million WW1 military records were destroyed by fire. We have managed to trace some information on the military service of the following:

Alfred Edward Bowles served as a corporal with the Hampshire Regiment in France, his service numbers were 1297 and 29421; Charles Bowles served as a private soldier in the Hampshire Regiment in Egypt, his service numbers were 2135 and 330651; Henry Charles Bright served as a private soldier in the Hampshire Regiment in France, service number 45577; William Loader served as a corporal in the Hampshire Regiment in Salonika, service number 21153; Clement Moore, aged nineteen, volunteered in Southampton for short service (for the duration of the war) on 4 November 1915, he served as a gunner in the Royal Garrison Artillery, service number 62694; Fred Peck enlisted on 14 March 1916 and served as a private soldier in the Hampshire Regiment, service number 241821 and the Royal Defence Corps, service number 95806, he saw service in India and Palestine; Kempton Shepherd served as a driver in the Royal Field Artillery, his service numbers were 24251 and 652668; George William Sherwood[2] served as a L/Cpl in the Army Service Corps, stationed at the Romsey Remount Camp, his service number was R4/095877 and William Tutt who enlisted on 12 April 1916, aged 31, into the Duke of Cornwall Light Infantry, service number 27110; he also served in the Labour Corps, service number 479754 and King's Royal Rifles, service number 58705.

As previously mentioned, out of the many hundreds of thousands of British lives lost in the Great War, Plaitford suffered the loss of three of its young men. They are commemorated on the memorial tablet in St Peter's church.

[1]The 1918 electoral roll for Plaitford is the only list we have found that records absentee military voters so we apologise if we have missed any one else from Plaitford who served. Robert Bowles who was lost his life in May 1918 at the age of 18, was below the voting age and is not listed.

[2]George William Sherwood came from Guildford. He married Mabel Elsie Tutt at Plaitford on 12 July 1917. He appears as a Plaitford resident on the 1918 electoral roll as an absent military voter.

Private, 10377, James Simmonds son of John and Eliza Simmonds, The Drove, was born in Romsey and enlisted as a volunteer soldier into the Hampshire Regiment[3] at Southampton in 1914. He served with the 10th Battalion, which formed part of the 10th Division at Gallipoli, landing in August 1915. This was the first Theatre of War which Pte. Simmonds entered on 5 August 1915. He was recorded as wounded and missing 4 months later on 7 December and is noted as presumed dead on his medal index card. His name appears on the Doiran Memorial, Northern Greece on the south east shore of Lake Doiran. James was 35 years of age. He was awarded the British War and Victory Medals and the 1914/1915 Star. James was listed with other fallen comrades in the Romsey Advertiser dated 28 January 1916.

Private, 1910, John Simmonds, elder Brother of James, enlisted into the Hampshire Regiment[3] in Romsey on or before 1914
He served firstly with the 1/5th (Territorial Force) Battalion and first entered a Theatre of War, which was in this instance India with this battalion on 26 August 1915. He then transferred to the 1/4th (Territorial Force) Battalion with which he served in Mesopotamia (Iraq). No date or reason for transfer can be found. He died (whether of sickness or wounding is unknown) in Mesopotamia on 21 May 1916 at the age of 42 and is commemorated on the Basra Memorial, Iraq. He was awarded the British War and Victory Medal and the 1914/1945 Star.

[3]The Royal Hampshire Regiment Museum

Private, 41263, Robert V Bowles son of Alfred and Sarah Bowles, Bowles Farm, served with the 1st Battalion Duke of Cornwall's Light Infantry[2]. He enlisted in Southampton and was killed in action on 1 May 1918 aged 18 years. He is commemorated at the Merville Cemetery Extension, Merville, Norde, France.

The 1st Battalion, DCLI War Diary entry for 1 May 1918 reads as follows:

"Rather dull day. Enemy artillery very quiet during the day but opened up at 9.15pm, and kept up heavy fire through the night.

Owing to heavy shelling by Trench Mortars the latter hours of the night, OC D Company decided to sideslip his company a little to the right in order to escape the shelling"

The casualty list for 1 May shows that Private Harris of HQ coy suffered from gas. The other casualties were all from D Company (already mentioned). Ptes. Miller, Harris Nash, Flew, Cook and Townsend were wounded, while Pt. Bowles was killed.

In March and April 1918, the German offensive had been fought to a standstill. That summer the British Army was content to merely hold the line while units were brought back to re-train for the coming advances which were planned for autumn 1918 – the advances that were to lead to final victory in November.

[2]The Duke of Cornwall Light Infantry Museum

Robert (Bob) Bowles 1899-1918

For two years, 1916/17 children of Plaitford school collected eggs for the National Egg Collection for Wounded Soldiers (NECWS). Over the two years they collected 1859 eggs and with money collected in lieu of eggs they purchased a further 353. The remainder of the money collected, including a collection box in the Shoe Inn, totalling three pound fourteen shillings and six pence half penny was sent to the NECWS head office. From the eggs collected in 1917 Lady Mond was asked to accept 39 for her Auxiliary Hospital at Melchet Court. Mr. Cook of Bridgefoot Farm kindly took on the responsibility for sending of the eggs by rail and bringing back the empty boxes thus saving carriage charges.

In May 1923, a War Memorial Tablet was placed inside Plaitford church on the south wall. The unveiling was recorded by the Romsey Advertiser on the 18 May 1923:

"This took place at Plaitford Parish Church on Sunday evening, where a marble tablet has been erected in memory of the men of Plaitford who were killed in the war. The unveiling took place in the evening service, when the preacher was Rev.Davis and special hymns were sung. Rev Davis preached a most interesting sermon on the supreme sacrifice of the men who were killed in the war. He said he was pleased that Col. Makin was there to unveil the memorial. Col. Makin then unveiled the tablet saying "I unveil this memorial to the honour and glory of god, in memory of those who gave their lives for us. Their names live for ever" The Rev. Davis then dedicated the memorial and the hymn "Oh Paradise, Oh Paradise" was sung. "Oh Valiant Hearts" was sung while the collection was taken, which was in aid of St Dunstan's National Institute for the Blind. At the close of the service the first verse of the National Anthem was sung. The inscription on the tablet was as follows:

"To the Glory of God and to the honoured memory of the men of this parish who gave their lives for King and country in the Great War
1914 – 1918
Robert V Bowles
James Simmonds
John Simmonds
All that was theirs to give they gave"

The following, taken from the Romsey Advertiser, is a fascinating story about a watch that belonged to Arthur Victor Dibden with a Plaitford connection.

The story of Arthur's watch was featured in the Romsey Advertiser and a special Remembrance addition of the Antiques Road Show on BBC television in November 2011.

Private Arthur Dibden was killed at the Battle of Villers Brentonneux in April, 1918, as his regiment, the Devonshires, fought to halt the Germans' last great offensive of the war.

Private Dibden's body was looted by a German soldier, who took his watch. The watch's new "owner" was himself killed when two Australian brigades launched a counter-attack. An Australian found the watch and read the inscription inside. On his way back to Australia via Tidworth, the Australian infantryman made a point of visiting Arthur's parents at Wellow Wood to return the watch.

Wind the hands forward 79 years and a small blue pouch containing the watch falls from the loft of a disused milking parlour at a farm belonging to Arthur's younger brother Les Dibden, at Belbins, near Romsey.

"Inside the back cover of the watch was a scratched inscription as clear as the day Arthur had written it. Ironically the inscription read "Steal not. A.V. Dibden, Wellow Wood, Hampshire".

Les Dibden's grandson, Danny Brown, took on the task of researching his great uncle's First World War records and some ten years after the discovery of the watch he responded to a BBC appeal for stories concerning wartime antiques for the Remembrance Special.

Arthur's parents, Harry and Ella, were married in Plaitford on 1 August 1897, both being 'of this parish'. Arthur was baptized at St Peter's church on the 4 September 1898. He attended Plaitford School and left on 10 July 1912, at the age of 14.

On the 1911 census, the family was living in a property near The Shoe Inn. The 1918 electoral roll shows Harry and Ella living at Wellow Wood and Arthur as an 'absentee voter'.

In 1930 and 1931, Harry and Ella were living at 1, Forest View, Church Lane Plaitford. Ella died in April 1931 and is buried at Plaitford. Harry continued to live at Forest View until 1934/35.

Arthur's mother was Ella Jennet Moore, youngest child of George and Eliza Moore, and her older brother, Charles, was the grandfather of the late Betty Sillence. Betty's father Clement Moore, who also saw action in WW1, was a first cousin of Arthur.

Chapter 14
The Second World War

Another major world catastrophe occurred just over twenty years after the war to end all wars had finished. Young men of the parish were again expected to do their bit and with the threat of an invasion the Home Guard was formed giving veterans of the first war another chance to volunteer to serve their country. Had the invasion taken place in 1940, Plaitford and the rest of the south of England would probably have taken the brunt of the initial attack. As it turned out we held on to our air superiority and the Germans decided not to invade. This was not the end; air raids on major cities, industrial areas, docks and military bases continued. In the battle of the Atlantic, enemy submarines attempted to starve us into submission by destroying shipping carrying vital food and supplies. With a shortage of food, clothes and other essentials, the government introduced rationing thus making life on the home front difficult. With many of the men-folk away in the services, the woman left behind had to do their best to look after the family, whilst in most cases doing some form of war work.

Like most rural communities, Plaitford was fairly self-sufficient with most people having a vegetable garden, a few chickens and in some cases a pig for meat and a cow for milk. We have been told by villagers who remember those times that everyone pulled together and helped one another and there was a great sense of community spirit. This can be seen when it came to fund raising for the war effort later in this chapter.

We have managed to obtain some memories of the home front during the Second World War from current and past residents of Plaitford. Our thanks go to the late Edith "Edna" Grayer and to Elrad Matthews. Both lived at Forest View, Church Lane during the war.

Elrad Matthews

At the time of the first air raid on Southampton, on the 19th June 1940, he was attending a dance at Sherfield English village hall and remembers the "flaming onions" the name given to anti-aircraft tracer shells.

A search light was positioned in various locations in and around Plaitford, such as Monkeys Jump, Tutts Bridge, Claypits on Plaitford Common and in the field opposite Forest View, Church Lane with its generator sited at the left hand end of Elrad's garden.

One evening he was sitting on his bicycle in the dark by Shoe Bridge whilst an air raid was taking place over Southampton. Local anti-aircraft guns were also in action. He heard an explosion somewhere in the direction of his home. Fearing the worst he rushed home to Forest View. The following morning he discovered that an anti-aircraft shell had exploded in Sherfield English Road and the tyre marks from his homeward dash the previous evening, were right on the edge of the crater in the road. The crater was alongside a farm gate that was full of shrapnel. The gate was on the left beyond Hobbs Copse Farm heading towards Bridgefoot.

Elrad also remembers a Lysander Aircraft landing in a field at Manor Farm and waiting whilst a senior army officer, with red flashes on his collar, walked off in the direction of Melchet Court. He re-appeared sometime later and the aircraft took off.

Melchet Court was requisitioned by the army in 1940 and the Ministry of Aircraft Production from 1941. More can be found in the chapter on Melchet Park and Court.

One particular night in the late summer of 1940, Elrad, his family and their neighbour George Stone and his family were sitting in a dug out shelter he and George had built in George's back garden at Forest View. The shelter consisted of a large trench with a Fir Tree trunk across it and sheets of tin laid from the side of the trench to the trunk, then covered with soil. There was a particularly bad air raid over Southampton at the time. Whilst they were sitting listening to the awful noise, home guard CSM Charlie Bowles arrived. He told Elrad and George, both members of the home guard, to report immediately, fully equipped to the Red Rover, which they did. That night the Home Guard was put on full alert and stood too for 24 hours. The only members allowed to leave were those who had cows to milk. Elrad recalls their rations were delivered to the Red Rover by lorry. To this day he has never discovered the reason why they were put on alert. At the time there were invasion rumours one of which involved Southend.

Edna Grayers

Edna, along with her Forest View neighbours, Mrs. Stone and Mrs. Cook with Mrs. Kemp from Compton Drive, attended First Aid Training at Plaitford House run by Miss Susie and Miss Belle Simmonds. Edna remembers that one of these meetings was the last time she saw Mrs. Kemp before she died as a result of an enemy bomb.

People from Sherfield English also attended the First Aid course. One night on their long walk home to Sherfield English, there was an air raid, and as a result they refused to attend further training. This did not go down too well with the two Miss Simmonds. Edna recalls that, due to the lack of attendance, the training was never completed.

To help with the war effort Edna was to have become a bus conductress but she found out she was pregnant with the first of her two sons, Melvin and Kenneth. She went on to work through the war for Fred Stone at Gauntletts farm, picking vegetables.

Edna's husband Jim was called up into the Royal Artillary – more later.

Other Memories

An anti-aircraft shell fell on a stable at Powell's Farm killing two horses. According to Keith Curtis, who now lives at Powell's Farm, the building still exists and is now part of Pyesmead Farm, and you can see where the repair was made to the brickwork.

After the Royal Tank Regiment and the Corps of Military Police, American Troops occupied Landford Lodge and grounds. Brian Curtis son of George Curtis (more later) was evacuated with his mother to the Shoe Inn and remembers American personnel using the pub.

In preparation for the D-Day landings, Canadian soldiers were camped in Mrs. Sparrow's field off Compton Drive. The field now forms part of Bracken Farm and the current owner, Tony Porter, has informed us that a well built and used by the troops is still in the field along with metal pipes that took the water around the camp.

Italian prisoners of war, held in a camp at Broxmore House, Sherfield English, were used in the parish to tidy along the banks of the River Blackwater, laying land drains and digging ditches and boundary banks that can still be seen on part of the boundary between Bracken Farm and Manor Farm.

To help towards the war effort, many trees with the exception of mature oaks and beeches were cut and taken from Plaitford Wood.

At the height of the blitz on Southampton, families would drive out of the city and park overnight along the main road (A36). They would sleep in their cars and return to Southampton in the morning.

Evacuees from the cities were sent into the country. Quite a few were billeted with families in Plaitford.

Civilian Casualty

The only known civilian casualty was as a result of a direct hit from a 150lb[1] bomb on Mary's Cottage in Compton Drive at 12.30am[1] on 9 July 1940. The cottage was occupied by George and Helen Kemp. Both were thrown into the garden, and Helen, aged 62, was killed by falling debris. George survived and was taken to the ARP head quarters at Plaitford House and later to hospital. The late Bet Sillence, who worked at Plaitford House, was woken by the commotion and remembered seeing him in the hall wrapped in a blanket

Edna Grayer and Elrad Matthews both remember hearing the explosion and seeing the devastation the following morning. They recall seeing curtains, clothes and other debris hanging from the surrounding trees.

The offending aircraft dropped three bombs[2] that night. The first fell in Plaitford Wood, the second on the Kemp's property and the third in the paddock, now containing the tennis court, at the rear of Manor Farm. This bomb did not go off and was taken care of by bomb disposal personnel.

With the help of the Southampton City Council Archives, it would appear the unfortunate destruction of Mary's cottage was not caused by an aircraft either lost or being chased away from larger raid on Southampton. Their records show that the first major air raid on the city took place on the night of 19th /20th June 1940, followed by the next on 13th August. The Civil Defence log of raids on Southampton records only one air raid in July 1940 which took place on the 12th on Hamble.

The Hants Control Incident Chart,[3] records an incident in the Romsey district at Plaitford on the 9 July 1940 *"Time of origin 0253hrs, 1 HE* (High Explosive). *Cottage demolished, one woman killed and husband taken to hospital"*. The report continues *"Romsey say there were several bombs around W' Wellow?"* The question mark would indicate some uncertainty.

The next line reports on the unexploded bomb at the rear of Manor Farm *"Time of Origin 1400hrs. One unexploded bomb reported 300yds from cottage, wrecked at about 0235hrs! Police have been informed and have reported to military"*. A later entry records the bomb was destroyed eight days later- *"1620hrs Bomb destroyed by Military pm 16 July"*.

It would appear that this incident was a one off hit and run by a single aircraft. There was some speculation at the time that it was an attempt on Melchet Court. The building was requisitioned by the army in July 1940 as head quarters of Southern Command. We have been unable to find the exact date the army moved in; we only know that General Montgomery took over from General Auckinleck on July 21.

In 1946, George Kemp applied for planning permission to build a semi-bungalow to *"replace house destroyed by enemy action"*. George continued to live in Mary's Cottage until his death in March

1970 aged 89. In his will he left Mary's Cottage to his lodgers and friends William and Phyllis Sparrow. William died in 1972 and Phyllis in 1976. The property was put up for auction and purchased by James Hill of Gunsfield Lodge. He went on to sell the property to Allan and Jane Wright who also bid for the cottage at the auction.

[1]The size of the bomb and the time 12.30am is taken from Plaitford Church Burial Records. The time in the Hants Incident Chart is recorded as 0235hrs.
[2]One bomb exploded in the area of grid reference SU217278.
[3] Hampshire Record Office Ref: H/EP1/1-June 1940-Dec 1943

Plaitford Home Guard
No 4. Platoon E. Company 10th Hampshire

On the night of 14th May 1940, Anthony Eden made his first speech as Secretary of State for War. In this speech he asked for volunteers for the newly formed Local Defence Volunteer force (LDV).

Many local men took up the call to defend their country, including veterans of the First War, men of military age waiting call-up into the services, men over military age and young men such as Elrad Matthews who at the age of 17 cycled to Romsey Police Station to put his name down. When asked if he had ever handled a firearm, he replied he had used a twelve bore shotgun at Manor Farm.

Plaitford platoon was formed as part of the Wellow Company under the command of Captain Burnett who lived at Chapman's Farm, Wellow. The Company head quarters were at the Red Rover Inn. Plaitford platoon had its own Nissan hut at Gardeners Farm in Flowers Lane. The hut is still there. The Platoon was later commanded by Captain Finmore.

The name was changed from "Local Defence Volunteers" to "Home Guard" in July 1940 on the instruction of Winston Churchill, as he felt the original name uninspiring.

The home guard also had a hut on Monkeys Jump, the high ground, on the border of Plaitford and Wellow. The hut contained a field telephone linked to the head quarters at the Red Rover and was manned every night from dusk to dawn. Members of the home guard took turns on watch for two hours at a time.

The Wellow company also had a Nissen hut at the rear of May Marshall's property, The Mount, (now demolished) on the rise opposite the Red Rover. The hut was used to store ammunition.

Elrad Matthews and Sergeant George Stone, who both lived at Forest View, operated a Browning Automatic Rifle (BAR). George was No 1 and Elrad No 2. Elrad later became a signaller learning Morse code. During the early days the LDV/home guard lacked uniforms and equipment. Later they became very well equipped with full uniform, water bottle, a belt with ammunition pouches, rifles, and machine guns, and Wellow/Plaitford even had a mortar.

Members of the Plaitford Home Guard

Back Row: CSM Charlie Bowles (WW1 Veteran), Bill Thornton, Wilf Biddlecombe, Hubert Bungay (WW1 Veteran) & L/Cpl Clem Moore (WW1 Veteran). Front Row: Fred Peck (WW1 Veteran), Charlie Crane, Peter Hayter (Later saw service in the Tank Corps), Edmond Robinson, Cpl. Jack Kench & Albert Hayter.

Other known members of the Plaitford Home Guard were Cpl. Derek Batson, Cyril Bowles (later saw service in the Coldstream Guards), Sid Fielder, Captain Hubert Finmore[1], Albert Hayter, Alan Jewell, L/ Cpl. Lister, Dudley Marlow (Later saw service in the Royal Navy), Elrad Matthews, Bill Rickman, Len Rudkin, William Scurlock, Sgt. George Stone, Denis Stone, and Fred Whetren.

If we have missed anyone it is because we have no record of their service.

The Home Guard was finally disbanded nationally on 31 August 1944, and Plaitford

Home Guard held a farewell supper as reported in the Romsey Advertiser on 1 June 1945:

"Members of the Platoon who had joined the Forces, there being two ex *The Plaitford Home Guard held their farewell supper in the Home Guard Hut on Saturday evening. Some 30 members and ex-members of the Platoon, sat down to an excellent supper; the refreshments*

*were catered for by Mr. Langford of Wellow. After supper the loyal
toast was proposed. C.S.M. Bowles proposing the principal toast said
he was glad to see so many present. He thanked the old boys of the
L.D.V and the present H.G's for the splendid way they had all
worked with him since May 1940. Captain Finmore, responding, said
he could not say much more than what the C.S.M. had just said, how
pleased he was to see the old faces again and he hoped they would all
keep up this spirit after the war. Sgt Stone proposed the health of the
Forces and ex members present (D. Marlow R.N and C. Bowles,
Coldstream Guards). D. Marlow. R.N. replied saying how glad he
was to be there. Mr. A Jewell suggested that this was made an annual
supper, as he thought it would keep them together. This was
unanimously agreed by all present. Cpl. Batson proposed a vote of
thanks to Mr. Langford and helpers for the excellent spread he had
provided in difficult times. The music was supplied by Cpl. Batson
and Pte.Whetren. A very enjoyable evening was spent."*
[1]Captain Hubert Finmore was 6feet 6inches tall.

Decoy on the common

In the summer of 1943 a [1]decoy site was situated in the middle of
Plaitford Common at map grid reference 274187 in the area of the
National Grid electricity pylon number 84. The decoy was part of an
unsuccessful operation - code name *Cockade,* a deception set up to
convince the Germans that landings were to take place on mainland
Europe in 1943. *Cockade* was divided into three sections code named
Starkey - a cross channel landing, *Tindall* - a landing in Norway and
Wadham - an American landing in Brittany. The site on Plaitford
Common known as 'Cadnam A' was part of operation *Starkey* and
was one of six sites around Southampton set up to give the
impression of a pre-invasion military build up. The Plaitford site was
an Assault Lighting Decoy (ASQL), which depicted a military dump
or convoy. The Germans didn't take the bait and the whole thing was
scrapped by November 1943.
[1]Fields of Deception by Colin Dobinson 2000

Some of the residents who saw service in WW2
Cyril Bowles: Served in the Coldstream Guards based at
Buckingham Palace. Some of his time was spent guarding the
Norwegian Royal Family.
Fred Cook lived at 3 Forest View, Church Lane and served in the
Royal Army Service Corps in the Middle East.

Thomas Gradidge was brought up by his grandparents, Alfred and Fanny Gradidge, at the Shoe Inn. He was orphaned after his father, Alfred, was killed in action in 1918, his mother Alice having died earlier. Thomas served in France at the beginning of the war and spent many days on the beach at Dunkirk until he was successfully evacuated. He spent the rest of the war in the UK serving with the Royal Engineers.

Arthur "Jim" Grayer lived at 2 Forest View, Church Lane and was called up into the Royal Artillery in 1940. He served in Italy where, whilst sleeping, he was wounded in the leg by an enemy grenade. The person next to Jim was killed and another badly injured. Unbeknown to his wife, Edna, Jim was invalided home to Colchester. This was around the time of the D-Day landings. According to Edna, Jim wanted to go to France but was not allowed. He saw out the rest of the war in England until his demob in 1946

After his demob, Jim returned to his job at Gunsfield Lodge. Two years before his death in 1990, he was the victim of a mindless attack in his own home. He was badly beaten and almost lost the sight in one eye around which he had 33 stitches.

Amongst the items stolen were Jim's precious war medals. Although the Royal British Legion replaced them, he found they didn't have the same sentimental value as the originals.

Peter and Roy Hayter though not Plaitford residents were brought up in a cottage just into Sherfield English Road, Landford on the right, where the bungalow Lyndale now stands. They both went to Plaitford School and Peter was an original member of the Plaitford Home Guard.

Peter Hayter After call-up he served in the Tank Corps in the Far East and reached the rank of Sergeant Major.

Peter's Brother **Roy** was called up in 1940 and joined the 5th Wiltshire Regiment based in Devises. He moved around the country, firstly to Scotland then to Aintree race course, Ireland and London where his regiment paraded in front of King George VI. The regiment later sailed to Madagascar then on to India where the ship was quarantined due to an outbreak of black water fever contracted in Madagascar from drinking river water. Many also suffered from malaria. The regiment lost a lot of men whilst in quarantine. When the ship was released from quarantine, Roy thought they would head for the Far East but instead they ended up in the Middle East and went through Iran and Syria to the Suez Cannel where they waited for General Montgomery's eighth Army. Roy was then involved in two invasions of Italy via Sicily and Salerno. He fought his way up through Italy to Rome. He was then due to come home but ended up in Germany when the war ended. After demob, Roy worked for Mr. Scrivans, (Mike Scrivans' father) Partridge Hill, Landford, then for Foster Wheeler at Fawley Oil Refinery. Roy was married to Peggy Kemish, who also attended Plaitford School, and they lived in Landford.

Charlie Hood lived at Bowles Farm and served in the Royal Artillery on anti-aircraft guns in Bethnall Green, London. Charlie and his wife Eva later lived at Poplars, the house behind the Shoe Inn

Des Pointer saw service in the Royal Navy, based in Gibraltar he served in motor torpedo boats in the Mediterranean. He lived in Evelyn Cottage on the A36 until his death in 2009.

Arthur Thornton lived at 1 Forest View, Church Lane and joined the Duke of Cornwall Light Infantry, later transferring to the Pioneer Corps. He spent the war in the UK. Arthur's wife, Margaret, (nee Skurlock) was a housemaid through the war years at Plaitford House for Miss Susie, Miss Belle and Mr. Sydney Simmonds.
Arthur lived with his wife in Wellow until hid death in 2012.

The Curtis Brothers were all brought up at Powell's Farm with the exception of **Cyril** who, only a toddler when his mother died, was raised by his grandparents, George and Ruth Grayer, a quarter of a mile away at Furze Farm. He stayed at Furze Farm until his war service in the Tank Corps and returned there to live until he married. He then lived in Canada Road, Wellow until his death.

George: At the outbreak of the war, George and his wife May were living in Midenbury, Southampton. George was working at Cundliffe Owen at Eastleigh Airport on Spitfire production. On September 11 1940, the day Brian, his son, was born, George had a narrow escape when eight German Bombers dropped 16 bombs on the Cundliffe Owen factory. Forty-nine people were killed and ninety-two, including George, were injured.

Later in 1940, George was called up into the Army and served in the Royal Artillery, and was also a member of the Royal Horse Artillery. A commissioned officer, he was for a time attached to the REME. He served in Palestine and was later posted to Madras, before going to Burma.

Whilst in Burma, he had a spell in charge of a detainee camp for Japanese prisoners of war. During this time he also met Lord Mountbatten, an association that was to continue long after the war with their connection to the Royal British Legion.

George was a long time member of the Romsey branch of the Royal British Legion. For eleven years he held the presidency of the

Wellow branch. He also served on Melchet Park and Plaitford Parish Council from 1954 until his death in April 1989, aged 71. George lived with his family including his daughter, Carol, at Gaymead, the Bungalow opposite Bridgefoot Cottages, where he ran a successful car breakers business for many years until his death.

Les stayed at home to help run the farm and served as an NCO in the Wellow Home Guard. He later lived at Bridgefoot Farm with his wife, Pat, and sons, Keith and Nicholas, until his death in April 2003. Les was a long time member and Chairman of Melchet Park and Plaitford Parish Council and Plaitford Village Hall Management Committee. A keen cricketer, he played for and captained Wellow and Plaitford Cricket club.

Les was also well known for his wine making, in particular his birch sap wine. At a certain time of the year numerous bottles could be seen hanging from the birch trees around his farm to catch the sap.

Maurice (Morry) the youngest, born in April 1926 a few days before his mother Hilda (nee Grayer) died as a result of complications during his birth, worked on his father's farm. Aged eighteen he enlisted in the Royal Field Artillery in Northampton on 2 November 1944. After his army service he returned to Powells Farm where he lived for the rest of his life.

Ron served in the Wellow home guard.

Walter (Walty) a well- known character in his suit, wellington boots, trilby hat and Reliant three-wheeler car. The story goes that Walty was called up into the Army and was posted to somewhere in Somerset. He got drunk one night and fell into a ditch and caught pneumonia and was sent home He lived at Powell's farm most of his life. He eventually moved to the Fordingbridge area and not long after he died in a motor accident.

Military Casualties

Many young men and women from Plaitford served in various theatres during the war. We know of one, Jim Grayer, who was seriously injured, others as far as we know came through unscathed. Our research has not found any wartime resident of Plaitford who lost his or her life serving the armed forces.

Sadly, however, there are two known servicemen closely associated with Plaitford who lost their lives.

Kenneth Harry Moody and his younger brother Malcolm Charles both served in the Royal Airforce Volunteer Reserve.

Although they were brought up just over the border in Landford, in the house on the other side of the A36 opposite the end of Sherfield

English Road, they both went to Plaitford School. Their parents were William Frank and Ethel Mary Moody.

923174 Aircraftman 1ˢᵗ Class, Kenneth served with 58 Squadron, Coastal Command, based at Linton-on-Ouse, Yorkshire, maintaining Whitley aircraft.

Kenneth died as a result of an accident on 12ᵗʰ May 1941, aged 28 years and is buried in Newton-on-Ouse (All Saints) Churchyard. He left a widow, Gwendoline Margaret Lilly.

920127 Sergeant Flight Engineer, Malcolm served with 76 Squadron, Bomber Command also based at Linton-on-Ouse, Yorkshire, flying Halifax Bombers.

Malcolm died as a result enemy action on 17ᵗʰ January 1943, also aged 28 years. 20 months after his brother. He left a widow, Millicent Joan, (nee Fanstone) who also attended Plaitford School.

A coincidence is that both brothers appeared to have been based at Linton-on-Ouse when they died.

The late Bill Robinson, who served as an RAF aircraft fitter during the war, and lived at Purley Way until his death in 2011, remembers meeting Malcolm on a training course early in the war. They did not know each other but discovered they came from the same area.

A report on the action in which Malcolm lost his life[1]:

"Captain (Pilot) Bjoern Naess, Royal Norwegian Air Force who along with the rest of his crew were reported killed in action when their Halifax 11, serial DT647, code MP-P from 76 Squadron took off from Linton-on-Ouse at 16.22 on 17/01/43 on ops to Berlin and were intercepted by Oberleutnant Paul Zorner some 45 kilometers northwest of the island of Juist and crashed into the North Sea at 21.54 on their return flight".

The other members of the crew were:

920127 (Flight Eng) Malcolm Charles Moody

Lieutenant (Navigator) Bjarne Indseth RNAF (Royal Norwegian Air Force)

1094107 Sergeant (Bomb Aimer) Leslie Lamb

1037399 Sergeant (Wireless Operator, Air Gunner) Alan Victory David Stinton.

1307696 Sergeant (W/op A.G) Alan Richard Saunders.

1397175 Sergeant (W/op A.G) Peter Harry Barrowclough P.Green.

[1]RAF - 76 Squadron Archive

Both Kenneth and Malcolm are commemorated on the brass processional cross in Landford church.

A report in the Romsey Advertiser in June 1940 mentions another loss of life with a connection to Plaitford:

"PLAITFORD PILOT OFFICER REPORTED MISSING
Received D.F.M. for Gallantry

Pilot Officer A.S.T Cargill, D.F.M., R.A.F.*, who was reported
missing end of June is the son-in-law of Mrs. Creath of the School
House, Plaitford. He received the Distinguished Flying Medal in
April last year when a Pilot Sgt., "for conspicuous gallantry in action
against the enemy"*

*The presentation was made by Air Vice Marshal C.D. Breese and
Mrs. Leonie Cargill the recipient's wife was the only woman on the
parade ground. Incidentally the ceremony took place on the first
anniversary of their wedding.*

*Pilot Officer Cargill, who is 27, was educated at Eagles House
School, Sandhurst and is one of the most experienced reconnaissance
pilots in Coastal Command. Since the war began he has been flying
over the North Sea hunting U-boats and guarding convoys. At the end
of last year he fought a duel with a Dornier 18 flying boat off the
Norwegian coast and damaged it seriously. Although his own aircraft
had a petrol tank shot through and a wing damaged, he brought his
crew home safely. The Dornier 18 flying boat was believed to have
crashed in Norwegian territorial waters"*

According to 224 Squadron records, Pilot Officer Cargill took of
from Leuchars, Scotland at 17.05 on 21/06/40 flying a Lockheed
Hudson 1, serial number N7287 ZS-P, borrowed from 233 Squadron
on Convoy Escort duty. He and his 3 man crew failed to return.
Arthur Sydenham Tremaine Cargill married Leonie Margaret Mary
Creeth at Plaitford Church on April 10 1939

Fund Raising

During the war the village took part in many local and national fundraising events in aid of the war effort:

In June 1940, pupils and parents of Plaitford School sent 150
children's garments to a Belgian refugee depot in London. This was a
very commendable effort for a small village. During the previous
week, one pound ten shillings was forwarded to the RNLI. This
amount was gratefully acknowledged by the secretary, who stated
more than 1,000 lives had been saved by the lifeboats in the nine
months of the war, a number which exceeded the total saved in the
previous four years of peace

During Warship week in December 1941, Plaitford adopted His
Majesty's Motor Torpedo Boat 30.

In February 1943, the Girls' Club (Founded by Mrs. Turner, Head
Mistress of Plaitford School) held a social in aid of the village Home

Guard. A sum of nine pounds was raised. Later in 1943, the Girls Club was affiliated to the National Council of Girls' Clubs.

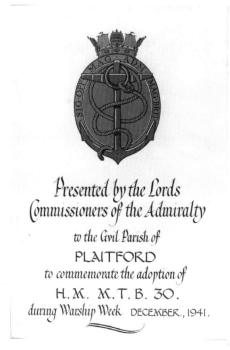

Presented by the Lords
Commissioners of the Admiralty
to the Civil Parish of
PLAITFORD
to commemorate the adoption of
H.M. M.T.B. 30.
during Warship Week DECEMBER, 1941.

Certificate presented to Plaitford, Warship Week December 1941

For "Wings for Victory" week in June 1943, Plaitford was given a target of £1,000. By wholehearted co-operation, the village (one of the smallest in Hampshire) raised £4,589.

In December 1943, a whist drive was held by the Home Guard in aid of the children's New Year party. In January 1944, a New Year party was given by the Home Guard in their hut for all the children in the village and the children of Home Guard members from outside the village. Each child was presented with a packet of sweets. The coupons for these were provided by the Home Guard members. The children also received a present and two shillings and six pence of saving stamps.

For "Salute the Soldier" week in May 1944, Plaitford's target was £1,250. The total raised was £7,510. This was the second highest amount raised by villages in the Romsey and District area and worked out at the astonishing figure of £36 per head of the population of this small village.

Various events were held in 1945 to raise money for the Home-Coming-Fund:

A whist drive was held at Plaitford School in May and raised five pounds. At this event Sgt. Stone of the Home Guard handed over a sum of nine pound five shillings and six pence. On 16 November, a social was held in Plaitford School room. This was to be the final effort for the fund and raised £40. The fund now stood at £227.14s.4d. In April 1946, a welcome home social was organized by the Home-Coming-Fund committee. A cheque for eight pound nine shillings was presented to each of Plaitfords ex-Servicemen and women.

The village held a Victory Celebration at Plaitford School on Saturday, 8 June 1946 with free refreshments, sports, fancy dress parade and a social evening. The celebration culminated with a bonfire and fireworks on the common.

Ticket for the Victory Celebrations in June 1946.
This ticket was given to Fred and Bertha Stone and their son John who lived at Gauntletts Farm

Chapter 15
Sport and Sporting Achievements

Cricket is recorded in Plaitford as far back as 1825 when two matches were played between Mr. John Henbest's team and Mr. C Cocks's team as follows from the Salisbury & Winchester Journal 25 July 1825:

'A well contested match of cricket was played on Monday last, at Stoney Cross, between Mr. John Henbest, of Bramshaw, and Mr. C Cocks, of Plaitford, for four sovereigns, which was decided in favour of the latter. The return match will be played on Monday next the 25th instant, on Plaitford Common'.

The return match is reported in the same newspaper on 1 August 1825:

'The return match of cricket between Mr. Henbest, of Bramshaw, and Mr. C Cocks, of Plaitford, was played on Monday last, on Plaitford Common, when the latter again beat his opponent at one innings, with four runs to spare'.

We know Plaiford had its own team from c1870s until 1906. The matches were played on the 'Shoe' field, opposite the Shoe Inn and the Shoe was used as the club house. The 1904 scoring book[1] records familiar names such as Brooke, Bungay, Curtis, Dibden, Fanstone, Hood, Hurst, Hutchings, Moore, Noyce, Peck and Tutt. The fixture of games for the 1905 season, home and away, were between Awbridge, Cadnam, Landford, Redlynch and Wellow. Matches were also played between teams from north and south Plaitford and Plaitford 1st IX versus Mr. Bungay and friends. Later the club merged with Wellow. The Wellow and Plaitford Cricket club still play today.

Les Curtis lived in Plaitford all his life, born at Savages Farm (now Redhouse Farm) in 1922. Unlike his brothers, Les went to Wellow School where his love of team sport was nurtured by his head teacher Mr. George Pierce MBE. Les played for both the school football and cricket teams and was playing when both teams won cups in 1936. Les's connection with Wellow continued for the rest of his life. He served as a corporal in the Wellow Home Guard during WW2 and in 1939 started playing for Wellow and Plaitford cricket club, captaining the team in the 1950s. A report in the Southern Daily Echo, 16 May 1984, sums up Les's long cricketing career:

"Wellow and Plaitford cricket stalwart Les Curtis put the swing back into the Sixties when he caned the Michelmersh attack for an unbeaten 101 in a recent clash between the village clubs. Les, 62 later this month, defied a cracked rib to pile up his third century for

Wellow. In partnership with John Lewis (107) he helped Wellow to 250-2 declared; Michelmersh replying with 204-9. All-rounder Les is something of an institution at Wellow. During 45 years service to the club, his medium paced bowling has produced two hat-tricks and he took all ten wickets in a match in 1962. Les topped the batting averages last season. He also plays for Calmore Wanders."

Later that same year, he was selected to play for the Hampshire Cricket Association team to play Sussex at Brighton. Unfortunately the game didn't take place due to Hampshire being unable to field a full team.

From the Romsey Advertiser, February 1928: *"The first prize (a BSA gun and a medal) in the Schoolboy Bisley, held at the recent Schoolboy's Own Exhibition in London, was won by* **Leonard Creeth**, *of Peter Symonds School, Winchester and son of Mrs. Creeth, Head-teacher of Plaitford School. With 14 targets, he made an average score of 36 out of a possible 40. The fact that over 1000 boys from most of the Secondary school across the country entered this competition makes this a really fine achievement. Creeth is the current holder of the Cadet Corps Musketry Challenge cup at Peter Symonds."* He retained the title in 1929 with a score of 291 out of 300.

Keith Curtis of Powells Farm, wanted to take up tennis as his main sport but a serious ankle fracture put pay to his ambitions. His other interest was motor cycles and this led to a successful spell (1975-1981) as a Trials and Grasstrack rider. Regular Motor Cycle Trials were held during the 1970s at Bridefoot Farm, where Keith was brought up. Keith had a winning success on his own track and other circuits in the area. As a novice in October 1975 he came second in a meeting at Broxmore, Sherfield English. He then moved up to Intermediate where he came 2nd out of 252 riders at a meeting at Bovington. Keith then moved to Motor Cycle Grass track coming 8th in the 500cc British Championship, 4th in the National held at the Lydden Circuit in Kent and 6th in the first Ace of Aces held in November 1979 at Winterslow.

Sally Ellis nee McDiarmid was brought up at Yew Tree Farm, Plaitford Green. A Marathon runner, Sally represented Great Britain in the 1991 World Athletic Championships in Tokyo where she finished 10th and the 1992 Barcelona Olympics finishing 25th. She also represented England in the 1990 Commonwealth Games in Auckland, New Zealand finishing 4th and the 1994 Commonwealth Games in Victoria, Canada finishing 8th.

Rita McGimsey nee Bowles, daughter of Harvey and Jean Bowles, Plaitford Wood Farm, started running when she was ten and a half years old. She continues:

I ran my first race at Wellow School sports day, and came in first place. Sally McDiarmid, who lived down the track from me at Yew Tree Farm, saw me and said I should come along to a running club that she went to called Southampton & Eastleigh Running Club. Sally's mum used to take us from Plaitford to Southampton Sports Centre on Tuesdays and Thursdays every week from then on.

During the 1970s and 80s I would spend weekends traveling all over the country to run for the club, wherever races were being held. I ran for Hampshire five times and was very proud to do so. I was also chosen to go to France to race for the club. We would go on a Friday and come back on Monday and I did this for a few years, it was a great experience.

I did most of my training around Plaitford, Melchet and Wellow. I stopped running for nine years when I had my three children. When I went back to it, it was mostly road running. I won a lot of road races including ten kilometer, ten mile and half marathons.

One of my favourite races, the Southampton ten kilometer took place in April 1996. I was in the lead from start to finish and had a police motor bike beside me all the way.

There is a ten mile race held over on the Isle of Wight which I won three times in a row from 1995 to 1997. I also held the course record of 62 minutes and 9 seconds.

After a lot of road races, I decided to try for a place in the London Marathon. I was accepted because of my history with the running club and I managed to raise a lot of money for Cancer Research. The first time I ran in 2004, I managed a time of 3:44:16 which I was really happy with. This gave me a qualifying time to be able run two more marathons, which I did in 2005 and 2006. I didn't get a better time, but I did manage to get three medals – one for each of my three children.

It took lots of training to do the London Marathons. I would cover between 50-80 miles a week, and would train in the early mornings in the villages. Because of where we live it was never a struggle to get up at five o'clock in the morning to start training.

Rita still lives in Plaitford in a property next to her parent's. She still runs, but now just for fun.

Boxer, **Henry Castle** of Plaitford Green won the ABA Featherweight title in May 2000 and soon after he turned professional. His first fight took place in Peterborough in January 2001 against Jason Nesbitt. Henry won with a KO in the sixth round.

His second fight in November 2001 saw another success with a second round KO against Eddy Navine. Success continued and in 2004 Henry was heading for a chance at the Featherweight title. He later lost the British lightweight title eliminator by just one point over 10 rounds against Gary Buckland in July 2009. Unfortunately Henry's career was brought to an abrupt end in 2010 after recording 20 wins out of 25 professional bouts.

On 31st May 1918 a Cricket match was held between Melchet Court and Sherfield English, as reported in the Romsey Advertiser:

'The wounded soldiers at present at Melchet Court Auxiliary Hospital engaged in a cricket match with Sherfield English at the mansion grounds in pleasant weather conditions on Saturday afternoon. The "Tommies", which included a number of capable English and Scottish players, gave a splendid account of themselves, despite the physical infirmities they played under, against the good bowling of H Hood, M'Kernan, Kellaway and Jones. They all exhibited good batting form which was only excelled by V Hacker on the visiting side who had more than half the total to his credit, his 19 including hits for 6 and 4. The bowling of the "Tommies" was too deadly for the comfort and effectiveness of the remaining batsmen. Pte. Grundie who has played for the Scottish County Championship had 4 wickets for 4 runs. Gunner M'Kernan 4 wickets for a slightly bigger average, and Bill Irvine, the ginger beer man at the hospital also bowled well'.

Melchet Court scored 45 runs to Sherfield English 32. A return match was played the following week. Sherfield English won by 24 runs. Sherfield English Team - Beauchamp, R. Dear, V. Hacker, H. Hood, S. Hood, R. O'Conner, H.M Olden, J. Pearce, B. Rogers, E Rogers and Private Kelly.

Chapter 16
Melchet Park and Court

At the time of the Domesday Survey, Melchet Wood belonged to the two manors of the Abbes of Wilton with rights to take wood and feed hogs.

In early times, the office of custodians of the park of Melchet belonged to the manor of Plaitford, a tradition that endured until the seventeenth century, though the owners of Plaitford seem to have lost the office from the middle of the fourteenth century until around 1524 when Sir William Compton, lord of the manor of Plaitford laid claim and obtained it as belonging of ancient right to the manor of Plaitford.

During the middle ages, Melchet Wood, Forest or Park formed part of the Royal Forest of Clarendon. Throughout the thirteenth century large grants and sales of timber were made from Melchet Wood. Much of the timber was used for works at Clarendon and Salisbury. A large quantity went to Queen Eleanor, wife of King Henry III, in 1276 to build Lyndhurst Manor. The Priors of Mottisfont, Breamore and Christchurch Twyneham and the Abbes of Romsey also obtained grants for timber from Melchet. In 1357, the Sheriff of Wiltshire received an order to make a lodge in the Kings Park of Melchet, and apparently about 20 acres around the lodge were enclosed.

In 1577, Richard Audley, chief ranger to the Compton family, who lived in the lodge, obtained leave from Queen Elizabeth to enclose 240 acres of Melchet Forest for twenty-one years. The enclosure remained undisturbed until 1610, when Sir John Daccombe, who succeeded Richard Audley and his son as chief ranger of the park, de-parked it of deer. He turned part of it into arable, part into pasture, and part into a coney warren. After this change, Anne Countess of Dorset, widow of Henry first Lord Compton, caused the park palings to be broken down as a protest against the common rights which she claimed as owner of Plaitford Manor.

In 1614, the park and forest were granted by the crown to Sir Laurence Hyde, attorney-general to Ann of Denmark, Consort of James I. After his death in 1641, his two sons eventually sold the forest and park of Melchet in 1664 to Richard Coleman. Richard Coleman's great niece obtained a license in 1775 by Act of Parliament to sell the estate which was purchased in the same year by James Lockhart, who with his wife Sarah sold the park in 1791-2 to Major John Osborne, who was responsible for planting California pine, cedar and other foreign trees in the park, some of which still stand today. In 1800, Osborne erected a Hindu Temple in the grounds dedicated to and containing a bust of his friend, Warren Hastings, who was Governor-General of Bengal (India) 1773–1785. It is believed the temple was demolished during the second half of the nineteenth century.

John Osborne died in 1821, and the following auction notice appeared in the Bath Chronicle and Weekly Gazette on 1 March 1821:

"HAMPSHIRE - MELCHET PARK, near ROMSEY, SALISBURY and SOUTHAMPTON.

Elegant HOUSEHOLD FURNITURE: about One Thousand Ounces of PLATE and Plated Articles; Library of Choice BOOKS; excellent Bed and Table Linen; handsome Services of China and Glass; fine PAINTINGS and PRINTS; WINES and BEER; a yellow bodied Phaeton (A light four-wheeled open carriage), *Carriage Horses; a leash of staunch Pointers, and four Spaniels; healthy Green and Hot-house Plants, fine Lemon and Orange Trees; a Boat; and various other Effects.*

To be SOLD by AUCTION, by MR. ROBINS
(Of Warwick-Street, Golden Square)
At the Mansion, Melchet Park, near Romsey, Hants, on Monday the 5ᵗʰ of March, 1821, and five following days, at 11 o'clock precisely.
The Property of the late JOHN OSBORNE, Esq; deceased"

A previous auction also carried out by Mr. Robins took place over six days from 26 February at the mansion and the farms of the estate at which all farm live and dead stock and farm equipment was sold.

It was not until 1823 that the mansion was advertised for sale by private contract, described as a *"Spacious Family Mansion with offices, gardens, pleasure grounds, hot houses, park, and enclosure containing upwards of 530 acres."* The advertisement in the Hampshire Chronicle, dated 7 July, goes on to mention the inclusion of the farms on the estate including some situated in Whiteparish and Sherfield English with a total of one thousand acres of arable, pasture and woodland.

The heirs of Major John Osborne conveyed Melchet Park to Alexander Baring, head of the famous firm Baring Brothers, who in 1835 was created Lord Ashburton. Records show that for twenty years, Alexander Baring leased Melchet Park to Richard Webb and his wife, Selina. Richard Webb, a land agent, is recorded as living at Melchet in 1824/25, he died in March 1837. His will, written in 1832, also makes reference to him living at Melchet Park. After her husband's death, Selina Webb continued to live at Melchet and she and her son, Richard, are recorded on the 1841 census. Richard junior, also a land agent, died in April 1844, aged 28. In October that year a notice appeared in the Salisbury & Winchester Journal: *Mrs. Webb is quitting the Mansion and an auction of all household furniture is to be held on 21 October 1844.*

An event that took place at the time the Webbs were at Melchet was the widespread uprising of 1830 and 1831 by farm workers against the introduction of new farm machinery known as the "Swing Riots", which saw an occurrence on 22 November 1830 when a mob of between 200 and 300 (numbers probably exaggerated) led by Charles Martin smashed a threshing machine at Melchet Park Farm, the property of Mr. Richard Webb.

Alexander Baring, 1st Lord Ashburton died in 1848 and was succeeded by his eldest son, William. Immediately after Alexander's death his second son The Hon. Francis Baring moved into Melchet Park. Newspaper articles and reports also record another son, The Hon. and Rev. Frederick Baring as living in the mansion from 1846 to 1862.

William 2nd Lord Ashburton moved to Melchet Park in 1862 and the work of demolishing the old mansion and rebuilding a new property was started. William died in 1864 and Louisa Lady Ashburton, his second wife, continued the building work which was completed in 1867.

Louisa Lady Ashburton was the daughter of James Alexander Stewart-Mackenzie, a wealthy Scottish politician and Governor of Ceylon. Besides her estates in Scotland and properties in London, she retained Melchet Park as a residence until her death in 1903.

Lady Ashburton was a prominent figure in the temperance movement and was local President of the British Women's Total Abstinence Union. She was responsible for the building of Sherfield English School, formerly known as Melchet Park School. During the last years of her life, she had Landford Wood Mission Hall built on part of her estate. The hall cost £300 to build and was opened in June 1899, and in1902-3 she built St. Leonard's church in Sherfield English, in memory of her daughter, Mary Florence Baring, the Marchioness of Northampton, at a cost of £6,000.

Melchet estate was advertised for sale in 1908, but was not sold. The estate remained in hands of the executors of Lady Ashburton until it was sold in 1911.

The sale catalogue produced in 1908 gives the whole estate as just over 2,478 acres including most, if not all, of Sherfield English. A map dated 1921 of Sherfield English Estate indicates that all parts of Sherfield English shown on the Melchet Park estate map and sale catalogue 1908/11 were bought as a whole. Some of the farms included in the 1908 catalogue included Manor Farm, Brices Farm, Sole Hill and Warren Farm.

In 1911, the estate was purchased by Sir Alfred Mond, a founder member of the chemical company ICI. Sir Alfred served as a minister in Lloyd George's government from 1916 to 1922 and was created 1st Baron Melchet of Landford in 1928. He died in 1930. His wife, Lady Violet Mond, died in 1945.

Records show that that Sir Alfred Mond bought Gunsfield, Boulder Wood and a large part of Plaitford Wood from the Earl of Ilchester when Plaitford Manor was split up and sold in 1911. By the time of the sale of Melchet Park in 1935, the Mond family had acquired other property in Plaitford including Manor Farm, Bridgefoot Cottages, Yew Tree Farm, and the following piece of land: A first for Romsey District Council Housing Scheme when, in October 1920, the first foundation stone was laid by Lady Violet Mond on the first of three double cottages to be built in the district. The land in Church Lane, Plaitford, now known as Forest View, was given to the council by Sir Alfred Mond.

The original north entrance lodge to Melchet Park from Sherfield English was a single story house that stood to the right of the entrance. Plans were drawn up in 1923 to build the arched gatehouse that stands today. The builders John Mowlem & Company started the work it would appear without planning permission early in 1924. The work was stopped by Romsey Rural District Council in a letter dated 31 March 1924. John Mowlen replied on 1 April as follows:

"G.W.P Dyson Esq. District Surveyor Romsey Rural District Council Thank you for your letter of 31st ulto. We send you the plans herewith and must apologise for not having forwarded them before, but the writer was under the impression, from former work done, that there was no Authority to whom plans would have to be submitted. As we have already started the work, we shall be grateful if you can kindly arrange to have the plans passed by your council at the earliest possible moment." Try getting away with that today!

In 1935, Henry 2nd Baron Melchet closed the house, and the estate was split and put up for sale. The Sales catalogue for 1935 gives the Melchet Estate as 1,719 acres compared to 2,478 in 1911. The estate was auctioned in July 1935; there were 57 lots of which 33 were sold making £29,760. Some lots were withdrawn and some including

Woodfalls and Melchet Court Farm were later sold privately. Melchet Court remained unsold until 1939.

Tithes and Boundary Changes

The extra-parochial district of Melchet Park has never had a church and its inhabitants were exempt from tithes. Most residents were in the habit of attending Plaitford church, where seats were provided for their accommodation. The non payment of tithes caused serious difficulties between the parson of Plaitford and the inhabitants of Melchet Park. A royal commission sent in 1619 to inquire into the subject reported that the former arrangement as to attendance should continue, and that Sir Laurence Hyde, then owner of Melchet Park, should on behalf of the inhabitants pay twenty shillings yearly at Easter in lieu of tithes and other dues. From the time of this arrangement up to the early 1900s Melchel Park was exempt of tithes Prior to the county boundary changes in 1895, Melchet Park was part of Whiteparish and was situated along with Plaitford and West Wellow in Wiltshire. In 1895, Melchet Park was a made a separate civil parish until 1932 when it was joined with Plaitford.

Melchet Court

No paintings or drawings exist, so nothing is known about the original Melchet Court other than it was thought to have been a typical eighteenth century mansion.

The present mansion, built in the Elizabethan style, completely replaced the original building and was completed by the widow of the second Lord Ashburton after his death in 1864. The architect was Henry Clutton, well known as a designer of several churches and country houses. A feature in The Builders Magazine of January 1863 reported that the construction costs amounted to £13,041. The interior was designed by Alfred Stevens, whose designs for the hall and staircase are now in the Victoria and Albert Museum. The following notice from the Salisbury & Winchester Journal dated 2 February 1867 gives an indication when building work was completed:

"MELCHET PARK
About 5 miles from Romsey and 2 from Whiteparish.
TO BUILDERS, CONTRACTORS, AND OTHERS
MR. JAMES JENVEY has been favoured with instruction from the Contractors for the Erection of the Mansion and Buildings at Melchet, to SELL by AUCTION, on the Premises, on FRIDAY, FEBRUARY 8, 1867 at Eleven o'clock precisely, on account of the great number of Lots, - A large assortment of exceedingly useful and

valuable SURPLUS BUILDING MATERIALS, sold in consequence of completion of the works"

The advertisement goes on to list various building materials and a large selection of builder's plant.

A fire destroyed part of the house in August 1872 causing an estimated £20,000 to £30,000 worth of damage. The restoration was again carried out by Henry Clutton between 1875 and 1879.

The census returns taken in the nineteenth century record the total population of Melchet Park estate, including the mansion, the lodge, farms and gardener's cottage as thirty in 1841 and 1851, and twenty-nine in 1861. After the re-building of Melchet Court was completed the population in 1871 was forty-one. Louisa Lady Ashburton was in residence at the time of the 1881 census that stood at fifty three. The record shows thirteen female servants comprising a cook, two kitchen maids, two laundry maids, four house maids, three ladies' maids and one general servant. There were also eight male servants comprising, a butler, one valet, three footmen, two general servants and a coachman. Only one of the ladies' maids was a local, Emilie Newman from Romsey. The rest of the staff came from all over the country. The population in 1891 was thirty-seven and thirty-one in 1901.

Melchet Court after the devastating fire of 1872. Blackened windows are devoid of glass blown out by the fire, Note the water, clock and bell tower.

Melchet Court Show

Melchet Court was host to The Sherfield English Fruit, Vegetables and Flower Show known to have taken place in the three years 1870 to 1872 by permission of Louise Lady Ashburton. The show held on a Wednesday afternoon in July was open to the inhabitants of Melchet, Sherfield English, Broxmore, Cowsfield, Whiteparish, Landford, Plaitford and Wellow Wood.

After the serious fire at Melchet Court in 1872, the show was forced to move to other venues. In 1873, it was held at Lt. Col Venner's park at Cowesfield House. Due to a lack of funds no show was held in 1874. The last show to be recorded in the 1870s took place in 1875 at Broxmore Park, the home of Mr. Robert Linzee.

The shows must have restarted in the grounds of Melchet Park around 1891 as the Romsey Advertiser records the fourteenth annual Sherfield English Flower Show in August 1904. The show was a popular event in the calendar year and was again held on a Wednesday with many people from Plaitford attending and entering exhibits in the various horticultural sections. We have few records of the continuance of these shows. We know from Plaitford School records that children from the school entered competitions held at Melchet Park shows into the 1930s.

Romsey Labourers Encouragement Society

As detailed in chapter 5, awards were presented annually from 1854 until 1878. Melchet Park was represented - here are just a few:

1854: George Martin of Sherfield for having worked at Melchet Park for 31 years and 'placed out' his children in respectable service, never having received parochial relief, awarded 60 shillings.

1870; Samuel Bell, Shepherd to Lady Ashburton, 125 lambs from 100 ewes with a loss of two ewes, awarded 20 shillings.

1878: Samuel Bell for long service (45 yrs) and Charles Sillence (42 yrs) at Melchet Farm both awarded 30 shillings each.

In July 1890, Henry Morton Stanley, the famous explorer and his bride, Dorothy Tennant, spent their honeymoon at Melchet as guests of Lady Ashburton.

Between 1912 and 1914, Sir Alfred Mond made extensive alterations, both internally and externally; most notably the removal of the water, clock and bell tower. There were no further additions or alterations until after the house was sold in 1939.

Before the First World War, Sir Alfred Mond employed one head gardener who was responsible for fifteen other gardeners. After the war started, women were taken on as gardeners to replace the men who had joined the forces.

During the First World War, Sir Alfred was chairman of Queen Alexandra's Hospital for Officers in London, and Lady Mond was Commandant of the Melchet Court Annex to the Hospital. She had turned the house into a 60 bed convalescent hospital for wounded servicemen. Lady Mond also opened her London home to Belgian refugees. For these services she was appointed Dame Commander of the Order of the British Empire in the 1920 birthday honours.

The 1918 electoral roll for Melchet Park the following are recorded as absentee military voters: Allan Brown, Wilfred Clipstone, Henry Mond and John Spalding. We have only managed to find service details for Henry Mond who served as a 2nd Lieutenant ACC with the 10th South Wales Borderers from 1915. He was later promoted to Lieutenant and was wounded in action in 1916.

A £5,000 jewel robbery took place in July 1926 when jewellery was stolen from Lady Mond's dressing room.

As mentioned previously, Melchet Park was split up for auction. The auction took place in July 1935 and it is recorded in the Western Gazette that *Melchet Court was unsold, there being no bidder*" It is thought it remained unsold until 1939.

Melchet Court c1915, after extensive alterations carried out by Sir Alfred Mond. The water, clock and bell tower has been removed.

From Stately Home to School

In March 1939, the house and grounds were purchased by Mr. Cecil. A. Ranger, who planned to transfer Pinewood Preparatory School[1], from Farnborough, Hants. Extensive changes were made to accommodate the school. The school started its life at Melchet in the Christmas term of 1939. The collapse of France in the summer of 1940 saw many boys leave for safer climes. The few remaining boys were joined by evacuees from Gosport.

In July 1940, the army requisitioned the school and it became the head quarters of 5 corps, Southern Command under the command of General Auchinleck and later Lieutenant-General Bernard Montgomery[2]. Montgomery took command on 22 July 1940. His area of responsibility for the defence against a German invasion stretched along the entire south coast from Bognor to Lyme Regis, including the Isle of Wight.

During this time the school moved to Devon. Melchet was de-requisitioned by September 1940. The returning pupils were joined at Melchet by pupils evacuated from Sandrock Hall School in Hastings.

Early in 1941, the house was requisitioned again by the Government, and taken over by the The Ministry of Aircraft Production and used as offices by Saunders-Roe[3] aircraft manufacturers. Melchet Court became the main office of the company together with works offices and records department which were transferred from East Cowes on the Isle of Wight. In addition to being the main centre for the control of production contracts, the control of some twenty smaller units was involved. Over 400 people were employed in the peak period. All the wartime board meetings were held at Melchet.

Many local people worked for Saunders-Roe including Eric Kemish from Wellow who worked in the central records office and recalls being taken to and from Melchet in a coach belonging to Skylark Coaches from Downton. The coach would travel via Plaitford, Landford and Whiteparish and was full when it reached Melchet. Eric also recalls Elizabeth (Betty) Rothnie who lived at Torran, Plaitford Common working in the same office and travelling on the same transport.

We have also found a reference that the premises also contained a drawing office for the MkIV Spitfire, unfortunately we have been unable to substantiate this.

In September 1941, Saunders-Roe Ltd placed an order with Test Road Materials Ltd. Kings Somborne for repair work to be carried out on the drive at Melchet at a quoted price of £479. The order also includes the following agreement:

"It has been agreed that owing to labour shortage we will supply five men at one farthing per hour with three at a subsistence charge of six shillings per day in addition. These costs are included in the quotation of £479."

From 1941 to 1946, Pinewood School now renamed Melchet School had relocated to Dartmoor in Devon. During this time Mr. Ranger died and in 1945, Melchet Court was sold and the school reverted to Pinewood and relocated to Bourton in Oxfordshire where it is today. In 1946, the new owners of Melchet Court now renamed Nazareth House were the Roman Catholic Poor Sisters of Nazareth who took over the building as a school responsible for looking after children orphaned by the war. A planning application dated 1946 for the proposed conversion of stables into a laundry and boiler room mentions the desperate need for these new facilities. They were needed to cater for 300 children from babies to boys and girls to the age of fifteen. Some of the children had been transferred from Wardour Castle School, Tisbury in Wiltshire, where they had spent the war years.

In 1947, some of the children were sent from Melchet and other parts of the UK to Australia. This was the subject of much controversy in later years, causing the British government to apologize to the children in 2010. It had also come to light that some of the children sent to Australia were not in fact orphans.

Early one morning in February 2010, Julian Clegg, the presenter of BBC Radio Solent's Breakfast Show, was doing a feature on the British government's apology to the children who had been sent to Australia in the late forties. On hearing the tail end of an interview with an Australian, who along with other children, was sent from Melchet Court. We contacted BBC Radio Solent, who were very helpful and put us in touch, via email, with the gentleman in question. His name is Laurie Humphreys and after sending him an email explaining about the book and asking him if he had any memories of his time at Melchet, this is his reply in his own words:

Here's a few thoughts on my time at Melchet Court. I left there in August 1947 at the age of thirteen to come to Australia. I believe I went there in early 1946 having been at Wardour Castle during the war for the period 1939-1946.

Compared with Wardour Castle, Melchet Court was luxurious with highly polished floors which we, as kids, used to polish with rags tied to our backsides and we dragged each other up and down the floors which was a lot of fun. It was the first time I had ever lived in a 'co-ed' orphanage in which girls had one half of the building and the boys the other. We attended school together on site. The classrooms were situated on the ground floor not far from the swimming pool. I recall learning to swim in that swimming pool and that included being thrown off the diving board by the teacher/priest which was a very quick way of learning to swim! It was rather a lavish pool – something we had never seen before. There was also a smaller, mosaic pond and I do recall seeing a snake trapped in it at one time. This was a bit scary at the time for me.

I made a great friend of the boiler attendant. He tended the coal-fired boiler situated in the basement. It was nice warm place to be and one where we made toast, with butter being supplied by the boiler attendant.

There was also a large greenhouse down the back where we grew tomatoes and I do recall there was a fair infestation of blackberry bushes which we attempted to dig out at one time.

I also recall Melchet Court as being a very spacious building. As far as I know we were sent there because Wardour Castle was being taken back by the Arundel Family. My fondest memory of Melchet is the lush green lawns – I used to love rolling on them. What a huge contrast it was to come to Australia!!!"

On a visit to the UK in the 1990s, Laurie visited Melchet Court where he met Larry Bartel, the headmaster of St Edwards School.

More changes were to take place - in 1954, Salesian Fathers opened the school as a theological college for the final stages of training before ordination took place.

Damage estimated at £20,000 (£320,000 today) was caused when a large fire broke out on the third floor of the west wing on 18 August 1961. Twelve appliances from the surrounding area attended the fire.

In 1962, the Salesian Fathers left Melchet, and in 1963, the Trustees of the Clifton Catholic Children's Society purchased the estate. In May 1963, the headmaster, matron, some staff and twelve boys arrived to start the school.

St Edwards School, as it is known today, is still owned and managed by the Roman Catholic Diocese of Clifton. St Edwards School celebrated its Golden Jubilee in 2013.

[1] Pinewood School webpage. [2] Monty-The making of a General by Nigel Hamilton. [3] Saunders-Roe-From River to Sea by Ray Wheeler

Back to the Melchet Park auction in 1935 - Hugh Quigley purchased 77 acres including 35 acres of woodland and the seventeen acre Yew Tree Farm in Plaitford for £1,175 (£15 per acre). In the late 1930s he created Melchet Park Farm (not to be confused with Melchet Park farm of the 1800s mentioned later in this chapter) that included a 50 acre apple orchard and erected a large farm house, built entirely out of wood. We do not have a record of when Hugh Quigley died. His son, Stephen, and daughter, Margaret, lived at the property. There were no apple trees left on the farm when it was sold in 1990. The new and current owners, Roland and Marie Chalk, built a new house a little further down the hill from the wooded structure which was demolished.

The 35 acres of woodland Hugh Quigley purchased in 1935 was dense with birch trees. He wrote in his book entitled Melchet in 1970: *"A sawmiller in Sway showed interest in the birch, a price was calculated to allow him to compete with broomheads from Estonia. In the event 12,500 birches were sold at 4½ pennies each. A small local industry was established and in the 30 years between 1936 and 1966, in all 30,000 birches, the last fellings being one shilling each were removed".*

Continuous Occupation

The following three properties have been occupied by the same families continuously for more that fifty years, from the date shown until 2013:

Newman[1] - Whitehouse Farm 1936 (77 years); Mitchell/Newman[1] - Woodfalls 1951 (62 years) and Blanchard - Sawpit Cottages 1960 (53 years), a combined total of 192 years.

[1]Unrelated

Melchet Court Farm

The earliest mention of a farm bailiff is that of Thomas Smith who was bailiff to Major John Osborne. Major Osborne died in 1821, and Thomas Smith is mentioned in an advertisement for the sale of farm stock that year and again in 1823 when the mansion, farms and buildings were sold.

For further information we have had to rely on the census returns from 1841 to 1911. From 1871 there appears to have been only one farm mentioned on the returns. It was addressed as Melchet Park Farm, Melchet Farm, Farmhouse or no address at all.

Thomas Brooke, aged 63, and his wife, Sarah, aged 45, are recorded on the 1841 census as living at Melchet Farm. Thomas's occupation is recorded as farm servant.

Their son, Oliver, went on to marry Sarah Hutchings from Gauntletts Farm, Plaitford, they eventually moved to Gardeners Farm in the same village.

On the same census, Samuel and Clarissa Short are living in the dairy house. In 1851, they are living at Park Small Farm and farming 52 acres and by 1871, they are at Little Farm farming 33 acres. There is no further mention of these farms after 1871.

To continue with Melchet Park Farm, the 1851 census records Susanna Frances, a widow, aged 46, dairy woman, born in Alresford. Her son, George, aged 24, born in Itchen Stoke was Bailiff of 200 acres. Of the 30 persons listed on the census only five were born locally including three born at Melchet Park. Twelve members of two families came from Dorset, including the Short family, and the eight members of the Frances family came from the Alresford/Itchen Stoke[1] area of Hampshire. Melchet Farm as it was known in 1861 was occupied by Isaac and Sarah Roberts who were living in Plaitford Wood in 1841 and 1851. And by 1871, Bailiff Joseph Cross and his wife, Mary, are recorded with no address shown. The 1881 census records William and Elizabeth Harris as bailiff of 620 acres employing twelve men and five boys. The 1891 and 1901 census records James and Emma Stephens and from a 1907 electoral roll and the1911 census, John and Annie Cooper. There are no individual addresses shown on 1915 and 1918 electoral rolls. From 1919 to 1930 Melchet Farm was occupied by David and Isabella Parker and from 1930 to 1935 they are recorded as living in the estate office. As there is no mention of a farm between 1930 and 1935, it is our guess that the estate office was situated at Melchet Farm.

Henry Mond, 2nd Baron Melchet, sold Melchet Park by auction in 1935 and Melchet Court Farm listed as 301 acres was purchased by Major Denys Angus Lambert Dwyer. From the electoral rolls held at the Hampshire Record office, we are able to place the following as occupying Melchet Court Farm: 1937/38, Walter and Dorothy Whitfield occupy Melchet Farm; 1939/40, Lyell and Dorothy Aylward at Melchet Court Farm;. There were no electoral rolls between 1940 and 1944; May 1945 Percy and Dorothy Batchelor are living in Melchet Farmhouse; 1946 to 1950 there is no mention of a farmhouse and six families are recorded as living at Melchet Court Farm: 1946, Albert and Joan Greenhalgh; 1946-1950, Robert and Winifred Hill; 1947 Reginald and Sarah Gooden; 1947, Ernest and

Annie Law; 1949, Billie and Kathleen Williams and 1950, George and Esther Hunt.

The only mention after 1851 of a second farm in Melchet Park comes from the 1937 and 1939/40 electoral rolls - that being Lower Farm occupied by Henry and Marion Daniels. [2]Known as Lower Farm, the Daniels lived in one of the Sawpit Cottages and farmed a few acres close by until just before the end of the Second World War.

[1]The Barings also had estates in Northington, Itchen Stoke and Itchen Abbas, all close to the Itchen Valley between Winchester and Alresford in Hampshire.
[2]Source: Julian Newman, Whitehouse Farm, Melchet.

Woodfalls

On 1 September 1927, Henry Mond, later 2nd Baron Melchet, made an application to the Rural District Council of Romsey to build a house in the grounds of Melchet Park. Although no approval date is shown, the house that would be become known as Woodfalls was built in1929. At the time of the 1930 electoral roll Henry Mond and his wife, Gwen, were in residence. The 1935 Melchet Court sale catalogue described Woodfalls as an attractive and modern South African style residence that included Woodfalls Farm, well timbered parklands and woods, a total of 194 acres.

When Melchet Park was divided up and sold by auction in1935, Woodfalls, Woodfalls Farm and Melchet Court Farm did not sell. At the auction Major Denys Angus Lambert Dwyer purchased Manor Farm situated in Plaitford. A report on the auction in the Western Gazette, 12 July 1935, records that lot 11; Melchet Court Farm was sold privately after the auction. There is no mention in the report of the fate of lot 22, Woodfalls and Woodfalls Farm. We are certain that Major Dwyer also purchased these properties privately after the auction. He and his wife, Audrey, are recorded on the 1936/37 electoral roll as living at Woodfalls. Major Dwyer formed Woodfalls Estate this included the Woodfalls house and farm, Melchet Court Farm and Manor Farm Plaitford, a total of 546 acres. By 1951 Major Dwyer had decided to move abroad. From an auction notice in The Times newspaper dated 19 February 1951 it would appear that Woodfalls Farm had become known as Home Farm. The notice lists the properties as follows: "*Woodfalls Estate, Sherfield English, 546 Acres. Modern country residence, Home Farm, 230 acres, with buildings and two modern cottages*". The notice continues: *Also - Melchet Court Farm, 160 acres and Manor Farm, Plaitford, 156 acres*". The auction took place on 28 March 1951.

The following announcement appeared in The Times on 3 April 1951:

"Messrs James Harris & Son of Winchester have sold by auction the Woodfalls Estate, Nr. Romsey with 546 acres, several farms and cottages for £45,000".

Woodfalls Estate excluding Manor Farm, Plaitford was purchased at the auction by Joseph Mitchell. The house was later occupied by his son, Aubrey, and daughter, Lillary, and her husband, Gerald Newman. Woodfalls house is still owned and occupied by the descendants of Joseph Mitchell.

Gerald Newman ran both farms followed by his son, Bradley. The farms now operate under the one name of Melchet Park Farm and is still owned and farmed by the Newman family.

Index